TRUE CRIME 2019

Homicide & True Crime Stories of 2019

Annual True Crime Anthology

By

Jack Rosewood
&
Rebecca Lo

DISCLAIMER:

This anthology of true crime stories from 2019 includes quotes from those closely involved in the cases mentioned, and it is not the author's intention to defame or intentionally hurt anyone involved. The interpretation of the events surrounding the stories are the author's as a result of researching each from a variety of different sources including newspaper stories and interviews, televised interviews and documentaries about the case. Any comments made about the psychopathic, narcissistic or sadistic behavior of the criminals arrested – some among the most prolific serial killers in the country - are the sole opinion and responsibility of the person quoted.

FREE BONUS!

Get two free books when you sign up to
my VIP newsletter at www.jackrosewood.com
150 interesting trivia about serial killers and the
story of serial killer Herbert Mullin.

Contents

Introduction 1

Chapter 1: JANUARY 3

Bottrop and Essen Car Attack.................................... 3

Sidewalk Terror 3

The Injured... 3

The Suspect 4

Tension in Germany.. 4

Children Attacked at A Primary School in China 4

The Attack.. 4

Unnamed Suspect 5

Similar Attacks... 5

Nevada Killing Spree 5

Home Invasion Murders 5

Finding the Killer Through Technology 6

Who is Wilber?... 6

In Custody 6

The Assassination of Pawel Adamowicz 7

Politician, Mayor and Lawyer................................. 7

The Assassination 7

Caught Red-Handed 8

Reactions and Vigils 8

The Funeral Service 9

Attack on the Nairobi DusitD2 Complex 9

Background 9

Under Attack 10

Claim of responsibility 12

Bogotá Car Bombing.. 12

The Conflict Behind the Scenes 12

Bombs Detonated 12

The Investigation and Responsibility Claimed 13

International Responses 14

Mass Shooting in Sebring Bank 14

How It Unfolded 14

Barricaded Within 15

Those Who Were Killed 15

Background of the Killer... 15

Behind Bars 15

Louisiana Mass Murder 16

Murderous Rampage.. 16

Dakota Theriot 16

Charges Laid... 17

Bombings of Jolo Cathedral 17

    Leading Up To The Attack 17

    The Bombings.. 18

    Identifying the Suspects.. 19

    Charges Laid 20

    Presidential Response.. 20

    Widespread Reaction 20

Terrorist Attacks in Brief 21

Chapter 2: FEBRUARY 23

Fatal Arson in Paris 23

    Deliberate Torching 23

    Criminal Investigation 24

    Paris in Mourning 24

Kaduna State Massacre 24

    A Turbulent Background 24

    Revenge By Massacre? 25

    Aftermath 25

Khash-Zahedan Suicide Bombing 25

    Iran's Revolutionary Guards.. 26

    Suicide Bombing.. 26

    Claim of Responsibility.. 26

    Reactions to the Attack.. 26

    Day of Mourning 27

Pulwama Convoy Attack 27

Behind the Conflict 27

Multiple People Killed 28

Investigation and the Perpetrator 29

The Aftermath 30

Legacy 30

Mass Shooting in Aurora 31

Reports of Gunfire 31

Those Who Were Lost 31

Disgruntled Employee 32

Politicians React 33

The Morrisville Family Murders 33

A Shocking Welfare Check 33

Dominique and Shana 34

A Disturbing Belief 34

YNW Melly on Trial for Murder 35

Who is YNW Melly? 35

Criminal History and Charges of Murder 35

Murder on My Mind 36

R. Kelly Arrested and Charged Again 36

An Illegal Wedding 37

Allegations of Child Pornography and Abuse 37

An Alleged Sex Cult 38

Arrest and Charges Made 39

Trial Date Set 40

Terrorist Attacks in Brief 40

Chapter 3: MARCH 43

Pollution of Kim Kim River 43

A Background of Illness 43

Further Pollution 43

Investigation and Arrest 44

Response by Government and Health Authorities 44

Government Criticized and Lawsuits Filed 45

Mass Shooting in a Mexican Nightclub 45

Under Fire 45

Identification of Suspects 46

Arrest of Cartel Leader 46

Murder of Christine Silawan 47

A Violent Death 47

Investigation and Suspect 47

The Death Penalty Argument 48

A Horrifying Confession 48

The Suzano School Massacre 49

How it Began 49

The Teen Killer 50

Planned Over Time 50

The Shooting Victims 51

Solemn Reactions 52

Terror Comes to New Zealand 52

Gunman on the Loose 52

Perpetrator Captured - Manifesto Discovered 55

The Innocent Victims 56

Legal Proceedings 67

Prime Minister Praised Around the World 67

Inspired Attacks 68

Video Distribution 69

Further Arrests 69

Tram Passenger Shooting in the Netherlands 70

Passengers Under Attack 70

Ten Victims 70

The Suspect Confesses 70

Reaction and Response 71

Ogossagou Massacre 71

The Herdsmen 72

Villages Attacked 72

The Aftermath 72

The Murder of Nipsey Hussle 73

Shot Down in a Parking Lot 73

Memorial Service 73

A Lasting Legacy 74

Alleged Suspect 74

Terrorist Attacks in Brief 75

Chapter 4: APRIL.. 78

Murder of Nusrat Jahan Rafi 78

Background of the Murder... 78

Revenge Attack 79

Suspects in Custody 79

Sentenced to Death 79

Attempts to Combat Sex Crimes 80

Guard Shot to Death Outside Prahran Nightclub 80

Deadly Night At Work 81

Who Fired the Shots? 81

Day in Court 82

Minatitlán Mass Shooting 82

Events as They Unfolded... 82

Official Response 83

Criticism of Government.. 84

Easter Church Bombings in Sri Lanka.......................... 84

Terrorism in Sri Lanka 84

Prior Threats 85

Churches Attacked.. 85

Further Bombings... 86

Investigations Undertaken 86

Multiple Arrests Made 87

Released on Bail! 88

Bombers Identified 88

Fallout Resignations... 90

Michael Cummins - Family Killer 91

Eight Killed By One Man... 91

The Victims 93

Who's Michael Cummins? 93

Awaiting Trial - Death Penalty Sought 94

Shooting at University of North Carolina 94

A Deadly Day.. 95

Killed and Wounded 96

The Shooter.. 97

Charges Laid 98

On Trial 98

University Response to the Attack 99

Terrorist Attacks in Brief 99

Chapter 5: MAY 102

School Shooting in Douglas County 102

The Charter School 102

Gunmen Enter the School...102

Victims: All Students 103

The Teen Suspects 103

In Court 104

Memorials, Rallies and Vigils 104

Deadly Riots and Protests in Jakarta..................................... 105

What the Protests Were About 105

Three Days of Violence 106

The Injured and the Dead 107

The Aftermath 108

Deadly Riot in Acarigua Prison 108

Overpopulated Prisons 108

Rioting Inmates 109

Mass Casualties 109

Reactions and Criticism.. 110

Children Killed By Parents in Shiregreen................................. 110

Gut-wrenching Discovery.. 111

Parents Under Investigation.. 111

Guilty Pleas 113

Fatal Kawasaki Stabbings 113

Students Attacked 113

Suspect Commits Suicide 114

Those Who Were Killed 114

Unhappy Employee Opens Fire in Virginia Beach.................... 115

Angry Man on a Rampage... 115

The Loss of Many...116

DeWayne Antonio Craddock.................................116

Vigils and Aftermath 117

Terrorist Attacks in Brief 117

Chapter 6: JUNE..119

The Darwin Mass Shooting 119

Shooter on the Move..119

The Suspect...120

The Victims 120

Unknown Motive...120

Murder of David Ortiz - Wrong Place, Wrong Time.................121

Who Was David Ortiz?...121

Mistaken Identity 121

Investigation and Arrests 122

Messages of Love 124

The Killing of Actor Rafael Miguel 124

A Child Star...125

A Disapproving Father 125

Killer on the Run 125

Sobane Da Massacre 126

The Fulanis and the Dogon 126

Seven Hour Massacre 126

Suspects and Aftermath......................................127

Amhara Region coup d'état Attempt... 127

    History of Conflict.. 127

    The Attempt to Take Control 128

    The Aftermath... 129

Terrorist Attacks in Brief 129

Chapter 7: JULY 133

The Torrid Tale of Jeffrey Epstein 133

    Epstein's Background... 133

    Hidden Video Cameras 134

    First Criminal Cases... 135

    Human Trafficking Charges 138

    Investigation in France... 139

    Epstein's Controversial Death 139

    Investigation Into His Death and Autopsy Results 139

    Guards Charged.. 140

Tacoma Firebombing... 140

    Detention Center Attacked 141

    Suspect - Willem van Spronsen 141

    The Manifesto 141

Northern British Columbia Murder Spree............................... 142

    Details of the Murders.. 142

    Suspects' Car Located 143

    Bodies Discovered 143

Law Enforcement Response 144

Arson Attack of Kyoto Animation 144

Background of the Studio 144

Fiery Explosion 145

Mass Casualties and Deaths 145

Suspect Injured in the Attack 147

Response and Impact on Production 148

Kidnapping and Murder of Alexandra Măceşanu 149

The Abduction 149

Location Identified 150

An Arrest and Confession 150

Was He Covering for Someone Else? 151

Criticism of the Case 152

The Nganzai Funeral Attack 153

Mourners Attacked 153

Presidential Response 153

A History of Conflict 153

Multiple Shot at Gilroy Garlic Festival 154

Background of the Festival 154

A Lone Gunman 154

Three Killed in Shooting 155

Shooter Identified 155

Unknown Motive 156

Markham Home Massacre 156

    Family Massacred 157

    Zaman the Perpetrator 157

    Statement from Perfect World Void 158

Terrorist Attacks in Brief 158

Chapter 8: AUGUST 160

El Paso Walmart Mass Shooting 160

    Random Gunfire 160

    The Victims 161

    Charges Laid Against the Suspect 162

    Manifesto by Crusius 162

    Aftermath and Memorial 163

Two Hours of Terror in California 164

    The Killing Spree 164

    Suspect Apprehended 164

    'Not Guilty' Plea 165

    Cairo Bombing Kills Twenty 165

    Hospital Targeted 165

    Group Responsible for the Attack 166

    Previous Attacks 166

    Operation to Rid Egypt of Terrorists 167

Nine Shot and Killed in Dayton 167

    Firing Into the Crowd 167

Collateral Damage 168

The Gunman with a Disturbing Past 169

Further Investigation 169

Morogoro Tanker Looting and Explosion................170

Massive Lethal Explosion 170

Official Response 171

Foiled Plot to Kill a Prime Minister 171

First Attempts at Assassination 171

The Plot to Kill the Prime Minister........................171

Suspects on Trial..172

Taualai Leiloa Changes His Plea...........................172

Killer Chased and Pinned by a Chair in Sydney..........173

The Knife Attacks..173

Bystanders Chase and Capture Suspect..................173

The Victims 174

Mert Ney - the Suspect.....................................174

Coatzacoalcos Nightclub Fire 175

Setting it All on Fire 175

The Response..175

Cracking Down 176

Midland-Odessa Spree Shooting...........................177

Drive-By Shooting Spree 177

Perpetrator Identified.......................................178

Investigation into the Killings 178

Aftermath 179

Stabbing Spree in Lyon 180

Under Attack 180

Suspect's Confused Statement... 180

The Mayor's Response... 181

Terrorist Attacks in Brief 181

Chapter 9: SEPTEMBER... 184

Another Attack on Children in China 184

School Children Targeted.. 184

Suspect - No Clear Motive... 184

Students Unsafe 184

Murder of Kathleen Jo Henry 185

Who Was Kathleen Henry? 185

Suspect Identified by Photographs and Video..................... 186

Smith Charged with a Second Murder 186

Deadly Riots in Johannesburg 187

Riots Break Out 187

Truck Drivers on Strike.. 188

How Nations Responded 188

Sanmatenga Attacks 189

Militant Attacks 189

Sanmatenga Explosion and Gunfire.................................... 190

The Immediate Aftermath 190

Murder of Derk Wiersum..190

Background of Wiersum 190

Shot at Home 191

Finding the Suspect 191

Aftermath of the Lawyer's Murder..................................192

Responses and Reactions 193

Hwaseong Serial Murders 193

Multiple Rapes and Murders..193

Identification and Confession..195

Wrongful Conviction..196

Known Victims...196

Gracious David - West - Serial Killer................................198

Early Life of David-West..198

Nine Murders 198

Killer's Confession 199

David-West Goes on Trial 200

Changes His Plea 200

Man Opens Fire in Bar in South Carolina 200

Patrons Under Attack 200

An Earlier Dispute...200

Searching for the Killer..201

Suspect Apprehended 201

Terrorist Attacks in Brief...202

Chapter 10: OCTOBER.. 204

Stabbing Attack at Kuopio School in Finland........................... 204

The Attack.. 204

Suspect identified and Arrested 205

Students Fought Back 205

Aftermath 205

Stabbing at Police Headquarters in Paris 206

Attacked By a Colleague 206

The Suspect and the Investigation...................................... 206

Political Reaction 207

Murder of Devan Bracci-Selvey... 207

Child Killed in Front of Mother 208

Devan Bracci-Selvey.. 208

Teens Arrested 208

School Response... 209

Far-Right Shooting at Synagogue in Halle, Germany 209

Unable to Gain Entry 210

Investigating the Attack 211

Gunman Stephan Balliet 211

Court Appearance 212

Truck Full of Dead Migrants Discovered in the UK 212

The Dreadful Discovery.. 212

Arrest of Mo Robinson... 213

Identifying the Dead 213

Widespread Investigation 215

Child Charged with Five Murders 216

A Deadly Fire is Lit 216

The Victims 216

Little Boy Lost..217

Legalities of Charging a Child with Murder 217

Russian Soldier Shoots Ten Colleagues..................218

How the Attack Took Place 218

Those Killed and Injured 219

Investigation and Suspect 219

Mental Health Motive 219

Contents of Serial Killer Ivan Milat's Final Letter......220

The Backpacker Killer..220

Terminal Illness and Death................................221

Milat's Final Letter...221

The Letter in Full..221

Orlinda Mass Shooting 222

Airbnb House Party...222

Multiple Gunshots Fired 223

The Investigation 223

The Response 223

Terrorist Attacks in Brief 224

Chapter 11: NOVEMBER 227

LeBarón Family Massacre 227

    A Religious Community 227

    Two Attacks on Three Vehicles 228

    Victims and Survivors 228

    Investigation into Criminal Cartel 229

    Response 230

Another School Shooting in California 230

    Student Shoots at Fellow Students 230

    First on the Scene 231

    The Casualties 231

    Shooter Had Turned 16 the Same Day 231

    Investigating Berhow 232

    Response and Aftermath 232

Fresno Football Party Shooting 233

    A Deadly Gathering 233

    Those Killed and Injured 233

    Unknown Identities, Unknown Motive 234

Dresden Royal Jewelry Heist 234

    The Green Vault Museum 234

    A Clever Plan 235

    Precious Pieces Stolen 235

    Still Under Investigation 236

Hyderabad Gang Rape and Murder..237

    A Violent and Abhorrent Attack 237

    Four Men Arrested 237

    Executed in Police Custody 238

    Second Body Found 238

    Local and Global Response 238

Stabbing on London Bridge......................................239

    Prisoner Rehabilitation Conference......................239

    Killer Khan Unleashes Terror.................................239

    Innocent Victims..240

    Usman Khan and Terrorism 240

The Hague Stabbing Attack.......................................241

    A Violent Spree..241

    Suspect Arrested 242

    Is There a Possible Link to the Earlier London Attack?..........242

Terrorist Attacks in Brief 242

Chapter 12: DECEMBER..245

Ten People Fired Upon in New Orleans 245

    Public Shooting..245

    Unknown Perpetrator...245

    Mayor's Response 246

Shooting at Pearl Harbor 246

    A Historical Place 246

U.S. Sailor Turns Killer 247

Unknown Motive 247

Robbery, Chase and Shootout in Miramar 247

Robbery of the Jewelry Store 248

Deadly Shootout 248

Victims 248

Perpetrators 249

Officers Stood Down 249

Family Response 250

Gunman Opens Fire at Naval Air Station Pensacola 250

Under Fire 250

Those Who Were Shot 250

The Gunman is Identified 251

New Jersey Mass Shooting 251

Shootings Begin 252

The Killed and the Injured 252

Suspects Identified 252

Hate Crime 253

The Aftermath 253

Gunman Takes Aim in Hospital Waiting Room 253

The Last Thing Anyone Expected 254

Police Arrive Within Three Minutes of Emergency Call 254

The Gunman 255

The Murder of Tessa Majors 255

    Fatal Robbery 255

    Investigation and Suspects 256

    Tessa Rane Majors 256

    The Aftermath 257

Hanukkah Stabbing in Monsey 257

    Background of Monsey 257

    Attack on Rabbi's House 257

    Suspect - Grafton E. Thomas 258

    Under Investigation 259

    Legal Proceedings 259

    Political Impact 260

West Freeway Church of Christ Shooting 260

    An Unexpected Shooting 260

    The Gunman 261

    Reaction 262

Terrorist Attacks in Brief 262

Conclusion 265

More Books by Jack Rosewood 266

Introduction

As each year passes, it's getting harder to ignore the level of violence, chaos, and crime that's presently besieging the world at an alarmingly increasing pace. School shootings are still tragically occurring, especially in America, and it seems that the message is still being lost. Perhaps they should be talking more to the students themselves to identify the issues before they escalate?

Mass killings have been a fairly regular occurrence in 2019, and there are many mentioned in this book. Michael Cummins, the family killer, the shooting at Pearl Harbor, and the deadly nightclub attack in Mexico are amongst the most terrifying. They serve as stark reminders that mass murders can happen anywhere at any time.

The most horrific event that occurred in 2019 was the mosque shootings in Christchurch, New Zealand. Never before had this country experience terrorism rock its core like it did in March. One man, numerous weapons, and a disturbing sense of beliefs ravaged the innocent while they prayed, and killed fifty-one people. Frighteningly, this event seemed to inspire a number of other terrorist attacks throughout the world, including France, England, and Europe.

Inside you'll also find information about the celebrities that have made major crime headlines - Jeffrey Epstein and R. Kelly. Both powerful men in their own right were charged with sex crimes. In today's world, we are becoming more alert and more men like these are no longer able to hide.

Robberies, a massive jewel heist, and the capture of serial killers, all have a place in this book. The tragic story of the young boy stabbed to death in front of his mother will tug at your heartstrings. And the truly horrific massacres that are taking place in African and Middle Eastern countries will make you realize how lucky you are.

Chapter 1:
JANUARY

Bottrop and Essen Car Attack

A car was deliberately driven into crowds of people in Bottrop and Essen on December 31, 2018, and January 1, 2019. Eight people were injured in the attacks. At first, it was thought to be a terrorist attack, but it became clear that the suspect had a mental illness.

Sidewalk Terror

The first attack was a near miss: the suspect was driving his silver Mercedes vehicle directly at a man who managed to avoid being hit. A few minutes later, the suspect then rammed his vehicle straight into a crowd at the Berliner Platz, Bottrop. Two men, a woman and a child, were struck and injured.

The suspect then drove to Essen and attempted to drive into a group of people who were waiting at a bus stop. He was stopped by police and arrested.

The Injured

Eight people in total were injured in the attacks, including a family from Syria. The family was comprised of the father, 48, the mother, 46, who was critically injured, and two daughters, 16 and 17. A Syrian boy, 4, and a woman, 29, from Afghanistan were also wounded.

The Suspect

During questioning by police, the suspect made several comments against foreigners. His name wasn't released, but the suspect, 50, had a history of mental illness. He'd no known ties to any extremist groups and hadn't been in contact with police prior to these attacks.

Tension in Germany

There has been increasing tension in Germany in recent years due to an influx of foreign asylum seekers entering Germany from Afghanistan, Syria, and Iraq. There have been a number of violent incidents that have escalated the high level of mistrust and friction between the Germans and the immigrants.

Children Attacked at A Primary School in China

In a disturbing attack, 20 young primary school children were attacked by a man wielding a hammer on January 8, 2019 in Beijing. Although violent attacks aren't common in Beijing, the number of incidences of violent attacks on children throughout China are increasing.

The Attack

On the morning of Tuesday, January 8, 2019, an angry man with a hammer decided to inflict his rage on innocent school children at a Beijing primary school. He struck numerous children: 20 required hospital treatment. Three of the children suffered serious injuries.

The suspect was quickly apprehended by police. While they conducted their investigation at the tragedy's site, anxious parents waited outside the school. One parent expressed concern about the impact on her child, "Even though they were on the same floor as the one where this took place, they didn't know anything about this. So I really don't want this information to be spread widely, so that he starts to feel scared."

Unnamed Suspect

The suspect has remained unnamed in the media, but he'd previously worked at the school. The 49-year-old man had been a maintenance worker at the school until his contract wasn't renewed. It's believed this was the trigger behind his anger. He was originally from northeastern Heilongjiang province.

Similar Attacks

In recent times there have been a number of attacks targeting children, involving axes, knives, and other weapons.

Twelve children were stabbed by a man wielding a kitchen knife in southern Guangxi Zhuang in January 2017. He was recently executed for the crime.

In April 2018, nine schoolchildren were killed on their way home from school by a 28-year-old man with a knife. The killer claimed that when he formerly had attended the school, He'd been bullied. He was executed in September for the crime.

Another attack occurred in late 2018 when a woman with a knife attacked 14 children at a kindergarten in south-western Sichuan province.

Nevada Killing Spree

A series of murders occurred in western Nevada after an intruder broke into homes of elderly people, robbed them, and then brutally killed them. For days the local people resided in fear until a manhunt by police finally led to the suspect's arrest.

Home Invasion Murders

On January 10, Connie Koontz, 56, was found dead in her home in Gardnerville. Jewelry had been stolen during the murder. The next victim was found just a mile from Koontz's residence. The body of Sophia Renken was found in her home in Gardnerville on January 13. She'd been shot to death.

On January 16, the bodies of couple Gerald, 81, and Sharon David, 80, were found in their house in Reno.

Finding the Killer Through Technology

The killer could have escaped even longer if it hadn't been for an Apple watch he stole from Koontz. Police tracked the killer for nine days using the watch. The killer, Wilber Ernesto Martinez-Guzman, had given the watch to a woman who then tried to connect a digital account to the watch. She was living with Martinez-Guzman at the time.

Police went to the location of the watch in Carson City. After surveilling the home of Martinez-Guzman and his mother, they followed him to a gun store and worried that he was going to purchase guns. In turn, they arrested him on January 19.

Who is Wilber?

Martinez-Guzman was just 19 years old when he committed the robberies and murders. He'd only been living in Carson City for about a year, and he was a citizen of El Salvador. He was arrested initially on charges of two counts of burglary, possession of stolen property and obtaining money under false pretenses.

In Custody

Martinez-Guzman was most likely in the U.S. illegally and was detained under an immigration hold. Because the crimes occurred in two counties, he'll be charged and tried in each county. On January 23, he made his first appearance in court to face the initial charges.

In court in February, he waived his right to a preliminary hearing. Subsequently, the judge approved for Martinez-Guzman to be transferred to Washoe County for four murder charges. The trial for the burglary and stolen property charges in Carson City was put on hold while he faces the more serious charges of murder.

The trial for the murders is expected to start in April 2020. The prosecution has already stated they'll seek the death penalty.

According to a detective during the Grand Jury hearing in March, Martinez-Guzman had claimed he committed the murders and the robberies because he wanted money to buy crystal meth.

The Assassination of Pawel Adamowicz

On January 13, while on stage at the Great Orchestra of Christmas Charity event in Gdańsk, Poland, Pawel Adamowicz was stabbed through the heart and later died in hospital. The perpetrator was quickly apprehended at the scene, after making statements over the microphone about false imprisonment and torture. The whole event was captured on video.

Politician, Mayor and Lawyer

In 1988, Adamowicz had been the head of the strike committee. In 1990, he was elected to the City Council in Gdańsk and chaired the council from 1994 until 1998. He became the Mayor in 1998, and in 2002 he was reelected. Adamowicz was known to be a progressive and liberal figure who supported immigration, minority groups, and LGBT rights.

He'd been married since 1999 to Magdalena Abranska, a fellow law student he had met while attending law school. She went on to become a law professor at the university. They had two daughters, born in 2003 and 2010.

The Assassination

While Adamowicz was on the podium at the event, the perpetrator launched himself onto the podium and directly at Adamowicz. He stabbed

Adamowicz multiple times before turning to face the crowd with his arms raised in the air in triumph. Security guards quickly tackled him, but not before he'd managed to shout out over the microphone that he'd previously been falsely imprisoned and tortured.

Adamowiccz was resuscitated by paramedics before he was rushed to the nearby hospital for treatment. He survived five hours of surgery but remained in a critical condition. He'd been stabbed in the heart and had stab wounds to his abdominal organs and his diaphragm. The following day, Adamowicz died from his injuries.

Caught Red-Handed

Because the perpetrator had been arrested at the scene, there was no denying he was the one responsible for assassinating Adamowicz. He was named as Stefan W., 27, but his full name wasn't released. He had an extensive criminal history, including attacking a police officer and four bank robberies.

Reactions and Vigils

Vigils took place across Poland on January 14, attended by thousands of people. President Andrzej Duda announced that a national day of mourning would occur on the day of the funeral.

EU Council President Donald Tusk made a statement: "Paweł Adamowicz, Mayor of Gdańsk, a man of Solidarity and freedom, a European, my good friend, has been murdered. May he rest in peace."

A minute of silence was held by the European Parliament to honor Adamowicz. The Mayor of London, Sadiq Khan, described the assassination as "devastating violence."

The Mayor of Prague appealed to the city council on January 17 for a street in Prague to be named in honor of Adamowicz, and on June 5, a promenade was officially named after Adamowicz.

The Funeral Service

Bearing the Gdańsk flag and decorated with white flowers, the hearse carrying Adamowicz's coffin was driven past significant landmarks in Adamowicz's life on January 18. The funeral was broadcast and watched by thousands of people. His coffin was transported to the Church of St. Mary, and following a mass, Adamowicz was cremated. His ashes were then laid to rest in one of the chapels.

His funeral was attended by several notable people, including:

- President of the European Council Donald Tusk
- President of Poland Andrzej Duda
- Prime Minister of Poland Mateusz Morawiecki
- Lech Wałęsa- former President of Poland, communist oppositionist and Nobel Peace Prize winner
- Former Polish Presidents Aleksander Kwaśniewski and Bronisław Komorowski
- Former German President Joachim Gauck

Attack on the Nairobi DusitD2 Complex

On January 15 and 16, a terrorist attack on the DusitD2 complex in the Westlands area of Nairobi resulted in the deaths of more than twenty people.

Background

Al-Shabaab, an Islamist militant group, has vehemently opposed involvement by Kenya in the Somalian civil war. There had been a previous serious attack in Westlands in 2013, during with the shopping mall at Westgate was attacked, leaving 67 people dead. Another attack in 2015 at Garissa University College resulted in the deaths of 147 students.

The DusitD2 complex is an upscale hotel and office complex. Inside the complex also houses the Commission on Revenue Allocation.

Under Attack

On January 15, 2019, attackers arrived at the complex in two vehicles, and it's uncertain whether there were four or six of the attackers. One of them, a suicide bomber, went near the Secret Garden Restaurant and detonated his explosives. Following the explosion, guards at the gates of the complex were forced by the attackers to let them in. The attackers shot at the guards and threw grenades at them as they entered.

In response, the anti-terrorism unit of the Kenya Police, the Recce Company, was sent in to combat the attackers. They were joined by private security groups, off duty police officers, and unarmed individuals. At the time, a British SAS soldier was conducting training in the country, and he also assisted with the response to the attackers.

The security detail of the Australian High Commission also fired at the terrorists as they entered the complex, injuring one of the attackers. Explosions and gunfire exchanges were heard until the early hours of the following day, January 16, 2019.

As a result of the attack, 21 civilians were killed, along with 5 of the attackers.

Victims Named:

- James Oduor, 34
  Killed on the eve of his birthday. Avid soccer player.

- Bernadette Konjalo, 31
  Manager at the Dusit Hotel

- Jason Spindler, 40
  Managing director of I-DEV International, a global consulting company.

- Feisal Ahmed, 31
  Employee at Adam Smith International a global project management company

- Abdalla Dahir, 33
  Employee at Adam Smith International, a global project management company

- Luke Potter, 40
  Africa Program's Director at the Gatsby Charitable Foundation

- Jeremiah Mbaria, 31
  Head of Hub, Cellulant

- Kelvin Gitonga, 28
  Hub Engineer, Cellulant

- Ashford Kuria, 31
  Head of Product Development, Cellulant

- Wilfred Kareithi, 23
  Implementation Engineer, Global Delivery Team, Cellulant

- John Ndiritu, 29
  Quality Assurance Tester, Cellulant

- Denis Mwaniki, 29
  Head of Information Security, Cellulant

- Japhet Ndunguja Nuru, 28
  Police officer who belonged to the General Service Unit

- Beatrice Mutua
  Personal assistant to general manager

- Erickson Mogaka, 30
  Chief Chef

- Trufosa Nyaboke
  Executive Housekeeper

- Dedricks Lemisi
  Security Officer

- Zachary Nyambwaga
  Security Officer

- UNNAMED AUSTRALIAN

Claim of responsibility

Immediately after the attack, Al-Shabaab claimed responsibility. They released a statement, claiming the attack was in response to President Donald Trump's "decision to recognize Jerusalem as the capital of Israel."

On January 19, five people accused of assisting in the attack appeared in court.

Bogotá Car Bombing

The General Santander National Police Academy in Bogotá, Colombia, was struck by a truck on January 17, 2019. The truck exploded, and numerous people were killed and injured. It isn't common for a suicide bombing to occur in Colombia, but it was the first terrorist attack in the capital since 2017.

The Conflict Behind the Scenes

The conflict in Colombia began in 1964, though there have been violent incidences tracing back to the Thousand Day's War at the end of the 19th century. In the midst of ongoing conflict, several key factions are involved: the National Liberation Army, the ELN, and the Revolutionary Armed Forces of Colombia, FARC. In 2016, a peace deal was brokered with the FARC and attacks have occurred less frequently.

Bombs Detonated

On January 17 at 9:30 am, a 1993 Nissan Patrol vehicle laden with 180 lbs. of pentolite was driven on to the campus of the General Santander National Police Academy after a passenger was left at a bus stop nearby.

The driver had entered the campus by using a side street that was usually used to deliveries to the campus.

During the entry to the campus, an explosives detection dog signaled that the vehicle was carrying explosive materials. At that point, the driver forced his way through the security checkpoint, striking security guards in the process. The truck stopped near the dormitories of the female students and detonated.

Authorities were unable to determine whether the bomb was detonated by the driver of the truck or the person who had been left at the bus stop. The driver was identified as José Aldemar Rojas Rodríguez, 57. He'd been involved in a previous bombing, during which he'd lost his hand. He'd allegedly been involved with ELN for 30 years and had served as intelligence chief for them. It was believed he' been teaching the construction of explosives to guerilla militants in Venezuela since 2011.

Records showed that in May 2018, Rojas had purchased the same vehicle used in the bombing at the police academy.

The Investigation and Responsibility Claimed

The identity of the bomber was further proven using fingerprints from his only hand and security camera footage to be Rojas. A day after the bombing, a second person was arrested in Bogotá, for his involvement in the bombing. He was identified as Ricardo Carvajal, and authorities were lead to him after intercepting a phone call he made during which he'd confessed to being involved in the bombing. When interrogated, he denied any involvement.

The authorities are still looking for other potential suspects that participated. Despite the ELN not claiming responsibility, which it has done in the past for other incidences, the authorities still believe they were behind the planning and undertaking of the bombing.

As a result, the peace dialogue between the Colombian government and

ELN leaders was officially halted by President Iván Duque Márquez on January 18.

Later the ELN claimed they were responsible for the attack, saying it was in retaliation for the ceasefire not being honored by the Colombian government, as ELN camps were still being attacked.

International Responses

Those that were killed and wounded came from a variety of counties, including the U.S., Ecuador, and Panama.

The Cuban foreign ministry stated: "Cuba will act with strict respect for the Protocols of Dialogue and Peace signed by the Government and the ELN, including the Protocol in Case of a Rupture in Negotiations."

The President of Ecuador Lenín Moreno announced the Vice President Otto Sonnenholzner was to be dispatched to Bogotá, along with the family members of Erika Chicó, a cadet who was killed during the attack.

The bombing was condemned by the U.S. and offered help by the U.S. Embassy to investigate the attack.

Mass Shooting in Sebring Bank

A gunman entered the SunTrust Bank in Sebring, Florida on January 23, and opened fire. Four employees and a customer were killed, all of whom were women. The suspect turned himself in to police.

How It Unfolded

When the gunmen entered the bank, he instructed all inside to lie face down on the floor. He then he approached each woman and shot them in the back of the head. All five women were killed.

After they were all dead, the gunman placed a telephone call to the police, explaining what he'd done. He identified himself as Zephen Xaver, 21, and waited for police to arrive.

Barricaded Within

Xaver stayed on the phone with the police. While he waited for them, he barricaded himself inside the bank. He told police he was wearing a bulletproof vest and was armed with a handgun. He refused to leave the bank so police used an armored vehicle to ram the doors of the bank, which were glass.

When police entered the bank, they found the five women deceased in the lobby. Each had been shot in the head and in the back. They then located Xaver in an office at the back of the bank and took him into custody.

One bank employee, who had been in the break room when Xaver entered the bank, managed to escape through the back door and was the only survivor.

Those Who Were Killed

The victims of the shooting were identified as:

- Debra Cook, 54
- Marisol Lopez, 55
- Jessica Montague, 31
- Ana Piñon-Williams, 37
- Cynthia Watson, 65 - customer

Background of the Killer

Xaver had been a former correctional officer trainee with the Florida Department of Corrections. He'd been training at the Avon Park Correctional Institution but resigned on January 9, 2019.

Behind Bars

Xaver is being held in custody awaiting trial for five counts of murder. Because of his lack of finances, he has a public defender appointed to him.

A not guilty plea was entered on February 22, and the prosecution is going to seek the death penalty.

Xaver didn't know any of the victims inside the bank and had no connection to that branch of the SunTrust bank. He hadn't planned to rob the bank, and it seems like he simply wanted to kill people.

Louisiana Mass Murder

Suspect Dakota Theriot allegedly killed three people and his parents in the Livingston and Ascension parishes in Louisiana on January 26, 2019.

Murderous Rampage

Theriot had been living with his girlfriend's family for a few weeks after his parents had kicked him out of their house. On January 26, he shot and killed Billy Ernest, 43, Summer Ernest, 20, and Tanner Ernest, 17, in Livingston Parish. Two young children from the home, aged 7 years and 1 year, managed to escape unharmed and alerted the neighbors who then called emergency services.

After stealing a truck, Theriot drove to the home of his parents, Keith and Elizabeth, in Ascension parish. He shot them both before fleeing, thinking they were dead. His father Keith, however, was able to call the police. When, they arrived at the house, both Keith and Elizabeth were still alive. Sadly they later died in hospital, but not before they identified their son, Theriot, as the shooter.

All of the victims had been shot in the face or head.

Dakota Theriot

Theriot had come into contact with law enforcement previously and had spent some time in mental health facilities involuntarily. He reported he heard voices' and at some point, he'd threatened to burn down his parent's house. According to Theriot's ex-wife, he was diagnosed as schizophrenic. She claimed he was abusive and had sought a protective order. He allegedly had broken her wrist, thrown her through a window, choked, slapped, and punched her during their relationship.

His ex-wife was unable to prove the abuse, so the temporary order of protection was dissolved.

Charges Laid

After chasing him for a day, Virginia State Police in Richmond County were able to locate Theriot at his grandmother's home in Warsaw. When they arrived, he was standing in the driveway and said he'd driven there to say goodbye to his grandmother and two aunts. He was subsequently extradited back to Louisiana.

Theriot was charged with two counts of first-degree murder and home invasion and three counts of first-degree murder in Livingston Parish. At a court hearing in March, he entered a plea of not guilty for all charges.

Theriot's lawyers requested the legal proceedings be halted until a source of funding could be identified as they'd been working for Theriot pro bono.

Bombings of Jolo Cathedral

Two bombs were detonated on January 27 at the Roman Catholic Cathedral of Our Lady of Mount Carmel in Jolo, Sulu, Philippines. The explosions killed 20 and an additional 102 were injured. The Islamic State claimed responsibility, which led. to the President of the Philippines, Rodrigo Duterte, to issue a war against Abu Sayyaf.

Leading Up To The Attack

On January 21, an autonomous plebiscite was held for the creation of Bangsamoro Autonomous Region, which would include the capital city of Sulu Province, Jolo. Abu Sayyaf group, ASG, had Jolo as its stronghold. The proposed government of Bangsamoro has plans to crack down on local private armies and decommission of their weapons.

The Bombings

At 8:28 A.M. January 27, the first bomb exploded inside the cathedral. Two minutes later, a second bomb was detonated in the parking area of the Cathedral as the 35th Infantry Battalion troops were responding to the first bombing.

The strategy of targeting first responders with the second bomb was similar to the attacks in Bali in 2002. The goal was to cause further casualties as emergency services responded. Authorities deemed that the bombs were detonated by a mobile phone with a triggering device, which was found near the site of the explosions. The bombs themselves were ammonium nitrate pipe bombs.

Named Victims:

Armed Forces of the Philippines:

- Sergeant Mark Des P. Simbre (Inf) PA- from San Isidro, Isabela
- Corporal John B. Mangawit, Jr. (Inf) PA- from Kalinga
- Corporal Minard Jann P. Ocier (Inf) PA- from Barangay Managok, Malaybalay City, Bukidnon
- Private First Class Alizon L. Ayoman (Inf) PA- from Kolambugan, Lanao del Norte
- Private Hernan U. Bulaybulay (Inf) PA- from Pagadian City
- Private Leomar P. Degumbis(Inf) PA- from Iligan City

Philippine Coast Guard:

- SN2 Jaypee M. Galicha PCG

Civilians:

- Leo Herbolario
- Bibing Perpetua

- Reynaldo Pescadera, Sr.
- Ridzmar Mukadil
- Romolo B. Reyes
- Albacora Perpetua
- Niseria Dela Cruz
- Cecilia Sanchez
- Daisy P. Delos Reyes
- Dolores S. Tan
- Fe Non
- Juliet Jaime
- Leah Angelica Reyes
- Chenly Rubio

Identifying the Suspects

Responsibility for the bombings was claimed by the Islamic State, who cited the bombings were undertaken by "two knights of martyrdom." The military believed the ASG was responsible because they'd previously intercepted intelligence that the ASG had planned to bomb other areas of Jolo earlier. The prime suspect was the brother of a killed leader of ASG, Kamah. Another prime suspect was Hatib Hajan Sawadjaan, a sub-leader of the ASG.

On February 1, the suicide bombers were identified as Abu Huda and his wife. Abu Huda had carried out the suicide bomb that went off secondly, while his wife was believed to have ignited the first suicide bomb inside the cathedral.

Kamah and four accomplices surrendered to police on February 4. Those accomplices were Rajan Bakil Gadjali, Albaji Kisae Gadjali, Salit Alih, and Kaisar Bakil Gadjali. Murder charges were filed against Kamah and the four accomplices, as well as 14 other accomplices who have yet to be apprehended.

Two further suspects were identified in July, as Rullie Rian Zeke and his wife Ulfah Handayani Saleh from Makassar, South Sulawesi. They'd traveled to the Philippines from Malaysia.

Charges Laid

Kamah denied having in part in the bombings and entered a plea of not guilty on all counts. However, according to eyewitness accounts, the prosecution maintained there was enough evidence for Kamah to be indicted for the murder charges, along with the accomplices.

Presidential Response

Soon after the bombings occurred, the palace of President Duterte released a statement that the perpetrators would receive no mercy. The spokesperson expressed, "We will pursue to the ends of the earth the ruthless perpetrators behind this dastardly crime until every killer is brought to justice and put behind bars. The law will give them no mercy."

The president ordered an 'all-out war' directive against terror groups, and the city of Jolo was placed on total lockdown.

Widespread Reaction

Murad Ebrahim, the chairman of the Moro Islamic Liberation Front (MILF), confirmed: "The MILF leadership joined peace-loving individuals in strongly condemning the twin bombing of the Cathedral." The peace panel chairman of MILF Mohagher Iqbal condemned the bombings, referring to the incident as senseless violence.

A statement was released by the Catholic Bishops' Conference of the Philippines who expressed sympathy for the victims and their families. They called for Christians to join with indigenous communities and Muslims to advocate for peace.

Pope Francis stated, "My strongest condemnation for this episode of violence that once again strikes this Christian community. I raise my prayers for the dead and wounded. May the Lord, prince of peace, convert the hearts of the violent and give the inhabitants of that region a peaceful coexistence".

Terrorist Attacks in Brief

January 1

Barsalogho Department, Burkina Faso: Ethnic clashes and jihadist attacks resulted in the deaths of 49 people.

January 15

Nairobi, Kenya: At least one suicide bomber stormed the luxury complex DusitD2 hotel in Nairobi and detonated his explosives. Several gunmen took hostages and attacked the hotel with firearms. At least 21 people were killed, including a British and an American citizen; 28 other people were injured and five attackers also died.

January 16

Manbij, Syria: A suicide bomb attack by ISIL caused 19 deaths, including four U.S. military personnel.

January 17

Bogota, Colombia: In the Colombian capital city of Bogotà, 20 people were killed, and 68 others were injured when a car entered a police school compound. When it was stopped by guards at a checkpoint, the driver accelerated and hit a wall, and the car exploded

January 21

Maidan Shar, Afghanistan; Taliban attack by suicide bombing and shooting on a military checkpoint killed 126 security personnel and injuries to approximately 70 others.

January 27

Jolo, Philippines: 22 people, were killed and 102 others were injured when two bombs exploded in a cathedral during Sunday mass in Jolo, Philippines. The Islamic State-related branch of Abu Sayyaf terror group, the Ajang Ajang faction, was behind the attack.

January 29

Loralai, Pakistan: Suicide bombers and gunmen attacked a Deputy Inspector General's office, killing 9 and injuring 22 Tehrik-i-Taliban claimed responsibility for the attack.

Chapter 2:
FEBRUARY

Fatal Arson in Paris

A fire raged through an apartment block on Rue Erlanger on February 5, tragically killing 10 and injuring a further 36 people. To make matters worse, police were quick to identify the fire as the result of arson that someone had deliberately lit that took so many lives.

Deliberate Torching

Earlier in the day, police had been called to the apartment building due to a domestic incident. They found a woman arguing with her neighbor who happened to be an ex-firefighter; and after the neighbor had left, police officers made a note that they were concerned about leaving her in the apartment building, but they left anyway. When the neighbor returned, the woman had vandalized his door and piled wood and paper against it. She confronted the neighbor saying, "So you're a firefighter? Here's a fire."

The fire was reported at about 1:00 A.M., and when the firefighters arrived, several floors were on fire. They immediately began evacuating as many as they could from the 9 story building, but the stairwells were obstructed by flames and smoke. Over 50 people had been unable to escape without assistance and were trapped. Ladders were used by firefighters to rescue them.

A total of 250 firefighters responded to the fire, and by 7:00 A.M., it had been extinguished. By that time, though, 10 had been killed, and 36 injured, including 6 of the firefighters. The area was described as a "scene of incredible violence" by firefighters. They had to complete more than 30 rooftop rescues as residents of the building fled to nearby building roofs.

Criminal Investigation

An investigation into the arson was initiated immediately. The fire had been started at the rear of the apartment building, which prevented the use of mechanical ladders from fire trucks due to the spread of the fire on the lower floors. The fire was the most violent on the bottom two floors, where the fire had been started.

Police arrested the woman who had been fighting with her neighbor near the burned building. She was intoxicated at the time. Investigators found that she'd been previously institutionalized in a psychiatric facility for several years and had only been released on January 23. She was charged with arson and murder.

Paris in Mourning

A month prior to the tragic fire, an explosion had occurred at a bakery that killed 4 people. Along with the fire, these two events highlighted a problem with the infrastructure in Paris in relation to fire. The Mayor of Paris Ann Hidalgo, announced that Paris was in mourning. French President Emmanuel Macron declared France had "woken up to tragedy."

Kaduna State Massacre

Just hours before the Nigerian general election, on February 10, more than 100 people were killed in a massacre in Kaduna.

A Turbulent Background

Political and civil turbulence had been boiling since the death of the leader of the Adara people, the Agom Adara III, HRH Dr. Maiwada Raphael Galadima. In October 2018, Galadima was kidnapped and held for ransom by the Fulani. Although the ransom was paid, Galadima was murdered anyway. That December, the state government divided the largely Christian chiefdom, creating two emirates. This angered the Adara people who refuted the Fulani from having any power due to their small population in the area.

Revenge By Massacre?

The attack began on February 10, resulting in 141 deaths, comprised of 130 Fulani and 11 Adara. However, Miyetti Allah, a Fulani group, estimated the numbers at 131 Fulani dead, 66 bodies recovered and another 65 missing. The Adara deaths supposedly occurred when Fulani gunmen launched an attack of Ungwar Bardi. In response, the Adara militia attacked Fulani settlements.

It was believed that the attacks were performed as revenge attacks following the violence that had occurred in October 2018. During that attack, approximately 55 were killed during clashes between Christians and Muslims in Kasuwan Magani, Kajuru. Of those killed, 11 were women and 22 were children.

In an attack in Karamai on February 26, 20 people were reportedly killed. This was suspected as a result of the Fulani retaliation against the previous attacks on their settlements. The death toll rose to 40 a few days later.

Aftermath

On March 18, a report by the Coalition Against Kajuru killings claimed 130 people had been killed due to revenge attacks for the massacre

Khash-Zahedan Suicide Bombing

A suicide bomb was detonated on the Khash-Zahedan road in Sistan and Baluchestan Province in Iran on February 13. The blast killed 27 Revolutionary Guards, and 13 more were injured. It was one of the worst terrorist attacks for years in Iran.

Iran's Revolutionary Guards

The Revolutionary Guards were formed to defend the Islamic system of Iran and acted as a counterweight to the country's regular forces. It was believed to be comprised of 125,000 troops and encompassed Special Forces, air force, navy, intelligence, and ground forces.

The Guards were allegedly stationed in embassies all over the globe to conduct intelligence operations. It also organized arms shipments and training camps for militant groups.

Suicide Bombing

A bus carrying personnel was targeted by the suicide bomber near the border of Pakistan. This particular area was often a refuge for drug smugglers and militant separatist groups. The soldiers on board the bus were returning after conducting a border mission when the car bomb was detonated.

Claim of Responsibility

A group connected to Al Qaeda, Jaish al-Adl, claimed responsibility for the suicide bomb attack. According to the commander of the Senior Revolutionary Guards, the bomber was a Pakistani, and the planner of the attack was also a Pakistani. Three other militant cell members were Iranian: and of those three, two were apprehended.

Reactions to the Attack

Mohammad Ali Jafari, the Iranian Major General, alleged that Israel and the U.S. had ordered the United Arab Emirates and Saudi Arabia to deliver the suicide bombing. He asked Pakistan to clamp down on Jaish al-Adl before revenge was sought by Tehran. Pakistan offered to cooperate in the bombing investigation.

Foreign Minister of Iran, Mohammad Javad Zarif, claimed it was linked to an ongoing U.S. sponsored Middle East meeting in Warsaw. He tweeted: "Is it no coincidence that Iran is hit by terror on the very day that

#WarsawCircus begins? Especially when cohorts of same terrorists cheer it from Warsaw streets & support it with twitter bots?"

Hassan Rouhani, the Iranian president, also insisted that the U.S. and Israel were behind the suicide bombing attack.

Overall, the U.S., Israel, and Pakistan were all blamed by various political heads in Iran.

Day of Mourning

The day after the attack, the bodies of the men killed were flown to Isfahan. There, the families and media were waiting. The Iranian media covered the mourning ceremony, and interviews with victims' families were broadcast across social media.

Pulwama Convoy Attack

A convoy of vehicles was attacked on the Jammu Srinagar National Highway on February 14. The vehicles were carrying security personnel, and 40 were killed by the suicide bomber. An Islamist militant group was quick to claim responsibility, and the bomber was swiftly identified. As a result, India blamed Pakistan, but Pakistan denied connection to the attack and condemned the action.

Behind the Conflict

Pakistan-based militants have increasingly conducted suicide attacks in Kashmir since 2015. These attacks have been aimed at the Indian security forces. In July 2015, they attacked a police station and a bus in Gurdaspur. Gunmen attacked the Pathankot Air Force Station in early 2016. That same year, another attack occurred in Pampore, and an Indian Army brigade headquarters was attacked, resulting in the deaths of 19 soldiers. Militants attacked the Commando Training Center at Lethpora in December 2017, thus killing five. Many of the attacks occurred close to the Jammu Srinagar National Highway.

Multiple People Killed

On the day of the attack, February 14, 78 vehicles were in convoy transporting 2,500 Central Reserve Police Force personnel to Srinagar from Jammu. The highway had been closed for two days, so there were more personnel being transported than normal. They'd left in the early hours and were expected to reach Jammu before the sunset.

A bus in convoy was rammed by a vehicle laden with explosives at Lethpora. The explosion killed at least 40 and many others were injured.

Released victims' names included the following:

Jammu sector:

- Naseer Ahmad (Jammu and Kashmir)
- Jaimal Singh (Punjab)
- Sukhjinder Singh (Punjab)
- Tilak Raj (Himachal Pradesh)
- Rohitash Lamba (Rajasthan)

Srinagar Sector:

- Vijay Soreng (Jharkhand)
- Vasantha Kumar VV (Kerala)
- Subramaniam G (Tamil Nadui)
- Manoja Kumar Behera (Odisha)
- GD Guru H (Karnataka)
- Narayan Lal Gurjar (Rajasthan)
- Mahesh Kumar (Uttar Pradesh)
- Pradeep Kumar (Uttar Pradesh)
- Hemraj Meena (Rajasthan)
- PK Sahoo (Odisha)
- Ramesh Yadav (Uttar Pradesh)
- Sanjay Rajput (Maharashtra)
- Koushal Kumar Rawat (Uttar Pradesh)

- Pradeep Singh (Uttar Pradesh)
- Shyam Babu (Uttar Pradesh)
- Ajit Kumar Azad (Uttar Pradesh)
- Maninder Singh Attri (Punjab)
- Bablu Santra (West Bengal)
- Ashvni Kumar Kaochi (Madhya Pradesh)
- Rathod Nitin Shivaji (Maharashtra)
- Bhagirathi Singh (Rajasthan)
- Virendra Singh (Uttarakhand)
- Awadhesh Kumar Yadav (Uttar Pradesh)
- Ratan Kumar Thakur (Bihar)
- Kankaj Kumar Tripathi (Uttar Pradesh)
- Jeet Ram (Rajasthan)
- Amit Kumar (Uttar Pradesh)
- Vijay Kr. Mourya (Uttar Pradesh)
- Kulwinder Singh (Punjab)
- Maneswar Bsumatari (Assam)
- Mohan Lal (Uttarakhand)
- Sanjay Kumar Sinha (Bihar)
- Ram Vakeel (Uttar Pradesh)

Investigation and the Perpetrator

The militant group Jaish-e-Mohammed claimed responsibility for the attack and released a video showing the suicide bomber. He was identified as Adil Ahmad Dar, 22, from Kakapora. He'd joined the militant group the year before, and his family hadn't seen or heard from him since March 2018.

Dar's family claimed he'd become radicalized by the group after being beaten by Indian police. He'd been arrested six times between September 2016 and March 2018 but was always released without any charges pending.

The investigation revealed the car had been carrying 660 lbs of explosives, including ammonium nitrate and 180 lbs of RDX, a high explosive. It was thought the explosives might have been stolen from a construction site because it wasn't possible to smuggle them across the border. However, he later stated he couldn't rule out the possibility of smuggling.

The Aftermath

Those killed in the attack were given State funerals. Each victim's family received a payment of US$17,000 in ex gratia compensation by the Punjab government. The next of kin of each victim was offered a government job.

Politically, India revoked the favored nation status of Pakistan. All goods imported from Pakistan to India received a customs duty hike of 200%.

General strikes, protests, and marches were held across India following the attack. In Jammu, there were a number of violent protests which resulted in a curfew. Protests were held in London outside the Pakistan High Commission.

A group of doctors who were meant to attend a conference in Pakistan canceled and refused to participate. An Indian broadcaster refused to broadcast the Pakistan Super League cricket matches, and Pakistani actors were banned from the Indian film industry.

A Pakistani prisoner, Shakarullah, was killed by other inmates in India's Jaipur Central Jail on February 20. He was beaten to death and stabbed allegedly during a brawl over the television. But, Pakistan claimed he was murdered in retaliation.

Legacy

During their third one day international match against Australia, the Indian cricket team wore camouflage caps instead of their usual blue cap as a tribute to those who were killed. Pakistan was angered by this and called for the International Cricket Council to ban the Indians for mixing politics with cricket. However, the Indian team had asked for permission to wear the changed caps beforehand as a fundraiser for the victims and permission had been granted.

Mass Shooting in Aurora

A mass shooting on February 15 at the Henry Pratt Company in Aurora, Illinois, resulted in five people being killed, along with the perpetrator, and several others injured. The perpetrator was identified as a disgruntled former employee of the company.

Reports of Gunfire

Reports of gunfire were first received by emergency services at 1:24 P.M. on February 15. The perpetrator had been seen by witnesses carrying a handgun with a laser sight. In response to the reports of the shooting, multiple agencies attended. On arrival of law enforcement, the perpetrator began shooting at the officers. They returned fire, and at 2:59 P.M., it was reported that the gunman had been shot and killed.

The event lasted for around an hour and a half. In addition to the civilians killed and injured, six police officers also received injuries.

Those Who Were Lost

All of the victims shot and killed were males and were employees of the Henry Pratt plant: the human resources manager, 32, a mold operator, 46, a forklift operator and stock room attendant, 55, and a student from Northern Illinois University, 21, who was on his first day as an intern at the company in human resources.

Four of the police officers injured received gunshot wounds, and another was struck by shrapnel. The sixth officer sustained an injury that wasn't related to gunshots. None of the officers received life-threatening injuries.

Disgruntled Employee

The gunman was identified at Gary Montez Martin, 45, who had previously been employed at the plant. He'd been released from his contract two weeks before he went on the shooting rampage. However, other reports stated he'd been fired that day and went on the shooting spree straight away.

Martin had a history of violence after he was convicted of felony aggravated assault in 1995. He went to prison for two and a half years for that conviction in Mississippi. According to police, he had a history of abusing a former girlfriend and had once stabbed her and struck her with a baseball bat. In total, Martin had been arrested six times by the Aurora Police Department, with the majority of arrests being related to violent acts.

Because he was a convicted felon, Martin couldn't own a gun legally in Illinois, but. he managed to obtain a Firearms Owners Identification Card in 2014. This enabled him to legally purchase a gun and ammunition in Aurora. Then, he applied for a concealed carry license, but this check included fingerprints, and so it was discovered he was a convicted felon. As a result, his application was denied, and his FOID card was canceled. He was instructed to return the gun, but he failed to do so.

Martin's home was searched after the shooting, but nothing was found to show he'd planned the shooting. But, they later discovered that he had indeed planned it. He'd made threats before he was fired to his co-workers that "If I get fired, I'm going to kill every motherfucker in here" and "I am going to blow police up." The employee who heard these statements didn't report it because he said Martin made similar comments regularly, so it didn't seem unusual.

Politicians React

Law enforcement was thanked for their response by U.S. Senators Dick Durbin and Tammy Duckworth. President Donald Trump and Governor J.B. Pritzker also thanked the police and law enforcement agencies involved. Condolences were also offered to the victims and their families.

Mayor of Aurora Richard Irvin stated: "It's a shame that mass shootings such as this have become commonplace in our country [and] that a cold and heartless offender would be so selfish as to think he has the right to take an innocent life. But we as a society cannot allow these horrific acts to become commonplace."

The Morrisville Family Murders

In February 2019, five members of a family were killed by two other family members in what was alleged to be some kind of cult or religious motivation, in Bucks County, Morrisville, Pennsylvania. Shana Decree, 45, and her daughter Dominique, 19, were responsible for the murders and had made suicide claims previously.

A Shocking Welfare Check

The Children and Youth Social Services Agency of Bucks County went to an apartment on West Bridge Street to perform a welfare check days earlier on Saturday, but nobody answered the door. In turn, they left a business card. The following Monday, they returned to the apartment in the afternoon; and again, there was no answer, so they contacted the maintenance worker of the apartment complex.

The maintenance worker opened the door to the apartment, and inside, he found Shana and Dominique in bed. They'd seemed disoriented and throughout the apartment, were signs of disarray. Police were called to the scene and the two women were transported to a hospital.

As they searched the apartment, police discovered four bodies inside a small bedroom. The fifth victim was later found underneath another victim. The victims included twin sisters Imani and Erika Allen, 9, Damon Decree Jr., 13, Naa'Irah Smith, 25, and Jamilla Campbell, 42, who was the mother of the twin girls. All but Campbell had died from asphyxiation. The coroner determined Campbell had been strangled to death.

Naa'Irah Smith and Damon Decree Jr. were children of Shana, and Jamilla Campbell was Shana's sister.

Dominique and Shana

After a thorough examination, Dominique was found to have injuries on her neck, but she denied knowing what had happened in the apartment at first. She then stated a man had hurt her, someone she didn't know, and repeated to police that she'd wanted to die.

When Shana was questioned, she also denied knowing what had happened. However, she then claimed two unknown males, and her sister's boyfriend had killed everyone. Dominique later made similar statements.

Later, Shana offer similar claims to police that all of the victims in the apartment had been talking about suicide and wanted to die, including the children.

A Disturbing Belief

Relatives of Shana and Dominique had their own suspicions about what had happened that day. The half-sister of the twins, Destiny Harris, had said the adults had been going through 'something religiously' and had dragged the children into it.

Damon Decree Sr. argued that the family in the apartment had talked about being surrounded by demons. He cited, "Apparently, they had dissected into some type of cult that they materialized online. I don't know how or what kind of cult."

These religious beliefs about demons had been prevalent for a month, and children's services had been called because of it.

Both women are facing murder charges, and the case is ongoing.

YNW Melly on Trial for Murder

YNW Melly is a rapper and songwriter who claimed a large following after he released songs 'Murder on My Mind' and 'Mixed Personalities,' which featured Kanye West. The song 'Murder on My Mind' was labeled his breakout single, and even more attention was drawn to it after Melly was charged with double murder.

Who is YNW Melly?

Melly was born Jamell Maurice Demons on May 1, 1999. His mother became pregnant with him when she was 14 years old, and she raised him as a single mother. At a young age, Melly joined the gang the Bloods and began posting songs he made on SoundCloud when he was a teenager.

While incarcerated in 2017, Melly released his first EP, which featured several well-known performers. His debut album, I am You, was released in August 2018. His second mixtape was released on January 17, 2019, and Melly was still behind bars. On Spotify, he has amassed over 200 million streams as of March 2019. The song that has been streamed the most is "Murder on My Mind."

Criminal History and Charges of Murder

Melly was arrested in 2015 for three counts of aggravated assault and one count of discharging a firearm in public when he was just 16 years old. He allegedly fired at three students near the high school they all attended. He claimed to have devised the chorus of "Murder on My Mind" while in jail for this crime.

On June 30, 2018, Melly was arrested in Fort Myers, Florida, for possession of a weapon or ammunition by a convicted felon, possession of drug paraphernalia and possession of marijuana. He was arrested again on January 3, 2019, for possession of marijuana.

Melly was charged with two counts of first-degree murder on February 12, 2019. Two of his friends, rappers Anthony 'YNW Sakchaser', 21, and

Christopher 'YNW Juvy' Thomas Jr., 19, were murdered in Fort Lauderdale in October 2018. They'd both been shot to death.

Authorities claim Melly had conspired with rapper Cortlen Henry, AKA YNW Bortlen, to stage the murder to make it look like it was a drive-by shooting. Henry drove the two victims to the hospital after the shooting but they both died. On February 13, Melly turned himself in, and made the following statement on Instagram:

"No I did not get locked up in Washington , but I am turning myself in today... a couple months ago I lost my two brothers by violence and now the system want to find justice.. unfortunately a lot of rumors and lies are being said but no worries god is with me and my brother @ynw.bortlen and we want y'all to remember it's a ynw Family I love you."

— @ynwmelly

It was announced on February 22 that both Melly and Cortlen were now considered suspects in the shooting murder of Indian River County Sheriff's Department Deputy Gary Chambliss, who was off duty at the time.

Melly entered a plea of not guilty in the double homicide and is still awaiting trial.

Murder on My Mind

The song "Murder on My Mind" has almost a diary feel to it and its lyrics include:

"His body dropped down to the floor, and he had teardrops in his eyes/He grabbed me by my hands and said he was afraid to die."

R. Kelly Arrested and Charged Again

Musician R. Kelly has been the subject of many investigations surrounding child pornography for decades. He has always denied all allegations and was acquitted of 13 counts of child pornography in 2008. A documentary series was released in January 2019 in which multiple women discussed allegations of sexual abuse committed by Kelly. As a result of public pressure, Kelly's record company dropped him.

Kelly was indicted on February 22, 2019, on 10 counts of aggravated criminal sexual abuse. In July 2019, he was arrested on federal charges of sex crimes and obstruction. In total, Kelly faces 18 federal counts, including child pornography, forced labor and kidnapping.

An Illegal Wedding

On August 31, 1994, Kelly illegally married Aaliyah, a 15-year-old music protégée in Cook County. Aaliyah had falsely stated she was 18 years old at the time. Demetrius Smith, Kelly's tour manager, claimed in an interview in 2008 that he'd obtained false identification for Aaliyah so the marriage could be performed.

Kelly had met Aaliyah when she was just 12 years old, after being introduced by her uncle. A video surfaced in 2019, showing Kelly state her age as 14, less than a year before they were married. This video validated that Kelly was fully aware of her young age.

In February 1995, the marriage was annulled as requested by her family. Both Aaliyah and Kelly denied they'd ever been more than just friends, and they hadn't been married. However, a lawsuit was filed by Aaliyah in 1997 to expunge any marriage records, claiming she was underage at the time of the marriage and she'd falsely signed the license.

At the time of the lawsuit, another was underway in which Tiffany Hawkins had wanted to use the marriage documents in her own case against Kelly. Later she accepted a settlement from Kelly of US$250,000.

Allegations of Child Pornography and Abuse

A video appeared on February 3, 2002, which allegedly showed Kelly engaging in sexual intercourse with an underage girl, during which he allegedly urinated on her. The story was sent to the *Chicago Sun-Times* newspaper and it became headline news on February 8. Kelly was scheduled to perform at the 2002 Winter Olympics opening ceremony at the time and denied his presence in the video.

Kelly was charged with 21 counts of child pornography in June 2002 in Chicago. He was then arrested later that month by Miami Police Department on a warrant. At the trial, the alleged victim on the video refused to testify, and Kelly was subsequently found not guilty of all counts in June 2008.

That same victim was later specified in new charges filed against Kelly in 2019. Police were investigating photos printed in the *Chicago Sun-Times*, which led to a search of Kelly's home in Davenport, Florida. While searching the property, a digital camera was located wrapped up in a towel and hidden in a bag. On the camera were 12 images of an allegedly underage girl.

According to the newspaper, the girl on the camera was the same girl who was in the video.

An Alleged Sex Cult

In July 2017, it was reported that three sets of parents had accused Kelly of holding their daughters in what was described as an abusive cult, but the alleged victims and Kelly all deny the allegations.

On April 17, 2018, Kelly was accused by a former partner of misconduct. She claimed he'd infected her with a sexually transmitted disease intentionally. Naturally, Kelly denied the allegations.

A news article by the BBC stated in January 2019 that a woman Kelly met in 2014, Asante McGee, claimed that while she lived with him, other women were residing there, too. She claimed he controlled every aspect of her life. She was able to l move out later.

Arrest and Charges Made

Kelly was arrested and charged on February 22, 2019, with 10 counts of aggravated criminal sexual abuse. Kelly allegedly sexually abused four women, three of whom were minors, from 1998 to 2010. Video evidence was provided that showed a new crime by Kelly. Kelly pleaded not guilty on all charges and was released on bail after spending two nights behind bars.

CBS This Morning broadcast an interview with Kelly on March 6, 2019, during which he continued to stress his innocence. According to Kelly, social media was to blame for the allegations. During the interview, Kelly exhibited an emotional outburst. Two women who lived with him defended him and declared their love for him. Their parents, on the other hand, claimed their children were captives and have been brainwashed by Kelly.

Kelly was indicted on July 12 on 18 charges. These include:

- child sexual exploitation
- kidnapping
- child pornography production
- forced labor
- obstruction of justice
- racketeering

Bail this time was denied. He received further charges on August 5, for soliciting a minor and prostitution in 2001 after allegedly inviting a girl to his hotel room and paying her to take her clothes off and dance with him.

A new charge was filed against Kelly on December 6, for bribing a government official to obtain a fraudulent identification document. The document was used to enable Kelly to marry a girl in 1994 who was underage. Although the girl was listed as Jane Doe in court documents, it is believed she was the late singer Aaliyah.

Aaliyah was 15 when she married Kelly, and he was 27. The identification certificate listed her age is 18 years.

According to investigators, Kelly and his associates ran a racketeering operation for 20 years, recruiting underage girls and women for illegal sexual activities.

The court documents filed in the latest charge reveal how Kelly paid the government official the bribe on August 30, 1994, the day before the marriage license to Aaliyah was obtained. The marriage was annulled within months because it was discovered she was underage.

Aaliyah tragically died in 2001 in a plane crash. Interestingly, her debut album was called "Age Ain't Nothing But a Number," and it was written and produced by Kelly.

Trial Date Set

For charges relating to sexual contact with five minors in Chicago, a trial has been set for April 27, 2020. Kelly's other trial for recruiting underage girls and controlling them is scheduled for May 18, 2020.

Kelly is also facing charges in Minnesota and Illinois and has also pleaded guilty to those.

Terrorist Attacks in Brief

February 2

Patikul, Philippines: Gunfire between more than 100 members of Abu Sayyaf and government troops resulted in the deaths of 5 Philippine soldiers and 3 militants.

February 4

Mogadishu, Somalia: A car bombing at a shopping mall in the city of Mogadishu left 11 people killed and 10 others injured. Al-Shabaab claimed responsibility for the attack.

February 11

Kajuru, Nigeria: An attack on an Adara settlement named Ungwar Bardi by suspected Fulani gunmen killed 11. Reprisal attack by an Adara militia targeted settlements of the Fulani. The death toll rose to 141 a few days later with 11 Adara and 130 Fulani dying per the government. The governor spoke that the motive was to destroy specific communities. The attacks took place in Kajuru LGA of Kaduna State. Miyetti Allah was reported to have published a list of 131 dead, but later clarified that 66 Fulani were buried and 65 remain missing.

February 13

Sistan and Baluchestan Province, Iran: A bus carrying Iranian revolutionary guard soldiers was attacked by a suicide car bomb. A total of 27 soldiers were killed, and a further 13 were injured. Responsibility was claimed by Jaish-al-Adl.

February 14

Pulwama, India: 40 personnel belonging to Central Reserve Police Force (CRPF) were killed when a suicide car bomber rammed an explosive-laden vehicle on a convoy in the Pulwama District. Around two dozen others were also injured in the attack. Jaish-e-Mohammed claimed responsibility for the attack. Several other vehicles were damaged in the powerful blast.

February 15

Spin Boldak District, Afghanistan: A security post was attacked by the Taliban, through shooting and suicide bombing, hence killing 32.

February 16

Maiduguri, Nigeria: An attack by 3 Boko Haram suicide bombers killed 8 and injured a further 15.

North Sinai Governorate, Egypt: A checkpoint was attacked by terrorists, and 11 soldiers were killed, along with 7 terrorists.

February 17

Turbat, Pakistan: A group named BRAS attacked and killed between 6-9 Frontier Corps personnel.

February 22

Madrid, Spain: The embassy of North Korea was attacked by a group of young Korean men with replica guns and knives. The staff members of the embassy were tied up while the invaders stole electronic equipment, which may have held secret information on North Korea's breaching of international sanctions. This information was given to the FBI. A woman managed to escape and warned the police. The perpetrators escaped. Three people sustained light injuries after the attack. A group named Free Joseon, led by Adrian Hong Chang, verified that it performed the attack.

February 24

Bangladesh: Biman Bangladesh Airlines Flight 147: A man who wanted to speak with Prime Minister of Bangladesh Sheikh Hasina tried to hijack the aircraft. The perpetrator was shot dead by Bangladeshi special forces. One flight attendant was injured.

February 28 - March 1

Mogadishu, Somalia: Two suicide car bombs were detonated in the street near a hotel in Mogadishu, along with grenade explosions and gunfire, which continued until March 1.

Chapter 3:
MARCH

Pollution of Kim Kim River

Illegal dumping of toxic pollution in the Kim Kim River in Malaysia resulted in 6,000 people being affected by the toxic fumes. A total of 2,775 people were hospitalized for treatment, many of whom were school students.

A Background of Illness

On March 7, canteen workers and several students from two schools near the Kim Kim River began complaining of feeling ill and having difficulty breathing. The schools were shut down and all those suffering from ill complaints were sent to the local hospital. The state health authorities were brought in to investigate.

Some of the victims required intensive care treatment. The symptoms included vomiting and fainting. There were 76 hospitalized as inpatients. On March 9, the police began to investigate.

Further Pollution

A further attack of air poisoning occurred on March 11, with another 106-207 people being hospitalized. This quickly escalated with more than 1,000 victims being treated at the hospital and 8 needing intensive care. Because the weather was so hot and there was a strong wind, the toxic fumes impacted a much larger number of people.

By March 19, there had been 76 reports made to police. On June 20, students from schools in Pasir Gudang began complaining of nausea and vomiting, and dizziness and this led to the schools being closed in the area. This was the third wave of toxic fume pollution.

Acheh's Well Village residents living near the Kopok and Daing Rivers that run from the Kim Kim River reported in August that the water in both rivers had turned oily and black and had a horrible foul stench.

Investigation and Arrest

The investigation discovered chemical waste had been illegally dumped into the Kim Kim River by a lorry tanker early on the morning of the first reports of sickness. Through the cleanup operation, 2.43 tons of chemical waste was collected on the day the pollution was reported. However, the contractor who was brought in to do the cleanup wasn't experienced in chemical waste, so the chemical reaction exacerbated.

The owner of a chemical factory in Kulai was arrested on March 10. Further arrests included the owner of a shredded waste factory and an employee in Taman Pasir Puteh. The dumped chemical was identified as marine oil, which emitted flammable benzene and methane fumes.

Another nine people were arrested on March 17. Two men who were believed to be responsible for organizing the transportation of the chemical waste were arrested on March 19.There had now been 11 people arrested.

Because of the chemical reaction during the cleaning process, other toxic gases were emitted. These included acrylonitrile, acrolein, hydrogen chloride, ethylbenzene, toluene, xylene and D-limonene. These chemicals can cause breathing difficulties, fainting, nausea, vomiting, and headaches.

Response by Government and Health Authorities

Sultan Ibrahim Ismail urged that immediate action be taken against those responsible for the pollution and endangerment of the public. He also stated that the stress on the medical facilities in the area from the incident showed a need for a government hospital to be built.

Prime Minister Mahathir Mohamad and the Deputy Prime Minister Wan Azizah Wan Ismail visited victims at the hospital.

Singaporean authorities are continuously monitoring the situation amid reports more illegal dumping sites in Pasir Gudang.

Government Criticized and Lawsuits Filed

Crown Prince Tunku Ismail Idris of Johor expressed on Twitter that a state of emergency should have been declared by the government on the first day they were aware of the situation. He stated the government should have relocated the local people to a safe area.

Mah Hang Soon, the Malaysian Chinese Association Deputy President, argued the preventive measures were incompetent and escalated hazard levels in the area.

It was reported in July that a young boy exposed to the toxic fumes had developed myokymia, a disease similar to Parkinson's. The Deputy Health Minister Lee Boon Chye said the boy had a history of seizures and was born prematurely. This resulted in 160 pollution victims filing lawsuits against the state government, and Johor Menteri Besar sought financial compensation for the boy.

Mass Shooting in a Mexican Nightclub

On March 9, a group of armed men stormed into a nightclub in Salamanca, Guanajuato, Mexico, and opened fire. The gunmen killed 15 people, the majority of who were later identified as Jalisco New Generation Cartel members.

Under Fire

A convoy of three vans arrived at the La Playa Men's Club, a strip club in Salamanca, in the early hours of Saturday, March 9. The entered the club and began firing bullets at people inside the club. Many club patrons tried to flee the scene in the chaos. Police officers and armed soldiers raced to the club when news reached them of the shooting.

A total of 15 people were shot and killed; and another 7 were wounded, and after being stabilized by paramedics, they were taken to hospitals for treatment. Two of those killed died on the way to the hospital, and the other 13 perished inside the nightclub.

When identifying those who had died, it was discovered that 14 of the deceased were members of the Jalisco New Generation Cartel.

Identification of Suspects

It was announced by the Mexican government that they believed the attackers were members of the Santa Rosa de Lima Cartel. Several attackers were identified. Just five days before the massacre, the government had announced an operation that was to crack down on the Santa Rosa de Lima Cartel.

There had been an ongoing bitter feud between the Santa Rosa de Lima cartel and the Jalisco New Generation cartel since 2017.

Two days after the massacre, a post was made on Twitter by the Santa Rosa de Lima Cartel that the main perpetrator was a member of CJNG, named Julio, and known as 'El Trompas.'

Arrest of Cartel Leader

Leader of the Santa Rosa de Lima Cartel, Agustin Medina Soto, was arrested on March 24, in relation to the massacre at the nightclub. The Mexican authorities seized all resources and property of the cartel and leader José Antonio Yépez Ortiz, also known as 'El Marro,' on July 16. The bank accounts of Yépez and those people who were linked to him contained nearly US$1.85 million.

During the arrest, six people who had been kidnapped and held by the cartel were freed. The cartel had paid residents of Santa Rosa to help them prevent the authorities from getting near them by blocking the roads with burning cars. It's estimated that approximately 300 people helped with the road blockages while others staged protests.

The government claimed the Santa Rosa de Lima Cartel was responsible for numerous oil and fuel thefts, costing billions of dollars each year. They'd been searching for Yépez for a long time, and it was a major coup to finally arrest him.

Murder of Christine Silawan

When the body of Christine Silawan, 16, was found in a vacant lot in Lapu-Lapu City, half of her face was missing, and she was naked from the waist down. She'd obviously been violently murdered, but the injuries to her face were unlike any that had been seen in the area before.

A Violent Death

Silawan was a school student at the time of her murder. It was discovered her boyfriend had set up a fake profile on Facebook and had convinced her to meet with him. On March 11, she was found dead with multiple stab wounds. Plus, and her face was so badly mutilated, it was down to the bone of her skull.

Her autopsy showed that there were further mutilations inflicted on her body. Her tongue, esophagus, trachea, her right ear, and parts of her neck were missing. On April 2, it was confirmed that Silawan had been raped, shown by bleeding in her genital area. It was also discovered acid had possibly been poured on to her face before the skin and flesh were removed. Silawan had been strangled to death by rope, and forensics believed up to 3 people were responsible for her murder.

Investigation and Suspect

A suspect who had been arrested for another murder, Jonas Martel Bueno, denied being involved or responsible for Silawan's murder. Bueno had killed a farmer in Danao City, Cebu, in a very similar manner, which led police to question him.

Police were able to track down the real suspect by assessing exchanges between the killer and Silawan on Facebook Messenger. He was arrested on March 17 at his house in Barangay Maribago, Lapu-Lapu City.

The forensic investigation found that Silawan had been killed on March 10, between 6:00-7:00 P.MCCTV footage showed her walking with a man early that evening. According to authorities, Siliwan had ended the relationship with her boyfriend a few days before she was killed, thus leading them to believe the motive was jealousy.

A relative of the suspect claimed he couldn't have committed the murder because he'd been playing basketball and doing chores at home on the day Silawan was killed. His mother said that if her son had killed her, he would've gone on the run, which he didn't. However, CCTV footage showed the suspect following Silawan at 6:12 P.M., the time it was claimed he was playing basketball.

The Death Penalty Argument

The murder of Silawan triggered political debate and controversy of the proposal of reinstating the death penalty for heinous crimes such as murder.

Many believe that the gruesome murder of Silawan would be the type of case that should elicit a death penalty sentence.

A Horrifying Confession

The suspect was identified as Renato Payupan Llenes. During his confession, Llenes, 42, told investigators that he'd scissors to inflict more than 30 stab wounds on Silawan's body and to remove the skin off her face.

He explained that he'd removed her face so she couldn't be easily identified. He stated he'd watched videos on social media sites to learn how to flay the tissue from Silawan's neck and face.

Llenes said he used the fake name CJ Diaz to meet Silawan on Facebook. He claimed they chatted often and became a couple. He further alleged: "We agreed to meet personally for the first time on March 10 at Sacred Heart Parish in Lapu-Lapu City. We fought on our way (to Barangay Bangkal) and that's when I killed her."

Apparently, the fight started because she wasn't happy that he was older than she'd expected to be and that he'd used a fake name. For Llenes, he was disappointed that she'd engaged in sexual intercourse with a previous boyfriend, so she wasn't a virgin.

Llenes said he was haunted by her death, and that a young suspect had been arrested for a crime that Llenes committed.

An arraignment hearing took place on June 7, during which Llenes pleaded not guilty. According to his lawyer, Llenes didn't deny his confession, but that he wanted the crime to be downgraded. The case is ongoing.

The Suzano School Massacre

The second major school shooting to occur in Brazil, the Suzano massacre occurred on March 13 in Suzano, São Paulo. Two former students of the school, Guilherme Taucci Monteiro, 17, and Luiz Henrique de Castro, 25, entered the school and opened fire, killing 7 people. But they had already killed earlier that day, with the murder of Monteiro's uncle, and Monteiro murdered again after the shooting.

How it Began

On the morning of the school shooting, Monteiro and de Castro went to a car shop near the school, where they a shot and killed Jorge Antônio Moraes, Monteiro's uncle. They then drove a rental car to the school, and the surveillance cameras at the school showed them entering at 9:40am. They entered one at a time, with about a 10-second gap in between.

As Monteiro walked into the school, he kept his face hidden from students and then pulled out a concealed gun, turned around, and started firing. Two staff members and several school students were just 3 feet in front of him when he started shooting at them. Then Monteiro began looking for more potential victims in the main patio before going to the linguistics center.

When de Castro entered the school, he was carrying multiple weapons including a bow that he ended up leaving on the floor. As he walked by dead victims on the ground, he attacked them with a hatchet. By now, students were running towards the entrance hall of the school, trying to escape the gunmen. But, de Castro was in the entrance hall, and they ran straight toward him.

Two staff members were killed along with 5 students, between ages 14 and 17 years. When police were alerted, they locked down the school. On searching the school for the shooters, they found a crossbow, a bow and arrow, Molotov cocktails, and a bag that was wired. It turned out to be a fake bomb.

The gunmen had fled the scene, and Monteiro killed de Castro before committing suicide.

The Teen Killer

Monteiro's mother had a drug addiction problem, so he'd been living with his grandparents up until the shooting. Both Monteiro and de Castro had previously been students at the school. The year prior to the shooting, Monteiro had dropped out of school because of bullying. The two young men had been friends since they were children.

Planned Over Time

The investigation showed that the two men had planned the massacre for about a year, and they'd been inspired by the Columbine massacre. They'd hoped their attack would draw even more attention than that given to the Columbine massacre.

Reports suggested they'd been influenced by a far-right image board, Dogolachan, that was renowned for inciting violence and terrorism. Monteiro and de Castro had left comments on the image board asking for support and the supply of weapons.

According to Monteiro's mother, he'd been bullied at school because he suffered from terrible acne.

A third suspect, who hadn't been involved in the massacre, said that Monteiro and de Castro had planned to rape some of their victims.

The Shooting Victims

The first person shot and killed was Marilena Ferreira Vieira Umezu, 59, who was the teaching coordinator. Four of the students killed died at the scene, and the fifth perished on the way to the hospital. Eleven students were injured and treated at the hospital, 2 of whom were in a serious clinical condition.

The victims were:

School staff:

- Eliana Regina de Oliveira Xavier, 38
- Marilena Ferreira Vieira Umezu, 59

Students:

- Douglas Murilo Celestino, 16
- Caio Oliveira, 15
- Samuel Melquíades Silva de Oliveira, 16
- Claiton Antônio Ribeiro, 17
- Kaio Lucas da Costa Limeira, 15
- Monteiro's Uncle:
- Jorge Antônio Moraes, 51

Solemn Reactions

The governor of São Paulo, João Doria, traveled to Suzano by helicopter upon hearing of the massacre. He was accompanied by the state Secretary of Education, Rossieli Soares, the Military Police Commander, Colonel Salles, and Army general João Camilo Pires de Campos. The governor decreed 3 days of mourning to take place.

President Jair Bolsonaro posted on Twitter four hours after the news broke of the shooting, labeling the attack by Monteiro and de Castro as an act of "an immeasurable monstrosity and cowardice."

Terror Comes to New Zealand

New Zealand had always been considered one of the safest places in the world, free from war and terrorism. But all that changed on March 15, 2019, when a lone gunman launched an attack on two Mosques in Christchurch causing mass casualties. Everything people loved about New Zealand changed overnight, and people suddenly had to come to terms with such a horrific attack taking place in such a peaceful place. Within days, more facts were uncovered about the gunman, and the Prime Minister stepped up to change gun laws almost immediately, which garnered international attention.

Gunman on the Loose

The gunman first approached the Al Noor Mosque in Riccarton, Christchurch, at around 1:40 P.M., while Friday Prayers were taking place. The first 17 minutes of this attack was live-streamed by the gunman on Facebook Live and included his drive to the mosque. While sitting in his car, he played a number of songs, including "Remove Kebab," a song that celebrated Radovan Karadžic, the Serb nationalist found guilty of genocide against Bosnian Muslims, and "The British Grenadiers," a British military song.

As the gunman entered the mosque, a worshipper greeted him with 'Hello brother,' and was immediately shot and killed. For several minutes, the gunman fired randomly in the mosque. Dozens were killed in a prayer hall, while three were shot and killed near the entrance. Attached to one of his guns was a strobe light that disoriented the victims, making it easier for him to target and shoot them.

Naeem Rashid, a worshipper, charged at the gunman and was shot, later dying from his wounds. When the gunman was done, he fled the mosque, while randomly shooting at people he saw outside. But he wasn't quite finished. Instead, he retrieved another weapon from his car and returned to the mosque. Many of those shot this time had previously been struck and were unable to escape the onslaught. Once again, the gunman left, killing a wounded woman on the footpath who was pleading for help. He fled the scene.

In total, he'd been at the Al Noor Mosque for around six minutes. As he was driving to his next destination, emergency services were arriving at the Al Noor Mosque and were greeted by a horrific scene.

At around 1:55 P.M., the gunman arrived at the Linwood Islamic Center, a mosque located about 3 miles from the first scene. The gunman apparently had difficulty finding the main door and shot at people gathered outside and through a window, which alerted those who were inside.

A worshipper inside the mosque, Abdul Aziz Wahabzada, realizing what was going on, grabbed a credit card reader and ran towards the gunman who was retrieving yet another gun from the car. He threw the credit card reader at the gunman, which elicited gunfire in return. Wahabzada hid behind cars and picked up an empty gun that had been dropped by the gunman. He tried to keep the attention of the gunman on him to protect those in the mosque, but the gunman continued opening fire inside the mosque.

The gunman returned to his car, and Wahabzada threw the empty gun at the car, which shattered the glass. Undeterred, the gunman drove off frantically.

When paramedics arrived at the scenes, they were faced with a gruesome task of trying to render help to those who were still alive but critical. Paul Bennett, one of the first paramedics to enter, recalled: "There was a river of blood coming out of the mosque. It was literally flowing off terra-cotta tiles."

He said it was a scene that wouldn't be forgotten. "I didn't go into the mosque because I couldn't get in ... because there were fatalities in the way. We ended up having to lift the bodies over top of other bodies on to our stretchers. Those people were bleeding, and there was a lot of blood."

Another paramedic spoke of having to step over bodies and the difficulty positioning themselves among the corpses and the blood to treat those still alive. An intensive care paramedic was placed outside the Deans Avenue mosque to direct St. John staff and ambulances as they arrived. He restricted how many paramedics entered the mosque because he didn't want too many to have to deal with the horrific scene inside.

After the chaos, a story of courage, one of many, emerged. Abdul Aziz was in the Linwood Mosque praying with his 4 sons when he heard the sound of shots being fired. Instead of running away from the sound, he grabbed the first thing he found, which happened to be a credit card machine. He threw it at Tarrant, which made him drop his shotgun. Aziz picked up the gun, aimed it at Tarrant and pulled the trigger, but the gun failed to fire. Tarrant took the opportunity to run to his car, where he had more weapons, and Azia followed. He threw the shotgun at Tarrant's car, smashing a window.

It's believed that Aziz's heroic actions may have been the reason Tarrant decided to drive away instead of rearming himself and going back in to kill more people.

Perpetrator Captured - Manifesto Discovered

Multiple attacks were reported, and at first, it was thought there were multiple gunmen perpetrating the attacks. Within 21 minutes of the first call to emergency services, the gunman was located and arrested. A police car was used to ram the gunman's vehicle against the curb, and he was dragged out of the vehicle at gunpoint.

It was later discovered the gunman had planned to travel to another mosque and continue his attacks. There were more weapons in his vehicle ready to be used at another location. Police ascertained there had been just one gunman all along.

The gunman was identified as Brenton Harrison Tarrant, 28, from Australia. He'd been living in Dunedin for a few years and was a member of a gun club in South Otago. From 2012, he'd been visiting many countries in Europe and Asia, and his visits to Bulgaria and Turkey were being investigated by the respective countries.

Tarrant was obsessed with Islamic extremist terrorist attacks in 2016 and 2017. Two years before Tarrant attacked the mosques, he'd been planning the attack. The targets were chosen three months prior to the mass shootings. Just before the mosque attacks, he sent a message to his mother that she was about to read and see terrible things about her son.

Tarrant allegedly wrote a manifesto called "The Great Replacement." The document was 74 pages long and detailed the planning of the attacks and the reason behind them. Just before he embarked on the attacks, the manifesto was emailed to 30 recipients, including media outlets, Twitter, and the prime minister's office.

The manifesto contained anti-immigrant sentiments, supremacist beliefs and hate speech, and many neo-Nazi symbols. Tarrant denies being a Nazi, instead referring to himself as an 'ethno-nationalist,' a 'kebab removalist' and an 'eco-fascist.'

The Innocent Victims

A total of 51 people were killed in the mosque attacks: the victims were predominantly male because Friday Prayer is customarily attended by mainly men. At the Al Noor Mosque, 42 were killed, and the other 7 were slaughtered at the Linwood Islamic Centre. One victim held on for 7 weeks before succumbing to injuries in the hospital on May 2.

The ages of the deceased ranged from just 3 years old to 77 years. A further 50 people were injured in the attacks, with 36 of these suffering from gunshot injuries. Dozens of people were reported missing in the following days.

The New Zealand Police released statements that the deceased were from many countries, including Bangladesh, Fiji, Indonesia, Jordan, India, Malaysia, Saudi Arabia, Mauritius, Palestine, New Zealand, Turkey, and Pakistan.

The victims were:

Mujaad (Mucad) Ibrahim - 3

Ibrahim was born in Hamilton, New Zealand. His parents were Somali immigrants who came to New Zealand in the early 1990s.

Lilik Abdul Hamid - 57

As an aircraft maintenance engineer, Hamid had worked for Air New Zealand for 16 years.

He is survived by his wife Nina and children Zhania and Gerin.

Sayyad Milne - 14

Sayyad was a student at Cashmere High School when he was killed in the shooting at the Deans Ave Mosque.

His father said he loved football and was brave.

Hamza Mustafa - 16

Als, a student at Cashmere High School, Mustafa, was the eldest son of Khaled Mustafa, who was also killed in the massacre. His younger brother was injured in the attack.

Khaled Mustafa - 45

Khaled was killed at the Masjid Al NoorMosque on Deans Ave, along with his son. They'd only been in New Zealand for a matter of months.

Syrian Solidarity New Zealand confirmed his death on Sunday.

Atta Elayyan - 33

Elayyan, born in Kuwait, was a gifted futsal player and award-winning app developer.

He played as a goalkeeper for the Futsal Whites, the New Zealand national team. He'd founded LWA Solutions, a tech company, providing mobile solutions for the likes of Microsoft and Trade Me.

His death was confirmed by New Zealand Football.

Tariq Omar - 24

Omar was a former student at Cashmere High School. He was killed in the Masjid Al Noor mosque attack.

He'd been dropped off at the mosque by his mother, Rosemary, who was still driving around looking for somewhere to park when the shooting began.

He played football, and his death was confirmed by his club Mainland Football.

Husne Ara Parvin - 44

Tragically Parvin was killed when she went back into the mosque to rescue her husband, Farid. They'd been married for 25 years, and he was in a wheelchair.

Farid described his wife was a "magnetic" presence who "could reach anyone."

Incredibly, Farid has forgiven the gunman who killed Parvin - he chose to forgive because he says that's what his wife would have wanted.

Ashraf Ali - 58

Ali, also known as Babu, was a regular worshipper at the Masjid Al Noor mosque, according to his sister.

Babu was a taxi proprietor and was a single parent to his daughter after his wife had died a year earlier.

Ashraf Ali - 61

Ashraf Ali, another Fijian man by the same name, was killed in the Al Noor shooting. He was a regular at the Al Noor Mosque.

According to his brother, Ashraf had migrated to New Zealand 17 years ago.

Syed Jahandad Ali - 34

Ali was a senior dynamics developer at Intergen, a software company, for over six years.

Ali's death was confirmed by the Pakistani Minister of Foreign Affairs.

Mian Naeem Rashid - late-40s

Pakistan's Prime Minister, Imran Khan, has labeled Rashid a martyr after he allegedly tried to tackle the Christchurch gunman and wrestle his weapon from his hands outside the Al Noor Mosque.

He later died of injuries at Christchurch Hospital, and his son Talha was also killed.

Khan said Pakistan would honor Rashid with a national award.

Talha Naeem Rashid - 21

Talha, son of Rashid, was shot and killed at the Al Noor Mosque.

the Pakistani Minister of Foreign Affairs later confirmed his death.

Farhaj Ahsan - 30

Ahsan was a software engineer who finished his master's degree at Auckland University in 2010 before moving to Christchurch.

He's survived by his wife, Insha, and his three-year-old daughter and seven-month-old son.

His death was confirmed by Indian MP Asaduddin Owaisi.

Syed Areeb Ahmed - 26

Ahmed was a chartered accountant from Pakistan, who had traveled to New Zealand on behalf of PriceWaterhouseCooper.

His uncle said he was very religious and would pray five times a day.

His cousin, Syed Abdur Rahim, confirmed the news on Facebook after a statement from the Pakistani Minister of Foreign Affairs.

Sohail Shahid - 40

Shahid was an engineer who worked for a resin manufacturer in Christchurch. He is survived by wife Asma, and two young daughters. "His daughters were his life," said his wife, Asma.

Shahid's death was confirmed by the Pakistani Minister of Foreign Affairs.

Maulana Hafiz Musa Patel - 59

Fijian Imam Patel was visiting Christchurch with his family when he was fatally shot at Linwood mosque.

He's survived by his wife, two sons and three daughters.

Fiji Muslim League Lautoka spokesperson Naved Khan said: "Patel was a highly respected member of the Fiji Muslim League and served selflessly as an Imam, teacher, mentor and was much sought after as a powerful orator and speaker."

Dr. Haroon Mahmood - 40

Dr. Mahmood was a tutor in economics at Lincoln University in Christchurch. He had previously worked in banks in Pakistan and had also been a business lecturer.

Dr. Mahmood is survived by a wife and two children, aged 11 and 13.

His death was confirmed by the Pakistani Minister of Foreign Affairs.

Haji-Daoud Nabi - 71

Nabi had previously worked for Canterbury Engineering and was a community leader. He was from Afghanistan.

He'd come to New Zealand more than 40 years ago as an asylum seeker.

His death was reported by the Afghan Association of New Zealand.

Dr. Abdus Samad - 67

Dr. Samad was a lecturer in Bangladesh's Agricultural Development Corporation until the end of 2012.

After that, he moved to New Zealand with his wife and two sons. He gained citizenship and taught as a professor at Lincoln University in Christchurch.

According to his brother Habibur Rahman, Dr. Samad would often lead prayers at the Deans Ave Mosque.

His death was confirmed by Bangladesh's state minister for foreign affairs.

Dr. Amjad Hamid - 57

Dr. Hamid was a senior medical officer at Hāwera Hospital in Taranaki. He'd migrated to New Zealand 23 years ago.

Osama Adnan Abu Kweik - 37

Kweik was originally from the Gaza Strip and had lived in Egypt. He was in the process of applying for New Zealand citizenship when he was killed.

The Palestinian Ministry of Foreign Affairs confirmed Kweik's death.

Muse Nur Awale - 77

Awale had been living in Christchurch for about thirty years.

He worked as a marriage celebrant for the Muslim Association of Canterbury until 2018. He's survived by his wife, Muhubo Ali Jama.

The Federation of Islamic Associations of New Zealand confirmed his death.

Mohsin Al Harbi - 63

Al-Harbi moved to New Zealand approximately 25 years ago. He worked in water desalinization, and occasionally gave sermons in the mosque.

He died in the hospital after the shooting.

The Federation of Islamic Associations of New Zealand confirmed his death.

Abdukadir Elmi - 70

Elmi and his family moved to Christchurch about 10 years ago from Somalia.

He lived in Halswell and is survived by his wife of close to 50 years, his four daughters, and five sons.

His death was confirmed by the Federation of Islamic Associations of New Zealand.

Mohammed Omar Faruk - 36

Faruk came to New Zealand from Bangladesh about two years ago. He'd been working as a welder. He's survived by his wife, who was four months' pregnant with his unborn baby at the time of his death.

Mojammel Hoq - 30

Hoq moved from Bangladesh to Christchurch over three years ago.

He worked in health care and had planned to go back to Bangladesh and marry his partner, start a family, and a dental clinic.

The Federation of Islamic Associations of New Zealand confirmed his death.

Hussein Moustafa - 70

Moustafa was of Egyptian origin.

His daughter-in-law Nada Tawfeek said he loved his mosque and was a happy and positive person.

"He trusted people's goodwill and wouldn't hurt a soul."

Abdelfattah Qasem - 60

Qasem moved to New Zealand from Palestine with his family in the early 1990s due to the Gulf War.

He was the former secretary of the Muslim Association. He'd also worked as an IT specialist in Kuwait.

The Federation of Islamic Associations of New Zealand confirmed his death.

Linda Armstrong - 65

Armstrong grew up in west Auckland and moved to Christchurch a few years prior to the shooting, so that she could be closer to her daughter and grandchildren.

She was credited with saving lives as the gunman attacked. She was known for her smile and kind heart.

Zeeshan Raza - 38

Raza, a mechanical engineer from Karachi, Pakistan, had moved to New Zealand in 2018.

He'd lived in Auckland for a while before moving to Christchurch for work. He's survived by his younger sister, who lives in Pakistan.

Ghulam Hussain - in his 60s

Hussain , Raza's father, was killed in the Linwood Mosque while in New Zealand visiting his son.

He's survived by his daughter.

Pakistan's foreign ministry confirmed his death.

Karam Bibi - in her 60s

Bibi, Raza's mother, and Hussain's wife was also killed in the Linwood Mosque during their visit to Christchurch.

She's survived by her daughter. Pakistan's foreign ministry confirmed her death.

Mohammed Imran Khan - 47

Khan, or Imran Bhai, as he was known by those close to him, had moved to New Zealand from India.

He was the owner of the Indian Grill restaurant in Christchurch.

The Federation of Islamic Associations of New Zealand confirmed his death.

Hussein Al-Umari - 35

Al-Umari moved to New Zealand 22 years ago from the UAE.

He'd worked in the travel industry and was a regular at the Deans Ave Mosque.

The Federation of Islamic Associations of New Zealand confirmed his death.

Junaid Ismail - 36

Ismail was born in Christchurch and was the owner of the Springs Road Dairy.

He's survived by his twin brother Zahid, who managed to escape the shooting, his wife, three children, and his mother, who he took care of.

The Federation of Islamic Associations of New Zealand confirmed his death.

Zakaria Bhuiyan - 34

Bhuiyan is from Bangladesh. He was getting ready to move to Auckland to start a job in engineering.

Abdul Fattah Qassim al-Daqqah - 59

Al-Daqqah was the former secretary of the Muslim Association in Christchurch. He was of Palestinian origin.

His death was confirmed by the Palestinian ministry of foreign affairs.

Ali Elmadani - 65

Elmadani was a retired engineer who had migrated to New Zealand more than 20 years ago from the UAE.

His death was confirmed by the Palestinian Ministry of Foreign Affairs.

Kamel Darwish - 38

Darwish migrated to New Zealand from Jordan only six months before the attack.

According to his brother, Darwish had been working on a dairy farm in Ashburton, and his family was still in Jordan.

He wasn't able to make it to the mosque very often to pray and was apparently excited that he was able to go to the Al Noor mosque on the day of the shooting.

Maheboob Khokhar - 65

Khokhar was the retired manager of a power station in Gujarat. He'd traveled to New Zealand for the first time the week prior to the shooting to visit his 27-year-old son, Imran.

His death was confirmed by the Indian embassy in New Zealand.

Asif Vora - 56

Vora, from Gujarat, India, was visiting Christchurch to see his son and daughter-in-law, and to meet his new grandchild.

His death was confirmed by New Zealand's Indian embassy.

Ramiz Vora - 28

Asif's son Ramiz was also killed in the attack. He and his wife had just experienced the birth of their child the week before the attack.

His death was confirmed by the Indian embassy in New Zealand.

Ansi Alibava - 23

Alibava moved from Kerala, south India to New Zealand a year ago along with her husband, Abdul Nazar.

She was studying agriculture at Lincoln University, a worked at Kmart Riccarton part-time, and interned at Lincoln Agritech.

The Indian Embassy in New Zealand confirmed her death.

Ozair Kadir - 25

Kadir was a student at the International Aviation Academy of New Zealand. He'd moved to Christchurch from Hyderabad and had planned on becoming a commercial pilot.

His death was confirmed by the Indian Embassy in New Zealand.

Munir Suleiman - 68

Suleiman worked at Scotts Engineering in Christchurch as a design engineer. He'd been in the job for more than 20 years.

He's survived by his wife, Ekram.

Egypt's Ministry of Emigration confirmed his death.

Ahmed Jamal al-Din Abdul Ghani - 68

Ghani was believed to have been running a donut food truck in Christchurch.

Egypt's Ministry of Emigration named Ghani as one of the victims.

Ashraf Morsi - 54

Morsi was survived by his wife Siham and children.

Egypt's Ministry of Emigration named Morsi as one of the victims.

Ashraf al-Masri - 54

Al-Masri worked in a shop and had two young children. He held dual citizenship in Egypt and New Zealand.

Egypt's Ministry of Emigration named Al-Masri as one of the victims.

Matiullah Safi 55

Safi came from Afghanistan to New Zealand around nine years ago.

He worked various jobs in Christchurch and is survived by his wife, six sons, and daughter.

Zekeriya Tuyan - 46

Was the last victim to die, surviving until May 2. Tuyan had been at the Masjid Al Noor Mosque on Deans Avenue when he was shot.

Legal Proceedings

In the days following the attacks, Tarrant was initially charged with one count of murder, to give time for all the information to be gathered. His face wasn't allowed to be shown in the media, but they were permitted to film the court process. Tarrant was taken in custody and taken to Auckland Prison, the only maximum-security unit in the country.

Police announced on April 4 that Tarrant had been charged with 89 counts, including 50 counts of murder and 39 counts of attempted murder. They were still considering other potential charges. He was ordered to have a psychiatric assessment to ensure he was fit to stand trial.

Commissioner Bush announced on May 21 that another charge had been pressed against Tarrant. The new charge was of engaging in a terrorist act. Another murder charge and one further attempted murder charge were also added.

Tarrant pleaded not guilty to all charges on June 14. The psychiatric assessments showed there were no issues surrounding his mental health and his fitness to stand trial. His court date has been set for June 2, 2020.

If Tarrant is found guilty of a terrorist act or the multiple murders, he faces life imprisonment with the possibility of parole. However, the presiding judge will have the power to extend the period of non-parole or remove the possibility of parole completely.

Prime Minister Praised Around the World

Following the attack, the terrorism threat level was raised to high for the first time in New Zealand history. Prime Minister Jacinda Ardern called the attacks an "an act of extreme and unprecedented violence" and referred to it as "one of New Zealand's darkest days."

Prime Minister Ardern stated she'd render Tarrant 'nameless' and urged the people of New Zealand to instead speak the names of the victims, not the terrorist. A directive was issued by Ardern that flags on all public and government buildings be flown at half-mast until instructed otherwise. The day after the attacks, Ardern traveled to the Phillipstown Community Hub in Christchurch and met with Muslim community members.

In the immediate aftermath, the gun laws in New Zealand were under scrutiny. Military-style semi-automatic rifles had been legal at the time, but after they were used in the Mosque attacks, Ardern vowed to change the laws. In essence, she succeeded. On March 21, Ardern announced a ban on the weapons. The Amendment Act was in front of the House of Representatives on April 1, and by the end of the week of April 10, the law had been changed.

Inspired Attacks

Escondido, California

Nine days after Tarrant attacked the mosques, a California mosque was attacked by arson. Graffiti in the driveway mentioned the Christchurch shootings.

Poway Synagogue Shooting

John T. Earnest entered the Poway synagogue on April 27 and opened fire, killing one and injuring three others. Earnest claimed he was responsible for the arson attack on the Mosque in Escondido and had written a manifesto in which he'd praised what Tarrant had done in Christchurch.

El Paso, Texas

On August 3, Patrick Crusius entered Walmart in El Paso and began shooting. He killed 22 and injured another 24. He also had a manifesto expressing his support for Tarrant and claiming motivation from the Christchurch mosque attacks.

A Mosque in Norway was attacked by Philip Manshaus on August 10, and fortunately, only one person was injured. Like Tarrant, he also tried to

Livestream the attack on Facebook. He'd even posted online supporting Tarrant, Crusius and Earnest, calling them heroes.

Video Distribution

On the same day of the attacks in Christchurch, copies of Tarrant's live-streamed video were reposted on numerous file-sharing websites, including Facebook, YouTube, and LiveLeak. Anyone who encountered the footage was urged to report it or delete it by the New Zealand Police. The video was quickly classified as objectionable so that distributing, exhibiting, or copying the video became a criminal offense.

Further Arrests

Eight people were arrested for either sharing the video or manifesto or for possessing the material. One teenaged man was charged with inciting racial disharmony and faces up to 14 years in prison if he's found guilty.

An Australian man was indicted on March 19 on one count of aggravated possession of a firearm without a license and four counts of possessing or using a prohibited weapon after he'd praised Tarrant's actions on social media.

Philip Arps was indicted on March 20 on two counts of sharing the live-stream video. In June, he was found guilty and sentenced to 21 months in prison.

A 16-year-old pleaded guilty to possessing the video footage on July 2. Initially, he was released on bail but was returned to jail on July 9 for breaching the conditions of his bail.

A man from Dunedin appeared in court on July 12 for possessing the video footage and other related charges. He was reprimanded and taken in custody.

Tram Passenger Shooting in the Netherlands

On the morning of March 18, a gunman entered a tram in Utrecht, Netherlands, and began shooting. Three were shot dead, and 7 were wounded, one of whom died several days later from his injuries. It was thought to be a terrorist attack, but that hasn't been confirmed.

Passengers Under Attack

The gunman boarded the tram near the 24 Oktoberplein junction in Utrecht at around 10:45A.M. He opened fire, shooting at the passengers on the train, killing 3 outright and injuring several more. He then fled in a vehicle, which resulted in a large scale manhunt by police for most of the day.

They eventually tracked down the suspect and arrested him. The suspect, a Turkish man who was 37 years old, admitted he'd completed the shooting.

Ten Victims

Three of those who were wounded suffered serious injuries and were taken to University Medical Center Utrecht. The deceased victims included 2 men, aged 28 and 49 from Utrecht, and a woman from Vianen who was 19 years old.

A crowd-finding action was started by the neighbor of the young woman killed to cover her funeral costs, but it raised so much money that it was turned into a fund for all of the attack victims.

One of the injured, a 74-year-old man, succumbed to his injuries on March 28, raising the number killed to 4.

The Suspect Confesses

The Turkish man arrested was a resident of Utrecht. He confessed that he was the only one responsible for the shooting. When police searched the suspect's stolen car, they found a letter that suggested the motivation for the attack was terrorism. Some of the surviving witnesses claimed they had heard him shout "Allahu akbar" as he fired at the passengers on the tram. Therefore, the prosecutor charged the suspect with murder with a terrorist motive.

In the letter was the following:

"I am doing this for my religion. You guys are killing Muslims and want to take my religion away from me. You will not succeed in that. Allah is great."

Reaction and Response

The attack raised the threat level in Utrecht to level 5, which was the highest level. Never before had the threat level escalated that significantly in Utrecht. Following the suspect's arrest, the level dropped to 4.

There was an increase in police presence at railway stations, including Rotterdam, Utrecht, The Hague, and Amsterdam in response to the attack. All tram services were canceled in the city. Jewish community buildings were guarded by elite police officers that were heavily armed with semi-automatic weapons. Mosques in Utrecht were evacuated, and others around the country had their security increased. This was in part due to the terrorist mosque shootings in New Zealand.

All national flags were flown at half-mast on government buildings and diplomatic posts around the world the day after the attack, as requested by the Prime Minister. A black banner was flown at Dutch royal residences to symbolize mourning.

Ogossagou Massacre

Multiple attacks on Fulani herders occurred on March 23 in central Mali. The violence was in response to government crackdowns on Islamic terror cells. The massacre delivered a major effect on the Mali government, leading to the resignation of the Prime Minister and his council.

The Herdsmen

There has been a history of conflict over land and water access for cattle between the Fulani herdsmen and other groups. As the climate changes and population grows, the conflicts between the herdsmen and others have been greatly increased due to competition for land and water. More violence between the groups has also occurred as well.

Villages Attacked

The villages of Ogossagou and Welingara, Fulani villages, were targeted and attacked. Dogon hunters armed with machetes and guns carried out the attacks. They believed the Fulani were in cohorts with jihadists, and claimed the attacks were revenge for the al-Qaeda attack on a military base in Mali a week before. During the attacks on Ogossagou and Welingara, almost every hut in the villages was burned down, a total of at least 220.

During the attack, at least 157 people were slaughtered. Men, women, and children, were killed, and around 65 others were injured. A total of 43 people were treated in hospitals, including 17 children.

Three mass graves were located by the United Nations team, with two holding 40 bodies each and the third grave containing 70 bodies.

The Aftermath

The Malian Chief of Staff General M'Bemba Moussa Keita was fired by the Mali president immediately following the massacre. Also fired was General Abdrahamane Baby, the Chief of Land Forces.

Those thought to be responsible for the massacre, the ethnic Dogon militia, were ordered by President Ibrahim Boubacar Keïta to be dissolved. The head of the Dogon group claimed they weren't responsible.

Mass protests took place over what was considered poor handling by the government to control the violence that was continuing to plague the country. As a result, the prime minister, along with his entire government, resigned on April 18.

The Murder of Nipsey Hussle

Born Ermias Joseph Asghedom, Nipsey Hussle was an American rapper, community activist, and entrepreneur. He founded the Marathon Clothing store in 2017, and was shot and killed in the store's parking on March 31, 2019.

Shot Down in a Parking Lot

Hussle was shot numerous times at around 3:19 P.M., while he was in the carpark of his clothing store. Among the 10 gunshots, he suffered were injuries to his right chest, his abdomen, a shot that severed his spine, a gunshot to his back that hit his lung, and another wound to the top of his head, injuring his scalp.

During the shooting, two others were wounded, and after all three were taken to the nearby hospital, Hussle was pronounced deceased at 3:55 P.M. Despite an announcement on an Instagram Livestream by rapper GBO Gaston claiming responsibility for the murder, police were quick to identify the true perpetrator.

Eric Holder, 29, was believed by the police to be the gunman. He'd known Hussle and apparently there had been some kind of personal issue between the two men. Police arrested Holder on April 2, 2019.

Hussle was buried at Forest Lawn Memorial Park in Southern California.

Memorial Service

The death of Hussle led to many celebrities offering their condolences through social media. Even the Mayor of Los Angeles, Eric Garcetti granted his sympathies to Hussle's family.

His memorial service took place on April 11 at the Staples Center in Los Angeles. It was open to the public at no charge. During the service, former

President Barack Obama stated, "While most folks look at the Crenshaw neighborhood where he grew up and see only gangs, bullets and despair, Nipsey saw potential."

The funeral procession traveled 25.5 miles through the streets of Southern Los Angeles, traveling past many of the players that had been important or relevant to Hussle. Many mourners gathered at the Watts Towers, and the streets were lined with people grieving the death of Hussle. It was a true demonstration of how largely Hussle had impacted the community.

A Lasting Legacy

Shortly after his death, a petition was created to rename the intersection of Slauson Avenue and Crenshaw Boulevard, near the store where Hussle was killed, to 'Nipsey Hussle Square.' The council agreed, with a few changes, and on the day he was buried, they announced the intersection would be renamed Ermias 'Nipsey Hussle' Asghedom square.

Within months of Hussle's death, more than 50 murals popped up around Los Angeles dedicated to him. In September 2019, Puma released the 'Marathon Clothing' collection. They announced that 100% of the net profits from the collection would be given to the Neighborhood 'Nip' Foundation. Also, in September, another clothing company AMB founded by Hussle with his friend Cobby Supreme was opened.

Alleged Suspect

Holder entered a plea of not guilty in April on the charges of murder and two counts of attempted murder. He was also charged with possession of a firearm by a felon, assault ,and assault with a firearm. On the day of the murder, former friends Hussle and Holder had many conversations during the day. Then Holder returned to the store and shot Hussle.

Allegations by witnesses claimed Holder had accused Hussle of being a snitch. During the Grand Jury hearing, it was claimed Holder was a gang member, and he'd been seen carrying a black semi-automatic gun and a silver revolver before the shooting. Bullet casings from the scene belonged to a .40-caliber pistol.

A woman told the grand jury she'd driven Holder to the scene and away after the shooting. She claimed she didn't know Holder was a gang member or that he'd been the one who shot Hussle, despite him running to her car after shots were fired and carrying two weapons in his hands.

The case is ongoing.

Terrorist Attacks in Brief

March 9

Salamanca, Mexico: A mass shooting occurred in La Playa Men's Club, a nightclub in Salamanca, Guanajuato, Mexico. Fifteen people were killed, and five more were injured.

March 13

Bay Region, Somalia: A bomb was detonated at a market, killing 8 and wounding 40.

March 15

Al-Baghuz Fawqani, Syria: Six people were killed when 3 ISIS suicide bombers hid among those who were leaving their Baghuz Village.

Christchurch, New Zealand: At 13:40 NZDT, an Australia-born self-described "Ethno-nationalist, Eco-fascist" "Kebab removalist" "racist" terrorist, who wrote a manifesto named after the far-right white genocide The Great Replacement conspiracy theory by French writer Renaud Camus, opened fire on Muslim worshipers attending Friday Prayer at Al Noor Mosque and Linwood Islamic Centre in Christchurch, New Zealand live streaming the attack on Facebook Live, killing 51 people and injuring 49 others. The shooter had announced the attack on 8chan and spread his manifesto on Twitter, Facebook and the aforementioned 8chan. Multiple improvised explosive devices were uncovered by police and successfully disarmed by the New Zealand Defense Force The Prime Minister of New Zealand Jacinda Ardern described the two consecutive terrorist attacks as "one of New Zealand's darkest days."

March 17

Ariel, West Bank: Two people, including a rabbi, were killed when a Palestinian gunman opened gunfire after fatally stabbing a soldier in the area of Ariel. Another soldier was seriously injured in the attack.

March 18

Utrecht, Netherlands: A man started shooting at random people in a tram. Three people died, and three others were seriously injured. Four people also sustained light injuries. One of the injured died of his injuries ten days later. The police arrested the 37-year-old Turkish suspect later the same day. Dutch prosecutors confirmed three days later that the attacker had a terrorist motive.

March 23

Mogadishu, Somalia: A suicide car bomb and shooting attack on a government building were carried out by Al-Shabaab gunmen. The deputy labor minister was killed, along with 14 others.

Mopti Region, Mali: 160 Fulani Herders were killed in an attack launched on the villages, Ogossagou and Welingara, near the town of Bankass. The attackers were dressed as Dozo Hunters and the attack appeared to have been ethnically motivated.

March 24

Escondido, California, US: Dar-ul-Arqam Mosque in Escondido, California, a city northeast of San Diego, California, was set on fire. When the police arrived, they also found graffiti referencing to the Christchurch mosque shootings in Christchurch, New Zealand that said: "For Brenton Tarrant -t /pol/" a reference to the Australia-born perpetrator behind the two terrorist attacks. The shooter of the Poway synagogue shooting at the Chabad of Poway in Poway, California one month later in April claimed responsibility in his manifesto that he posted on 8chan.

March 28

Mogadishu, Somalia: A car bomb was detonated outside a restaurant, killing 15 people.

Chapter 4:
APRIL

Murder of Nusrat Jahan Rafi

Bangladeshi student, Nusrat Jahan Rafi, 19, had gone to the authorities to report a brutal sexual attack she'd suffered. Little did she know that by identifying and reporting her attacker, she'd be further targeted and murdered.

Background of the Murder

Rafi was a student at the Sonagazi Senior Fazil Madrasa. On March 27, she complained that she had been sexually harassed by Siraj ud-Daula, a head teacher. Following her report to the police, a video was leaked, showing the police chief taking her complaint but referring to it as not 'a big deal.'

However, ud-Daula was arrested and taken to jail. His family put pressure on Rafi's family to make her drop the complaint, but she refused.

On April 6, Rafi was at the school for an exam, and a fellow student, Poppy, convinced her to go to the roof of the building. Once there, she encountered five other students, three of whom had been in her class. They used a scarf to tie up her hands and feet, and then set her on fire.

The attackers had hoped it'd be seen as suicide by Rafi, but the scarf tying her was burned through, and she miraculously managed to escape the roof and summon help. In the ambulance on the way to the hospital, her brother recorded a video statement by Rafi about the attack.

Rafi sustained burns covering 80% of her body. Five days after the attack, on April 10, she succumbed to the devastating injuries and died.

Revenge Attack

The investigation determined that the attackers had been ordered to perform the horrific assault by the headmaster, ud-Daula, from behind bars. Two of his accomplices were local ruling Awami League, party leaders. They instructed the students to kill Rafi if she refused to retract her complaint against ud-Daula.

Suspects in Custody

Sixteen suspects, including the two politicians, were arrested and charged with Rafi's murder on May 29. The suspects are:

- SM Sirajuddoula
- Ruhul Amin
- Shahadat Hossain Shamim
- Nur Uddin
- Imran Hossain Mamun
- Hafez Abdul Quader
- Iftekhar Uddin Rana
- Maksud Alam
- Kamrunnahar Moni
- Saifur Rahman Mohammad Zobair
- Javed
- Umme Sultana Popy
- Mohiuddin Shakil
- Mohammad Shamim
- Abdur Rahim Sharif
- Absar Uddin

Sentenced to Death

All of the 16 suspects were eventually sentenced to death. Of the suspects, 12 had confessed when questioned about the murder; the other four claimed innocence.

The trial was fast-tracked, and the courtroom was packed when the sentences were announced. Afterward, the prosecutor declared, "The verdict proves that nobody will get away with murder in Bangladesh. We have the rule of law."

Because of the fear of reprisals after the death sentences were announced, police were deployed around the home of Rafi's family for protection.

Attempts to Combat Sex Crimes

As a result of Rafi's murder, the prolific culture of sex crimes against children and women were exposed, and the fear of reporting any crimes became well-known. Violence inflicted on women is still a major problem, despite the 'Suppression of Violence Against Women and Children Act that was passed in 2000.

It isn't common for prosecutions to proceed in cases of sexual assault and rape. In the aftermath of Rafi's murder, schools in Bangladesh were ordered by the government to set up committees to help prevent sexual crimes.

The South Asia director at Human Rights Watch, Meenakshi Ganguly, insisted: "The horrifying murder of a brave woman who sought justice shows how badly the Bangladesh government has failed victims of sexual assault. Nusrat Jahan Rafi's death highlights the need for the Bangladesh government to take survivors of sexual assault seriously and ensure that they can safely seek a legal remedy and be protected from retaliation."

Guard Shot to Death Outside Prahran Nightclub

When you work as a security guard outside a nightclub in Melbourne, Australia, you might expect to be involved in a scuffle or fight occasionally. But you don't anticipate to be gunned down in a drive-by shooting, which is exactly what happened in the early hours of April 14.

Deadly Night At Work

On duty, that night was Aaron Osmani, 37, a security guard working the door of the LOve Machine nightclub in Malvern Road, Melbourne. He was standing outside the club, along with two other staff members, and a patron who was waiting to enter the club.

At around 3:20 A.M., a stolen black Porsche drove past the group outside the club and began firing. Osmani was killed at the scene, and the patron, Richard Arow, 28, later died in hospital. Four others suffered injuries, including a young woman who fell and hit her head in the chaos.

The stolen, burnt vehicle was later found in the suburb of Wollert. Police investigated a number of theories, including that the shooting was in relation to a bikie gang who were apparently extorting the nightclub. It was a known haven for bikies, strippers, and other various criminal elements.

Who Fired the Shots?

The investigation led detectives to Moussa Hamka, 25. When they searched his home, they located the weapon that had been used in the shooting. Although it was clear Hamka hadn't been the trigger man, police believed he knew who had been behind the incident.

Following his arrest, Hamka claimed he'd been told to collect a package at a nearby park, which he thought was drugs; in reality, it was the gun. He was charged with being an accessory after the fact of murder, possession of a prohibited firearm, threatening to kill, and stalking.

With the help of CCTV footage from the night of the shooting, police were able to identify other vehicles that were seen to leave the scene along with the stolen Porsche. That helped lead them to who they believed was the main shooter.

On July 1, police arrested Jacob Elliott, 18, at his construction work site. Elliott is the son of Nabil Moughnieh, also known as Nabil Maghnie, an underworld figure in Melbourne. It is believed that he acted on orders from a notorious crime family. Allegedly the daughter of Moughnieh and his son had been ejected from the nightclub three weeks prior.

Day in Court

When Elliott (who goes by his mother's surname) went to court, he was charged with two counts of murder and attempted murder on the others who were injured in the shooting. As his lawyer told the court how it was the first time he'd been in police custody, Elliott openly wept.

If he's found guilty of the murders, each count will carry a 25-year prison sentence. His lawyer requested that any information pertaining to the supporters of Elliott be suppressed in fear of retaliation, and the judge agreed. The names of the surviving victims were also withheld.

A third person was later arrested and charged with the two murders as well as three counts of attempted murder. Allan Fares, 22, was understood to be an associate of Elliott's.

The case is ongoing.

Minatitlán Mass Shooting

Minatitlán, in Veracruz, Mexico, was the scene of a mass shooting on April 19, during a birthday party. The party was for a 52-year-old woman, and the gunmen were heard to ask for 'La Becky' before they opened fire. La Becky was the manager of a gay bar in the area.

Events as They Unfolded

While people were celebrating the birthday at a bar in the city, three men burst into the party around 9:00 P.M. After asking for La Becky, they started shooting at everyone there, including a one-year-old baby.

Most of the party attendees were females, including older women, many of whom were dancing when the gunmen entered. The baby was shot multiple times, even while on the ground after falling. The mother of the baby was also shot, and the father was killed.

Overall, 13 people were massacred, including five women, seven men, and the baby. Those who had survived the hail of bullets were tortured psychologically, having been made to watch as the gunmen shot others. They kept telling the survivors to look at the bodies as they brutally shot them.

The sister of the woman's party recalled , "It was my sister's birthday, she was 52, I was coming from the bathroom when the thundering began, I did not see how many they were because I did not leave. I lost my son, my only son, and you can imagine the pain I have to see my only son dead. I'm standing here, with my pain, because you cannot say anything else, he was 32 years old."

Another surviving victim revealed, "I do not know how many they were, what I did was to throw myself under the table, they pointed me out, but I entrusted myself to God and said: Forgive me, Sir, and let your will be done. It seemed eternal to me, I thought it was not going to end. We were like 50, we were all ladies."

To date, the perpetrators haven't been identified.

Official Response

A lot of criticism was directed at President Andrés Manuel López Obrador over his response to the attack. Instead of commenting on the tragedy, he posted a tweet against his political opponents immediately following it.

It was announced through social media by the region's governor Cuitláhuac García Jiménez that they'd held an emergency meeting in response to the shooting. It resulted in an operative to find those who were responsible to be activated and assurances that there wouldn't be any impunity.

Support for the state agencies was given by the Secretariat of Security and Civilian Protection.

Criticism of Government

Criticism of the president was fueled further following the response by another presidential candidate, José Antonio Meade, who called for the responsible criminals to be punished and that the victim's families should be certain that an investigation would take place. Obrador, instead, made no response. This resulted in protests being organized demanding the President's resignation.

Other former presidents of Mexico Vicente Fox and Felipe Calderón also directed criticism over the current President's attitude. Calderón claimed the corrupt regime of the current president and the insecurity it created had led to the shooting.

Vicente Fox stated in response to the President's tweet following the massacre, "What a shame that even tragedies are used by you as a springboard for aggression. It's not all about you, AMLO. To speak about the people does not mean to govern them, but to take care of them. No more violence! #Minatitlan."

Easter Church Bombings in Sri Lanka

Easter Sunday was a devastating day in Sri Lanka as multiple localities were targeted by terrorist suicide bombings. Three luxury hotels and three churches were attacked on April 21, and smaller bombs were detonated in a housing complex. In total, 259 people were killed in the bombings, and 500 at least suffered injuries in the attacks.

Terrorism in Sri Lanka

The Liberation Tigers of Tamil Eelam (LTTE) had historically been behind terrorist attacks against the army and government in Sri Lanka. In 2009, the LTTE was defeated after it tried to take control of the eastern and northern coasts from the ethnic majority.

A number of threats and attacks were made in the 2010s against Christian congregations and individuals. There were also attacks against other religious minorities and monks. A large increase in attacks against Christians occurred in 2018.

Because Easter Sunday is such a holy day for Christians, the churches on this day are usually full.

Prior Threats

A warning had been made by Hilmy Ahamed, Vice President of the Muslim Council of Sri Lanka, three years earlier that the National Thowheeth Jama'ath was encouraging attacks against non-Muslim communities.

In early April, information was given to the authorities by Indian intelligence agencies that contained the potential locations and methods of an attack. The warnings were repeated up to two hours before the churches were bombed.

Churches Attacked

The bombings were well planned, with the coordination and sequence of the attacks orchestrated in such a way as to create maximum devastation. The first explosion occurred at the Shrine of St. Anthony, a Catholic church. The suicide bombing resulted in the deaths of more than 50 church-goers.

The second bombing took place in St. Sebastian's Church in Negombo, north of Colombo. At this site, more than 100 people lost their lives. Because of the location of the church, close to the main airport, security services were increased at the airport in case it was targeted.

In Batticaloa, the Protestant evangelical Zion Church was the next target. The suicide bombing there killed 30 people. The bomber had tried to enter the church pretending he wanted to film the service, but he wasn't allowed inside. In turn, he detonated his explosives in the churchyard. Many of the dead were children who were taking a break from Sunday school.

Further Bombings

The Shangri-La Hotel was struck by the bombers during breakfast time. On the third floor, the Table One Restaurant was serving breakfast, with most of the clientele comprised of mainly foreign tourists.

Next to be attacked was the Cinnamon Grand Hotel. The suicide bomber had checked in under a false identity the night before. In the morning, he entered the Taprobane restaurant at the hotel and detonated his bomb while standing in the breakfast line.

The Tropical Inn, a guest house in Dehiwala, was targeted by the bombers later in the day. Later it was discovered that the Inn wasn't the preferred target, with the original location being the Taj Samudra Hotel in Colombo. The bomber had entered the dining area and made a few attempts to detonate but failed so left.

When police were searching a suspect's house later the same day, a bomb detonated, killing three police officers, the suicide bomber and four others. The suicide bomber had been a pregnant woman, and her three children were also killed in the explosion. She'd been the wife of the Shangri-La bomber, Ilham Ibrahim. The bomber at the Cinnamon Grand, Inshaf Ahmed Ibrahim, had been her brother in law.

Among the dead were 45 foreigners from countries all over the world. Also killed were Shantha Mayadunne, a TV chef in Sri Lanka, and her daughter. Three of Anders Holch Povlsen's children were killed. Povlsen is the multi-billionaire CEO of Bestseller, a Danish clothing company.

Forty-five children were killed: nine of whom were foreigners.

Investigations Undertaken

Prime Minister Ranil Wickremesing admitted that they'd been warned about the impending attacks and stated that the government would investigate why precautions weren't taken.

An investigation into the bombings was launched, and it developed into a major transnational investigation. Scotland Yard, the FBI, Interpol, and three other international authorities joined forces to track down the bombers and who was behind the attack.

The bomber at the Shangri-La Hotel was identified as a factory owner, Insan Seelavan, and nine of his employees had been arrested. The bomber at the Cinnamon Grand Hotel had registered under the false name 'Mohamed Azzam Mohamed.'

It was announced on April 23 that a national of Syria had been held for questioning over the bombing attacks. The same day, the defense Minister said that investigations had identified that Islamic extremists "carried out the attacks in retaliation for a March attack on two mosques in New Zealand." However, Prime Minister of New Zealand Jacinda Adern and analysts thought this was unlikely and deemed that the bombings had likely been planned long before the attack in Christchurch. The investigation uncovered information suggesting the bombers had been given military training by a man called Army Mohideen, and they had received weapons training overseas.

On April 28, it was announced that four homes in Palakkad and Kasaragod had been raided in connection with the bombings.

Multiple Arrests Made

On the same day as the bombings, police arrested eight people in Dematagonda, Colombo. Overnight, a further five more people were apprehended. Within 24 hours, the police had identified and arrested 24 people.

The number of people arrested rose to 40 by April 23, and by the next day, the number increased to 60. On April 26, police announced they now had 70 suspects in custody held on suspicion of terrorism, aiding and abetting and conspiracy to commit terrorism.

Police eventually identified the nine suicide bombers. The suspected mastermind of the attacks, Hayathu Mohamed Ahmed Milhan, was deported to Sri Lanka from the Middle East along with four others.

Released on Bail!

Nine of the suspects arrested on April 22 appeared in court on May 6 and were formally charged with supplying equipment used in the act of terrorism. Remarkably, they were released on bail, and the court had considered the case against them was weak. An investigation was undertaken which found the local police had made a number of mistakes, and several important facts hadn't been presented to the court.

Bombers Identified

The majority of the bombers had come from either middle or upper-middle-class families; they were all well-educated. All had been financially independent, with at least one bomber who previously studied in the United Kingdom and Australia.

The bombers were identified as the following:

Mohamed Ibrahim Ilham Ahamed:

- From Dematagoda
- Attacked Shangri-La Hotel
- Brother of Inshaf
- Husband of Fathima

Mohamed Ibrahim Inshaf Ahamed:

- From Dematagoda
- Attacked Cinnamon Grand Hotel
- Owner of Colossus Copper
- Brother of Ilham

Abdul Lathif Jameel Mohammed:

- From Gampola
- Attacked Tropical Inn
- Bomb failed at Taj Samudra
- Studied in the UK and Australia

Alawdeen Ahmed Muad:

- From Mattakkuliya
- Attacked St. Anthony's Shrine
- Brother also arrested

Atchchi Muhammadu Muhammadu Hasthun:

- From Valaichchenai
- Attacked St. Sebastian's Church
- Wife Pulasthini Rajendran, wanted by CID, killed in a police raid at the house

Mohamed Nassar Mohamed Asad:

- From Kattankudy
- Attacked Zion Church
- Original target was St. Mary's Cathedral, but the service had finished by the time he arrived

Mohamed Azam Mohamed Mubarak:

- From Colombo
- Attacked Kingsbury Hotel
- Member of NTJ
- Wife arrested

Fathima Ilham:

- Detonated bomb during police raid at her home
- Killed herself, three children
- Murdered three police officers
- Pregnant wife of Mohamed Ibrahim Ilham Ahamed

Mohamed Cassim Mohamed Zahran:

- Attacked Shangri-La Hotel
- Founder of NTJ
- Suspected ringleader of the attacks
- Wife and daughter injured at home during the police raid
- Father and 2 brothers killed at home during the police raid

Fallout Resignations

Following the bombings, President Sirisena announced on April 23 that there were plans to change the people in charge of the defense forces. Secretary of the Ministry of Defense, Hemasiri Fernando, tendered his resignation on April 25, after the President had requested the resignation.

The President requested the resignation of the Inspector General of Police (IGP) Pujith Jayasundara, but by April 29, the IGP hadn't responded to the President's request and was sent on leave. Because the IGP is appointed by the Constitutional Council, the President cannot dismiss him.

On July 2, the former defense official and the former police chief were arrested and charged with crimes against humanity due to the alleged security lapses that led to the bombings.

Governor of Western Province Azath Salley and the Governor of Eastern Province M.L.A. M. Hizbullah tended their resignations on June 3. An announcement was made the same day that all Muslim Ministers would resign from their portfolios. This included the following:

- Cabinet Minister, Kabir Hashim
- Cabinet Minister, Rauff Hakeem
- Cabinet Minister, M.H.A. Haleem
- Cabinet Minister, Rishad Bathiudeen
- State Minister, Faizal Cassim
- State Minister, H. M. M. Harees
- State Minister, Ameer Ali Shihabdeen

- State Minister, Seyed Ali Zahir Moulana
- Deputy Minister, Abdullah Mahroof

The Chief of National Intelligence, Sisira Mendis, resigned on June 8, claiming it was due to health reasons. His resignation came a few days after he'd testified that the Parliamentary Select Committee inquiries into the bombings, which had angered the president.

Michael Cummins - Family Killer

When officers responded to an emergency call to a house in Sumner County, they were horrified to find the bodies of four deceased people, along with a fifth person with injuries. Inquiries led police to other locations where they found more bodies. The tally would eventually end at eight murder victims, and the trail led straight to a family member, Micahel Cummins.

Eight Killed By One Man

On the afternoon of Saturday, April 27, police were called to a mobile home in a rural area of Westmoreland following a call from a relative of those who lived in the home. But it would be hours before they were able to enter the mobile home because they'd to wait for a search warrant, and for animal control to come and remove the multiple dogs and cats that lived there.

As soon as they were able to enter the home, they found the first victim. On the couch in the living room was the body of Marsha Nuckols, who was still hooked up on the oxygen machine she'd needed due to poor health, but it was clear she hadn't died of natural causes.

Beneath the love seat in the room was Sapphire McGlothlin-Pee, 12. Her body was found because one of her feet was sticking out from under the seat. Near her was a serrated knife.

Two further bodies were discovered in a bedroom doorway. Rachel

McGlothlin-Pee, Sapphire's mother, and Charles Hosale. On the bed, Mary Sue Hosale lay barely clinging to life.

One of the other bedrooms was blocked by furniture, which prevented the officers from gaining entry to the room straight away. Once they were able to clear the doorway, they found the body of David Cummins, covered by a comforter. Underneath a recliner chair that had been overturned was the body of Claire Cummins.

All of these victims had been struck in the face and the head, and it was initially difficult to determine how they'd died because they were all covered in so much blood.

Police identified their main suspect so quickly they hadn't even finished counting the victims. They believed that Michael Cummins, 25, had killed his parents, his uncle, the girlfriend of his uncle and two members of her family, and had also tried to murder his grandmother, the only survivor.

Cummins had run from the vicinity of the mobile home once his relatives started screaming at the discovery of the bodies. When police found him, there was gunfire exchanged, before Cummins was shot in the leg, and then was arrested.

The discovery of murder victims wasn't finished, however. In a creek bed nearby where Cummins was known to frequent, a black Kia Forte was found. It had been stolen, and police followed the lead to the home of Shirley Fehrle, who lived within a mile from the Cummins family mobile home.

On entering her home, police found the body of Fehrle with injuries to the face and head, and her arm had been 'spun around.'

At the Cummins home, pieces of a broken rifle were found to belong to a stolen firearm, and they traced it back to its owner in Sumner County and found a link to yet another terrible murder.

On April 17, before the Cummins family murders, authorities had been called to a cabin in Westmoreland that belonged to James Fox Dunn Jr.

While searching the area outside the cabin, Dunn's decapitated body was found in some thick brush.

The Victims

The family relationships to Cummins were as follows:

- David Carl Cummins, 51 - father
- Clara Jane Cummins, 44 - mother
- Charles Edward Hosale, 44 - uncle
- Rachel Dawn McGlothlin-Pee, 43 - uncle's girlfriend
- Sapphire McGlothlin-Pee, 12 - Rachel's daughter
- Marsha Elizabeth Nuckols, 64 - Rachel's mother
- Shirley B. Fehrle, 69 - unspecified relative
- James Fox Dunn Jr., 63 - unspecified

The autopsies on the eight family members all showed similar injuries, with multiple lacerations and bruises to the head, limbs, and torso. The wounds had been inflicted with both sharp and blunt-force instruments, but the exact nature of the weapons wasn't disclosed.

It was determined that none had died from a single blow, that it'd taken multiple strikes with weapons to cause death. The majority of the victims had over a dozen wounds on their heads and faces.

Who's Michael Cummins?

At just 25 years of age, Cummins had a long history of criminal activity in Sumner County. These included convictions for domestic assault, aggravated assault, and aggravated arson. At the time of the murders, he was on probation.

In 2017, Cummins was arrested for attacking his neighbor and setting her house on fire. He stated he would 'finish the job' after he was arrested and charged. He was released on probation after serving just 16 months of his 10-year sentence, but he constantly violated the terms of his release.

He was required to obtain a mental health evaluation, but he failed to do so. He was also supposed to have no contact with his previous victim, but he broke that term of his probation as well. When a probation officer tried to visit him at home on April 10, Cummins fled through the back door and into the woods. Yet he still wasn't recalled to prison.

Authorities decided to arrest him for the violations of his probation days after the attempted home visit, but they were too late - by then, Cummins was committing the murders.

A former girlfriend had posted on social media in 2017 that Cummins, who she had a child with, was dangerous. She cautioned that if he wasn't stopped, he'd end up killing someone. She'd previously had him arrested for stalking.

Awaiting Trial - Death Penalty Sought

When Cummins appeared in court, he still had a cast on his leg from the gunshot and was in a wheelchair. During the hearing, he constantly bobbed his head back and forth. The matter of his probation violations was dealt with, and Cummins was ordered to finish the rest of his 10-year sentence.

Cummins was charged with multiple counts of first-degree murder, and when he appeared in court in August to enter a plea, he entered not guilty. He was remanded in custody, and his trial is set for March 5, 2020. The prosecution is seeking the death penalty.

To date, no motive has been given for the murders.

Shooting at University of North Carolina

The University of North Carolina, located in Charlotte, USA, was the scene of yet another tragic school shooting on April 30, 2019. With two killed and three in a critical condition, it was the deadliest school shooting that far in 2019.

A Deadly Day

April 30 was the last day of classes at the University of North Carolina for the Spring semester. In room 236 of the Kennedy Building, students who were enrolled in a course on anthropology and the philosophy of science were giving their final group presentations. There were around 60 students in the room, which had entrances in the rear and in the front. Adam Johnson, Professor of Anthropology, was the instructor for the course.

Each group of students had been given 10 minutes to deliver their short video on a topic of their choice, and the first group began their presentation at 5:33 P.M. Just a few minutes later, the gunman burst into the room and began shooting with a pistol.

The gunman allegedly smiled before he opened fire, and seemed to shoot randomly, not aiming at anyone in particular. Throughout the attack, the gunman displayed no emotion. Johnson immediately began helping students move toward the exit, pausing only to help a fallen student. He led them to another room, the anthropology department office, and they barricaded themselves inside while emergency services were called.

With the gunman still shooting, a student, Riley Howell, bravely tackled him, knocking him to the ground, shouting for other students to flee. As a result, Howell was shot multiple times, the final bullet entering his brain through his jaw and ear.

When the gunman's pistol was empty, he simply sat down and told a student that he was 'done.'

The emergency call was dispatched by the university through Niner Alerts on Twitter, telling students to run, hide, and fight. At the time of the shooting, numerous police officers were in a meeting about security plans for a concert that was meant to be taking place that evening on campus. This enabled the police to respond immediately to the emergency call.

Police Sergeant Richard Gundacker entered the building where the shooting had taken place and summoned the students to identify who the gunman was. Surprisingly, the gunman identified himself, and he was quickly disarmed and arrested.

By 6:15 P.M., the gunman was in custody and had been identified as Trystan A. Terrell.

Killed and Wounded

Two of the victims died from their injuries and four were injured, three of them critically.

One of those who lost his life was Ellis Parlier, who had previously graduated from the Central Academy of Technology and Arts. The other deceased victim was Riley Howell, from Waynesville. His major was environmental studies and he was a Reserve Officer Training Corps cadet. He received full military honors and an honor guard at his funeral, which took place on May 5. More than 1,000 people attended his funeral, and he posthumously received the ROTC Medal for Heroism, a Purple Heart, and a Bronze Star.

Drew Pescaro was shot in his back just an inch from his spine. The bullet entered his abdomen, missing his liver and stomach, but he required multiple surgeries. When police officers attended Pescaro at the scene, they determined there wasn't enough time to wait for an ambulance, so they picked him up and transported him to hospital in a police car. Following his discharge from the hospital, he developed a complication, was readmitted, and was then discharged again on May 26.

Rami Al-Ramadhan was an international student from Saudi Arabia and had been sitting at the front of the class when the shooting began. He was shot twice, one hitting his stomach and the other grazing his arm, and he was released from the hospital on May 2.

Other students injured were Emily Houpt, and Sean DeHart. Houpt was from Charlotte and was studying global studies. DeHart was from Shelton, Connecticut originally, but had lived in Apex. DeHart was the first to be discharged, leaving the hospital on the same day as the shooting.

96

In response to their actions and the loss of their lives, the Chancellor of the University, Phillip Dubois, announced that both Howell and Parlier would be awarded 'degrees in memoriam.'

The Shooter

The shooter, Terrell, 22, had been a former undergraduate student at the university studying history but had withdrawn from studies on February 14, 2019. Authorities found no record of prior criminal activity, and he'd purchased the weapon legally.

Terrell and his family had moved to North Carolina in 2015. His grandfather Paul Rold descried Terrell as autistic and socially reserved. He'd lost his mother in 1999 due to breast cancer and was devastated by the loss. Terrell had apparently dreamed of working in South America and had used a language learning program to teach himself how to speak Portuguese and French.

Rold stated Terrell had never shown any interest in weapons, including firearms, and that he was in fact critical of the gun culture in America. Terrell had said it was too easy to get firearms in America and had spoken of the gun law changes in New Zealand following the mosque shootings in Christchurch.

While Terrell attended the University, he sat in the very classroom that would become the scene of the shooting. A former student in the class with Terrell stated Terrell hardly ever spoke but would blurt statements out occasionally. He also said Terrell often seemed strangely angry at times.

After his arrest, Terrell stated to the media that he "just went into a classroom and shot the guys." During questioning by investigators, Terrell made a full confession and stated he'd been planning the attack for a number of months. He told investigators where he'd purchased the pistol, how he decided where the shooting would take place, and the research he'd undertaken on mass shootings. He'd apparently researched the Sandy Hook Elementary School shooting at some length.

On the day of the shooting, Terrell had dressed all in black and taken the light rail to the campus. He entered the Kennedy Building; and before beginning the attack, he went into a restroom to load his weapon. Terrell stated he hadn't fired at anyone specifically, instead firing at random. He told the investigators he'd used his phone to record the event.

Charges Laid

Following his confession, Terrell was charged with two counts of murder, along with four counts of attempted first-degree murder, four counts of assault with a deadly weapon intending to kill, one count of discharging a firearm on education property, and one count of having a firearm on educational property.

When police searched his apartment, they located paper targets, a laptop, six boxes of ammunition, three handgun magazines, and a magazine loader. They were unable to identify a motive for the attack, didn't believe anyone else was involved, and concluded that Terrell had worked alone.

On Trial

On May 6, the grand jury formally indicted Terrell. In court on September 19, Terrell pled guilty to the counts of murder, attempted murder, and discharging a firearm. The prosecution dropped the assault charges.

Terrell's attorneys testified that he was under stress from his student debt and inability to find a job. They further claimed that because of his autism, he became obsessed and panicky about his situation. Terrell had chosen the university because he was familiar with it and was in debt to it.

A plea bargain was reached, resulting in two consecutive life sentences without the possibility of parole, hence avoiding the death penalty.

University Response to the Attack

Responding immediately, all activities that were due to take place on the evening of the shooting were naturally canceled, along with the final exams that were meant to take place on May 5. Students were given the option of taking other exams and projects. The concert that was to occur that night, the Waka Flocka Flame concert, was canceled.

A vigil took place on campus on May 1, with around 7,500 people attending. Counseling was offered to any students that felt they needed it. Security was enhanced with the implementation of metal detectors, both handheld, and walkthrough, and bags were to be inspected.

The university developed a permanent online memorial, 'Niner Nation Remembers,' to honor the victims and the survivors. A Remembrance Commission was founded by the university, with 14 members, included Emily Zimmern, who headed the Commission. The members were comprised of staff, faculty, alumni, student body representatives, the uncle of Reed Parlier, and other community leaders. The main objective of the Commission was to decide the best way of memorializing the victims.

Terrorist Attacks in Brief

April 2-4

Louisiana, US: After the burning of a church on March 26, two other churches were burned down in St. Landry Parish. The Greater Union Baptist Church on April 2 and the Mt. Pleasant Baptist Church on April 4. The son of a St. Landry Parish sheriff's deputy has been charged with the arsons.

April 3

Arbinda, Burkina Faso: Attacks by terrorist militants and subsequent clashes resulted in the deaths of 62 people.

April 9

Sheikh Zuweid, Egypt: A suicide bomber attacked a market, killing 7 people, including bother civilians and officers. Responsibility for the attack was claimed by the Islamic State.

April 12

Quetta, Pakistan: A suicide bomb killed 20 people at a vegetable market.

April 18

Makran Coastal Highway, Pakistan: Buses were stopped by Baluchistan separatists and the people on board who they believed were Pakistani Navy officers were shot. Fourteen were killed.

April 19

Minatitlan, Mexico: Forty people were killed, and two were injured, including a one-year-old baby, while they were celebrating a birthday party for a 52-year-old woman. The assailants asked for a woman who was the manager of a gay bar in Minatitlán, and they started shooting. Several citizens criticized the attitude of Mexican President Andrés Manuel López Obrador, accusing him of not responding in a timely manner for the massacre.

April 21

Al Zulfi, Saudi Arabia: Islamic State members attacked a Saudi police station. The attack was foiled, four attackers were killed. Three policemen became injured.

Colombo, Negombo, Batticaloa, Sri Lanka: A series of explosions were reported at three churches, three hotels, and two other places in several cities in Sri Lanka, including the capital Colombo. At least 253 people, including dozens of foreign nationals, were killed and more than 500 were wounded in the bombings. The church bombings occurred during Easter mass in Negombo, Batticaloa, and Colombo; while the three hotels targeted were the Shangri-La, Cinnamon Grand and Kingsbury hotels in Colombo. Two other attacks occurred in Dehiwala and Dematagoda, while authorities were conducting their investigations following the morning attacks. 76 suspects have been arrested in connection with the attacks.

April 26

Kalmunai, Sri Lanka: During a police raid on a suspected jihadist safe house, at least three suicide bombers detonated their explosives, and more militants opened fire on police officers. Six terrorists were killed during the raid, along with nine of their family members. A civilian was shot dead during the battle, and two others were injured.

April 27

Poway, US: A man started shooting at Jews in the Chabad of Poway synagogue in Poway, California (a city near San Diego, California). One woman was killed, and three other persons became injured. The suspect published an anti-Semitic and racist open letter on 8chan, where he blamed Jews for a supposed white genocide and other ills. He was inspired by Austrailian-born terrorist Brenton Harrison Tarrant and Robert Bowers, the perpetrators of the violent Christchurch mosque shootings at Al Noor Mosque and Linwood Islamic Centre in Christchurch, New Zealand and the Pittsburgh synagogue shooting at Tree of Life – Or L'Simcha Congregation in Pittsburgh, Pennsylvania, United States respectively.

Kumbo, Cameroon: SDF leader John Fru Ndi was abducted in Kumbo by separatists. He was released shortly afterward, and the SDF claimed that the whole affair owed to a "misunderstanding" that was quickly solved. The next day, a video of John Fru Ndi conversing with his captors surfaced online, thus shedding light upon the abduction's motive.

Chapter 5:
MAY

School Shooting in Douglas County

A shooting at STEM School Highlands Ranch, a charter school in Douglas County, Colorado, left one student dead and several others injured on May 7.

The Charter School

The number of students enrolled in the school at the time of the shooting was 1,850. Unlike many schools that have police officers on-site, the charter school utilized a private security company instead.

A phone call by a concerned parent to the school in December 2018 documented the violence and bullying that was occurring there. The School Executive Director was urged to investigate the concerns and, take any appropriate action, if necessary.

Threats were made against all schools in the Denver area on April 16 by a woman who had flown in from Florida and purchased a firearm. All of the schools were canceled on the day until the threat passed.

Gunmen Enter the School

On May 7, two gunmen entered the school at 1:53 P.M., carrying guitar cases loaded with weapons, including handguns. They began shooting in two different areas of the school and struck several students, resulting in the school going into lockdown.

Within two minutes of receiving the first 911 call, the police responded.

When they were inspecting a suspect's vehicle, they discovered tactical gear, so they brought in a bomb disposal robot to investigate.

The suspects were taken into custody, without any further gunfire exchanged .Yet a private security guard fired on a sheriff's deputy as he came around the corner, mistaking him for a suspect. Fortunately, the officer wasn't shot.

Police recovered three handguns and a rifle at the scene. When they searched one suspect's home, they found a car that had 'Fuck Society,' a '666,' and pentagram graffiti on it.

Victims: All Students

As one of the suspects pulled out a gun and ordered everyone t to freeze, one student reacted. Kendrick Ray Castillo, 18, jumped onto the suspect to prevent the shooting but was shot and killed and a bullet penetrated his chest. Two other students, Joshua Jones and Brendan Bialy, quickly moved toward the gunman and were able to disarm and subdue him.

Jones received two gunshot injuries to the hip and leg, butBialy was eventually able to disarm the shooter.

Of those injured, two were seriously wounded: the other six surviving victims sustained less critical injuries. The youngest victim was just 15 years old.

The Teen Suspects

The two suspects had been students at the school, and they were taken to different locations for questioning. Neither of the teen killers had been in trouble with the law previously, and it was believed they'd stolen the weapons from one of their parents.

Devon Michael Erickson, 18, was identified as one of the gunmen. He'd allegedly made jokes regularly about school shootings and had apparently told those he knew well not to come to school. Erickson was charged with one count of first-degree murder and 29 counts of attempted first-degree murder. He was taken in custody.

The second gunman was identified as Maya Elizabeth McKinney, 16, who is a transgender male who goes by the name 'Alec.' During the interrogation, McKinney claimed he'd been planning the shooting for weeks, and Erickson had learned about it the night before while they were talking on Snapchat.

According to Erickson, he'd gone along with it because of threats McKinney had made against him, and Erickson was afraid he'd be killed. McKinney claimed that he'd planned on killing two particular students who had continuously ridiculed him about his gender identity.

McKinney stated how he "wanted the kids at the school to experience bad things, have to suffer from the trauma like he has had to in his life."

Both McKinney and Erickson told investigators that they'd used cocaine before going to the school and initiating the shooting.

In Court

At the court appearance on May 15, both were charged with 48 criminal counts. These included first-degree murder after deliberation, burglary, and arson. Because of his age, McKinney was charged as an adult, but his lawyers are trying to have his case moved to the juvenile court.

The judge who had been appointed to both cases recused herself on June 14 from McKinney's trial but proceeded with Erickson's case.

Memorials, Rallies and Vigils

Many community gatherings took place after the attack and included a community service, dinner, and an interfaith memorial vigil. A protest occurred during the vigil and people reportedly heard students saying, 'mental health.' Many of the students left the event after hearing speeches from politicians and community members, and the students deemed the politicians as more interested in the issue of gun control than the support needed for the victims.

An article written by one of the students recalled, "many who attended this vigil desired to exploit our pain to support political agendas" and that there should have been more focus on "honoring Kendrick, 18, who rushed the shooter and was fatally shot".

Deadly Riots and Protests in Jakarta

For three days in May, violent protests and riots erupted around Central and West Jakarta. The reason behind the protests, like so many others, was political, following the Indonesian presidential election. As a result of the riots, eight people lost their lives, and hundreds more were injured.

What the Protests Were About

Immediately following the April 17 Indonesian presidential election, the losing candidate, Prabowo Subianto, and his team cited claims of cheating that caused the election of Joko Widodo as president.

The election was deemed free and fair by international observers, yet Prabowo proclaimed himself as victorious. Before the official results were even announced, supporters of Prabowo had begun protesting in front of the General Elections Commission.

The announcement of the successful candidate was to occur on May 22, so Prabowo's campaign team and supporters planned to protest outside the General Elections Commission on that date, declaring that all protests would be executed in a peaceful manner. Prabowo said he wouldn't accept the results and his team demanded a stop for a recount.

Throughout the month of May, many endorsers were questioned by the Indonesian National Police with suspicions of treason. They arrested 29 people who were mainly former members of ISIL under suspicion that were planning terror attacks at the political rallies. Because of the risk of terrorists infiltrating the protests, police asked that they not take place.

Soenarko, a Prabowo supporter and former commander of Kopassus, was arrested and charged with possession of illegal firearms. He'd been video recorded previously instructing supporters of Prabowo to besiege the General Elections Commission building and the Merdeka Palace.

The day before the announcement was due, May 21, the election result was formally announced, saying that vote tallies had shown Jokowko winning 55.5% of the vote. Prabowo quickly announced he was rejecting the result and later said he'd take the case to the Constitutional Court.

Around 45,000 armed police officers, armed, were brought in to guard the General Elections Commission and the Election Supervisory Body offices in Central Jakarta in anticipation of the scheduled protests. Armored personal carriers and Mobile Brigade Corps with rifles were deployed to the location.

A police spokesman stated the officers weren't carrying firearms but instead were wearing and carrying riot gear, water cannons, and tear gas. Along the road that led to the building of the Election Supervisory Body, barbed wire was installed to help police control the crowds.

Three Days of Violence

On May 21, protestors were told they couldn't hold their rally directly in front of the Election Supervisory Body building, and the opposition complied. It was a generally peaceful protest, leading to permission for the protest granted to continue until after Tarawih prayers, finishing around 9:00pm.

About a half an hour later, another large group of people had congregated in front of the building, and they remained until approximately 10:45pm. Around 11:00pm, a group of protestors tried to force their way inside the building but were driven back by the police and the Army. They pushed the group to Tanah Abang, at which time the officers were attacked by a group with stones and fireworks, which resulted in police deployment of tear gas.

The unruly mob of people set fires to wooden objects and trash, which were extinguished by water cannons by police. The police arrested around 100 of the protestors.

Early on the day of May 22, two cars were set on fire by a group of unidentified people in front of a Brimob dormitory in Tanah Abang. Nobody was injured in the incident, and the people gathered were dispersed with water cannons by the police.

Later that day, the large group of protestors had returned to the Election Supervisory Body building, but another group gathered at the Sarinah intersection. Small clashes took place in the Slipi area of West Jakarta, resulting in tires being burned and stones being thrown. A claim was made by some protestors that they'd discovered hollow-point bullets in police cars, but the police denied this claim. The police, in turn, said they'd confiscated envelopes of money from protestors who had been arrested, but this was denied by the protestors.

To try and prevent the spread of provocative media content and hoaxes, the authorities stated that sending of video and images through social media applications would be temporarily restricted.

As the night approached, riots were still continuing. A fire truck was hijacked, and the crew onboard were forced to spray the anti-riot police with the hoses. The next day, Prabowo finally called upon his supporters, telling them to go home, put their trust in the law and rest, and promised to contest the results of the election.

The Injured and the Dead

According to Anies Baswedan, the Jakarta Governor, six people had died during the protests and riots, and 200 had been injured. This was by 9:00am on May 22. One of the victims had been shot in the chest and died in hospital. A hospital that had treated the injured noticed that some of their victims had been shot.

On May 23, Baswedan updated the death toll to 8 and more than 600 injured, ranging from mild to serious injuries. The event would later be described as the worst political violence in Indonesia in 20 years.

The Aftermath

In an official address to the country on May 22, Jokowi stated there wouldn't be any room for rioters who "ravage the country." Prabowo made a statement around the same time, calling for his supporters and authorities not to use physical force. He'd claimed beforehand that any rioters would not be his supporters. According to the Indonesian Coordinating Minister for Political, Legal and Security Affairs, the riots were planned by 'paid thugs' and that the government had been aware of who the mastermind was.

Deadly Riot in Acarigua Prison

On May 24, yet another violent prison riot occurred in Acarigua, Venezuela. The riot took place in the overcrowded police station cellblocks, allegedly following the murder of an inmate and amidst days of protests by relatives who were denied visitation.

Overpopulated Prisons

It's common knowledge that the prisons in Venezuela are terribly overpopulated, and many are run by gangs, leading to a lot of violence. There have been a number of violent and deadly riots in the prisons in Venezuela, but this time it took place in the police station cells.

The cells in the police station are designed to hold up to 60 inmates, but they often hold up to 500, which is a staggering statistic of overcrowding. Prisoners are only meant to spend 48 hours maximum in the police station cells, but they're often left there for much longer periods.

For many days before the riot, the inmates had asked the ombudsman to ensure they wouldn't be transferred to prisons far away from their relatives who would be unable to visit. Apparently, the prison had planned to move them distantly to try and prevent gang wars within the inmates. Tension began to rise on Mother's Day when visits by family members to the police station cells had been denied.

Before the riot took place, an inmate with his face covered managed to record videos asking for the violence to stop and for the guards to stop shooting at them. He was seen waving a weapon and exclaimed he was 'willing to die' if he fought the guards. Following the riot, these videos were released on social media. The inmate was identified as Wilfredo Ramos Ferrer, who had been bargaining for better conditions with the prison.

Rioting Inmates

On May 14, the initial rioting began, and by May 23, it had escalated to the point where inmates were taking visitors, hostage. Troops started entering the prison. At first, an official said it was an attempted escape: that the inmates had tried to flee through a hole in the wall but ended up fighting.

However, the understanding is that the violence escalated when Wilfredo Ramos Ferrer was shot by prison officials during the protests. Ferrer was known as the inmate's leader.

The violence lasted from 5:50 A.M. on May 23, and ended at 10:00 A.M. on May 24, after the prisoners surrendered. The National Guard, local police and a specialized prison unit attended the riot to try and bring back control. Explosions were heard by those nearby, and there had been a lot of gunshots.

Mass Casualties

The conflict between inmates and officers during the riot resulted in at least 29 inmates shot and killed. Several victims had been shot through the head, and it was reported that the body of Ferrer had been horribly destroyed, with large facial injuries. He had to be identified by a tattoo on his shoulder. Officials claim he was shot and killed because he had a grenade in his hand.

Of the officials, 19 guards received injuries.

Reactions and Criticism

The official story by the local government was that an escape had been attempted by rival gangs in prison, and they were killing each other. When the guards tried to stop it, they inflicted injuries on the guards. The report also claimed there were fewer inmates than other reports, alleging there were 355 present not 500.

However, a police report of the incident stated there were 540 inmates at the police station cells. Many inmates were arrested for inciting the riot, and photographs showed them lying on the ground, naked, lined up in rows.

Because of a large number of deaths, extra scalpels and gowns had to be brought in from over 200 miles away to perform the autopsies. Some of the family members of those killed ended up supplying equipment just so their loved ones' autopsies could be completed.

The violence at the police station was condemned by the Inter-American Commission of Human Rights. They called on the State to "adopt immediate measures to guarantee the life and integrity of detainees."

Because the prisoners were under state custody, Erika Guevara-Rosas, Director of Amnesty International, blamed the government for the deaths.

Other human rights groups queried the accuracy of the official report into the incident. In a telephone interview, Humberto Prado of the Venezuelan Prisons Observatory, stated: "How is it that there was a confrontation between prisoners and police, but there are only dead prisoners? And if the prisoners had weapons, how did those weapons get in?"

Children Killed By Parents in Shiregreen

Calls were made to the police in South Yorkshire, England, that several children were in danger at a home on Gregg House Road on May 24. The family living at the home had been the subject of welfare concerns before; and due to the nature of the calls on this day, they arrived enforce at the residence, including 15 police cars. Inside they found it was too late for two children, and four others were in need of medical care.

Gut-wrenching Discovery

At 7:30 A.M. on May 24, police rushed to the house on Gregg House Road and inside found six children, all unconscious. They ranged in age from 7 months to 14 years, and the Yorkshire Air Ambulance was summoned to the scene to transport the most critically ill children to the hospital. The others traveled in four ambulances.

The two eldest children Blake Barrass, 14, and Tristan Barass, 13, died in hospital. The other children had regained consciousness and were classed as non-life threatening.

It was later discovered that the first attempts to kill the children had occurred the night before, but when that failed, the suspects tried again and strangled and suffocated the two older boys. They then tried to drown one of the other children in the bathtub.

Police quickly identified the main suspects to be Sarah Barrass, 35, the children's mother, and Brandon Machin, 39, and they were taken into custody.

Parents Under Investigation

Although police and authorities knew Barrass was the children's mother, they discovered that Machin, her half-brother, was allegedly the father of the children. They'd been conducting an incestuous relationship for many years. Machin lived at another home but spent a lot of time at the house on Gregg House Road.

During the investigation, they found Barrass had made a note on her cellphone that Machin was the father of the children. The children, though, had been led to believe their father had died.

Questioning of Barrass uncovered the motive of the murders and attempted murders. Back in November 2018, an accusation had been made towards Blake of committing a sexual assault on another child. This had resulted in social services becoming involved with the family. Two years beforehand, he'd been diagnosed with ADHD (Attention Deficit Hyperactivity Disorder), but the accusations didn't stop there.

Just before the murders in early May, another accusation of sexual assault had been made against Tristan. A meeting with social services occurred on May 22, of which Barrass wasn't included, and this is believed to have been a crisis point for Barrass. The investigation uncovered messages she'd written that showed she was concerned about losing her children to care.

Following the social services meeting, Barrass was told the status of the children as 'child in protection,' which involved a more active intervention by social services.

Then, on May 23, yet another sexual assault allegation was made against Tristan, and Barrass received a phone call from a local stating they were going to report the matter to the authorities.

On the night of May 23, Barrass and Machin tried to poison the four oldest children using ADHD medication that had been prescribed for Blake. When this failed to kill the children, Barrass grabbed a cord from a dressing grown and began strangling Tristan. Machin used his hands to strangle Blake. Once they were unconscious, they placed plastic bags over their heads to suffocate them. Then they tried to drown one of the other children in the bath.

Shortly after 7:00 A.M. on May 24, Barrass sent a text message to a friend claiming Machin was going to kill her and that two of the children, Tristan and Blake, were already dead. Both the friend and Barrass called the police.

Guilty Pleas

When Barrass was arrested, she told police that she would rather see her children dead than in social services care. She also stated, "I gave them life, and I can take it away."

In court on September 27, Barrass and Machin pled guilty to the two murders and charges of conspiracy to murder all six of the children. Barrass was actually charged with five counts of attempted murder, despite only four children surviving, because she'd tried to kill one child twice.

The sentencing hearing was scheduled for November 12. On this day, Barrass and Machin received sentences of life imprisonment with minimum terms of 35 years.

Fatal Kawasaki Stabbings

A 51-year-old man went on a stabbing rampage at a bus stop in the Tama ward of Kawasaki City, Japan, on May 28. The morning attack left two dead and an additional 18 injured.

Students Attacked

An emergency call was placed at 7:44 A.M., informing authorities that a man had attacked numerous students waiting at a bus stop. The attacker had targeted largely female students and was using long and thin knives that were typically used to prepare nigiri sushi and sashimi.

The attack was witnessed by a bus driver who stated he'd seen the man carrying two knives walking towards the bus. The perpetrator then began attacking the young students as they lined up to board the bus.

The rampage resulted in injuries to 16 elementary students and three adults.

Suspect Commits Suicide

The attacker, later identified as Ryuichi Iwasaki, stabbed himself in the neck to commit suicide following the attack. There were two knives covered in blood near him, and another two knives were found in his backpack that He'd left at a FamilyMart near the scene.

Iwasaki was still alive and was transported to a local hospital for treatment, but he subsequently died from his self-inflicted injuries.

He was described as unemployed and a 'hikikomori,' a person who withdraws from society in an extreme manner. He'd been living in the home of his elderly uncle. There had been a dispute between Iwasaki and the neighbors, but he refused to tell his uncle what it was about.

Those Who Were Killed

The two victims who were killed were Satoshi Oyama, 39, an employee of the Foreign Ministry who worked as a diplomat in Myanmar, and Hanako Kuribayashi, an 11-year-old student.

Both deceased victims had been transported to the hospital where they were declared dead. The surviving victims had been transported to three hospitals, including Kawasaki Municipal Tama Hospital, St. Marianna University School of Medicine, and the Shin-Yurigaoka General Hospital.

The students were from a Catholic school, Caritas Gakuen, in Kawasaki City. Oyama was believed to be the father of one of the female students.

No motive was identified for the attack. According to the school headmaster who was near the bus stop at the time of the stabbings, Iwasaki didn't say anything during the attack. However, other witnesses thought they heard him say he was going to kill the girls.

This type of violent crime isn't common in Japan, but there have been a number of stabbing attacks in the last several years. A knife-wielding man attacked 19 patients at a disabled facility in 2016, killing them all. Another attack occurred in 2010, when a stabbing spree took place on a commuter bus and a school bus, resulting in more than a dozen children and adults being stabbed.

Unhappy Employee Opens Fire in Virginia Beach

A mass shooting occurred on May 31 at a municipal building in Virginia Beach, Virginia, America. The actions of a former employee would result in the deaths of twelve people, and the wounding of four others before the perpetrator was shot and killed by police.

Angry Man on a Rampage

On the afternoon of May 31, the disgruntled employee shot someone sitting in a car in the parking lot of the Virginia Beach Municipal Center. He then shot another person on the steps as he entered the building. Inside the building were the offices of the city's public works, planning departments and utilities. Although security passes were needed to enter employee areas, there was no security at the entrance of the building.

The gunman opened fire randomly as he moved through the three floors of the building. It didn't seem as though he was targeting anyone, just firing at anyone he saw. Alerts were sent out through the building through text messages and phone calls, urging people to take shelter or evacuate.

Because renovations were being undertaken, many employees thought the gunshots were nail gun sounds, so they hadn't been aware there was a problem until the alerts occurred.

When police responded, along with the FBI, ATF, and Department of Homeland Security, they had difficulty entering through the electronic security doors inside the building. The gunman and the law enforcement officers exchanged gunfire once they were inside, resulting in the death of the gunman.

The Loss of Many

Eleven of the 12 killed were employees of the city, and the other victim was a contractor who had come to the building to get a permit. Among the employees, their combined years of service amounted to 150 years. One of the victims had been an employee for an astonishing 41 years.

Six of the victims had worked alongside the gunman in the public utilities department. Of the five people injured, three were critical, and four were treated in hospital. One of the police officers was shot, but fortunately, it struck his bulletproof vest, thus saving his life.

DeWayne Antonio Craddock

The gunman was identified as DeWayne Antonio Craddock, 40, who was born DeWayne Antonio Hamilton in October 1978. He had worked in the public utilities department as an engineer but sent an email to city management a few hours before the shooting to offer his resignation.

Because his resignation was the same day, and they felt he wasn't a risk, so he hadn't been forced to return his security badge immediately. This enabled him to gain access to the employee areas during the attack.

Leading up to the resignation and attack, Craddock had allegedly been involved in some physical altercations with fellow employees and he'd been threatened with disciplinary action.

During the three years prior to the shooting, Craddock had legally purchased a total of six firearms, including:

- 2x Glock 21 .45-caliber pistol
- H&K USP Compact Tactical pistol with a suppressor
- Bond Arms Backup Derringer .45-caliber
- Just Right Carbine .45-caliber
- Ruger rifle

The two weapons used in the attack were one of the Glock 21 .45-caliber pistol and the H&K USP Compact Tactical firearm with a suppressor.

Craddock had previously served as a cannon crew member in the Virginia Army National Guard between 1996 and 2002. He didn't see any combat time but was ranked a Specialist with the First Battalion, 111th Field Artillery Regiment at the time of his discharge. During his service, he obtained a degree in civil engineering.

Vigils and Aftermath

In the aftermath of the shootings, many organizations and churches held vigils for the victims. At the crime scene, the Courthouse Community United Methodist Church provided food for the police officers once the scene had been secured.

During the police official announcement the following day, they only mentioned Craddock's name once, saying it'd be the only time they'd say his name. Instead, they focused on the victims, including where they were from, their backgrounds, names, and ages.

Terrorist Attacks in Brief

May 1

Gadchiroli, India: An explosive device was triggered by Naxalites near a police vehicle, killing 15 police personnel and the driver.

May 3-6

Southern Israel Gaza - Israel: Clashes escalated between Israel and Gaze after a Palestinian Islamic Jihad sniper shot two Israeli soldiers and Gaza militants fire over 600 rockets into Israel. A total of at least 19 were killed, along with 10 militants. Injuries were in the hundreds.

May 8

Lahore, Pakistan: Female visitors were targeted by a suicide bomber at the Sufi Data Darbar shrine. Thirteen were killed, plus the bomber. A splinter group of the Taliban in Pakistan, Hizbul Ahrar or Jamaat-ul-Ahrar, claimed responsibility.

May 11

Gwadar, Pakistan: Gunmen dressed in security uniforms attacked a hotel, resulting in a shootout that lasted hours. Eight people were killed, along with the 3 gunmen.

May 24

Kabul, Afghanistan: Three people, including a senior Muslim preacher, were murdered and at least 20 wounded after an explosion in a mosque during Friday prayers in the Afghan capital, Kabul.

Lyon, France: A 24-year-old Algerian man riding a bike dropped a bomb in front of a bakery. Minutes later, the bomb exploded, injuring 13 people. The suspect told investigators that he'd pledged allegiance to the Islamic State.

May 26

Kathmandu, Nepal: Three separate bombings, all accidental, resulted in the deaths of the 4 perpetrators.

Chapter 6:
JUNE

The Darwin Mass Shooting

Four people were killed and another injured in a mass shooting on June 4 in Darwin, Australia. Beginning at 5:39 P.M, the shooting occurred across several locations, and one man was eventually captured and charged with the crimes.

Shooter on the Move

The shooter started his rampage near Finnis Street, close to the central business district, before moving onto other locations. These included the Buffalo Club, the Palms Motel, Gardens Hill Crescent, and a Coles Express and Jolly Street in Woolner, Darwin.

Witnesses near one of the locations saw the gunman enter the Palms Motel, located on McMinn Street. He proceeded to shoot through the door of a guestroom using a pump-action shotgun, and approximately 20 shots were fired. As the gunman moved from room to room, witnesses heard him screaming out the name 'Alex.'

When police responded, the area was locked down. Reportedly 100 police officers attended the incident, including members of the Territory Response Group. The suspect fled the scene of the shooting at the motel in a vehicle and was at large for around an hour. He then told police where he was: at the intersection of Daly and McMinn Streets, so he was then taken into custody.

The Suspect

The perpetrator was a suspected motorcycle gang member, Benjamin Glenn Hoffman, 45. He had been incarcerated until January, at which point he was released with an electronic monitoring bracelet as part of his parole terms. During the attack, he'd suffered a knife wound and had been tasered, so he was taken to hospital for treatment.

When Hoffman had been released in January, he'd been serving a 6-year sentence and 4 years had been eligible for parole. After he was released, he violated his parole conditions by breaking his curfew. Even though it was only broken by less than an hour, he was returned to prison for another two weeks, before being released out again in May.

After his arrest for the mass shooting, police revealed Hoffman had been stopped hours beforehand for speeding.

The Victims

Hassan Baydoun, 33, was a taxi driver taking his meal break at the Palms Motel when he was shot and killed by Hoffman. An unidentified woman, 23, received gunshot injuries to the legs at the motel.

In Gardens Hill Crescent, a short distance away, Nigel Hellings, 75, was shot and killed. Then in the Buff Club carpark, Michael Sisois, 57, was shot and killed. Hoffman then traveled to Woolner and attacked Rob Courtney, 52, a casino security guard. Courtney fought back with a knife, resulting in Hoffman's injuries before he was shot to death.

Unknown Motive

Charges of murder and attempted murder were formally expedited by June 5. The motivation behind the attack hasn't been identified by police or Hoffman. But, because he'd been heard calling out for 'Alex,' the belief is that he was looking for someone in particular. However, according to police, the 'Alex' he was looking for was out of the state at the time of the mass shooting.

Murder of David Ortiz - Wrong Place, Wrong Time

David Ortiz was a retired professional baseball player. On June 9, he was shot while sitting in a bar in Santo Domingo, Dominican Republic. It was later announced that the shooting was a case of mistaken identity, and Ortiz had simply been in the wrong place at the wrong time.

Who Was David Ortiz?

Born in the Dominican Republic, Ortiz later resided in a variety of places throughout his baseball career. Since 2017, he'd lived with his wife and two of their children in Miami, but continued to keep a home in the Dominican Republic.

During his career, Ortiz had played for the Minnesota Twins and the Boston Red Sox. Despite his fame, Ortiz would often go to popular clubs at night in the Dominican Republic without any security. His friends claimed Ortiz believed his fans would always protect him.

Mistaken Identity

At around 5:40 P.M., on June 9, suspect Alberto Miguel Rodriguez Mota was seen arriving at the Dial Bar and Lounge, East Santo Domingo. For several hours he waited for the man he intended to shoot, Sixto David Fernandez, who happened to be a friend of Ortiz.

Fernandez arrived and took a seat at the same table he usually sat at. Mota photographed Fernandez and sent it to a prison inmate, Jose Eduardo Ciprian. The photograph was quite blurry, and a white object was obscuring the black pants Fernandez was wearing.

The photo was sent by a text message by Ciprian to Gabriel Alexander Perez Vizcaíno. 'He'd met with a number of other suspects at a gas station and showed them the texted photo.

Meanwhile, Ortiz had arrived and took a seat next to Fernandez. Ortiz was dressed in a shirt similar to the one Fernandez was wearing, and a pair of white pants.

Footage from a security camera later showed two men outside the bar on a motorcycle talking to a man in a vehicle. At around 8:50 P.M. a man got off a motorcycle and entered the bar. He mistakenly identified Ortiz as the man in the photo and shot him, striking him in the back. A TV host, Jhoel López, had been sitting with Ortiz, and he suffered a gunshot wound to the leg from the same bullet that had hit Ortiz.

Following the attack, Ortiz was rushed to a hospital and went into surgery. Three doctors performed a six-hour surgery which resulted in the removal of his gallbladder and part of his colon and to repair damage to his liver.

The Boston Red Sox organized for a medical flight to transport Ortiz to Bostom on June 10 so he could receive top quality treatment at Massachusetts General Hospital. Another surgery was performed, after which he was said to be making a good recovery. A third surgery was completed on July 11. After spending six weeks in the hospital, Ortiz was discharged on July 26.

Fortunately for López, the injury to his thigh he received from the gunshot didn't require any surgery.

On September 9, Ortiz appeared in public for the first time at Fenway Park to throw the ceremonial first pitch.

Investigation and Arrests

Immediately after the shooting, one of the suspects, Eddy Feliz Garcia, fell off the motorcycle outside the bar. He was subsequently beaten by bar patrons until police arrived and arrested him.

Six suspects were arrested by June 12, and police were searching for still more. According to Police Major General Ney Aldrin Bautista Almonte, the attack organizer had been offered the equivalent of $7,800 USD to orchestrate the attack.

The number of suspects arrested rose to 9 by June 14, including 1 woman and 8 men. The gun used to shot Ortiz was also located. The same day, another suspect turned himself into police. An 11th suspect was identified as Franklin Junior Merán on June 18 and taken into custody. Police alleged he'd rented one of the vehicles that had been involved in the planned attack.

One of the suspects was Rolfi Ferreira Cruz, 25, and police believed he was the actual gunman. He'd previously been wanted for multiple robberies and charges relating to firearms in New Jersey.

Following his arrest, Cruz stated that Ortiz was not the intended victim. He said that he had been hired to carry out the killing and used the given clothing description based on the blurry photo.The named suspects included:

- Rolfi Ferreira Cruz - alleged gunman
- Alberto Miguel Rodriguez Mota - allegedly took the photo
- Víctor Hugo Gómez Vasquez - allegedly solicited the attack, also charged in Texas with federal drug trafficking
- Jose Eduardo Ciprian - an inmate who received the photo and passed it on
- Gabriel Alexander Perez Vizcaíno - allegedly showed the photo to other suspects
- Luis Alfredo Rivas Clase - aka 'The Surgeon' - met with Vizcaíno before the shooting also wanted in connection with attempted murder in Pennsylvania
- Eddy Feliz Garcia - allegedly was on the motorcycle
- Franklin Junior Merán - allegedly rented a vehicle used in the attack
- Maria Fernanda Villasmil Manzanilla - aka 'The Venezuelan' - was allegedly in the car when Rivas Clase met Vizcaíno

Messages of Love

As soon as the news of the shooting was made public, numerous messages of support and love were conveyed to Ortiz. Some of the baseball players who sent messages were:

- Pedro Martínez
- Alex Rodriguez
- Mike Trout
- Marcus Stroman
- David Wells
- Travis Shaw
- Nelson Figueroa

A statement by Eduardo Núñez, player for the Boston Red Sox, argued that it was 'unimaginable' for the shooting to take place in the Dominican Republic and that it was an "international shame."

A tweet was created by former President Barack Obama which reminisced how Ortiz had helped Boston heal from the Bostom Marathon Bombing, so Obama a wished him a speedy recovery.

Following the official announcement that the shooting was the result of mistaken identity, many were skeptical. The supposed original target Fernandez claimed he'd no enemies and that he didn't even look like Ortiz. Despite there being many doubts about the government's claim of mistaken identity, people also doubted that Ortiz had actually been the number one target that night.

The Killing of Actor Rafael Miguel

In a tragic case of domestic violence, young Brazilian actor Rafael Henrique Miguel was shot and killed on June 9 alongside his parents. The family had gone to the home of Miguel's girlfriend's family to discuss the relationship when the girl's father opened fire on them.

A Child Star

Born in 1996, Miguel began acting as a child in a variety of commercials, one of the most well-known in Brazil was an advertisement for a nutritional supplement, Sustagen.

From there, he acted in a number of TV films and TV series on Brazilian television, and he became highly acclaimed, particularly with younger people.

Miguel made his first major debut in JK, a miniseries, in 2006. Later that year he starred in a telenovela, *Cristal,* playing the part of Bentinho. During 2006 and 2007, he acted in *Pé na Jaca*, depicting the son of Murilo Benicio and Flavia Alessandra.

He continued to have acting success in *Cama de Gato* in 2009 and playing the part of Paçoca in the telenovela *Chiquitita*s between 2013 and 2015, this most prolific role.

A Disapproving Father

Miguel and his parents went to his girlfriend's house on June 9 to discuss the progression of their relationship with her father. Soon after, Miguel and his parents were shot and killed by the father, who allegedly blamed Miguel for his daughter, Isabela Tibcherani, suffering from depression.

On June 10, Miguel and his parents were buried, a customary quick burial, in Cemitério Campo Grande, located South of São Paulo. Meanwhile, their killer was on the run from authorities.

Killer on the Run

The killer was identified as Paulo Cupertino Matias, and police still have no clue where he's hiding. There has been much speculation that Matias may have left the country, while others believe he's still seeking refuge within the city.

His whereabouts are still unknown.

Sobane Da Massacre

The Dogon village of Sobane Da, Mali, was attacked on June 10 in a massacre that lasted for several hours. The attack was blamed on a Fulani militia group, and the death toll was 35 with many others missing. About 50 attackers drove into the village and began killing in a massacre the government believes was undertaken by terrorists.

The Fulanis and the Dogon

Traditionally, the Fulanis are herders and the Dogon farmers, and there has been a long-standing historical dispute between them over grazing land and water supply. The conflict has been worsened by the increase of jihadism in the area.

The Fulani have been accused by the Dogon of supporting terrorist groups including Al-Qaeda. In return, the Fulani have accused the state of supporting the Dogons in their attacks upon them. Between January 2018 and May 2019, there have been 488 Fulani deaths and 63 Dogon deaths during attacks.

Seven Hour Massacre

On June 9, attackers arrived at Sobane-Da on motorbikes and began killing people and setting fire to their homes. They shot every person they came across while shouting, "Allahu Akbar." Animals were stolen and buildings completely destroyed in the attack, which lasted for 7 hours.

At first, the government announced 95 people had been killed as they were going by what was said by soldiers that were there and the mayor. Eventually, the official toll was dropped down to 35. Part of the confusion about the death toll was that people weren't aware that nearly 100 women had managed to escape the massacre.

Suspects and Aftermath

During the investigation, police arrested 6 suspects they believe were involved in the massacre.

A week after the tragedy, 2 other Dogon villages were attacked and 41 people were killed.

President Ibrahim Boubacar Keita announced there'd be 3 days of national mourning.

The governor of the central Mopti region was sacked followed the attack on the Dogon group. General Sidi Alassane Toure stated, "Drawing lessons from this tragedy, the cabinet had dismissed Mopti's regional governor."

Of those killed in the massacre, 24 of them were children.

Security forces were deployed to the region.

Amhara Region coup d'état Attempt

A coup d'état was attempted against the regional government of the Amhara Region, Ethiopia, on June 22, resulting in the assassination of the Amhara Region President. The man suspected of being behind the attempt later escaped and was shot and killed.

History of Conflict

There has been a long history of conflicts between ethnicities in Ethiopia; and as a result, the government created a system of ethnic federalism under the 1995 Constitution. This resulted in the establishment of the Amhara Region as a subnational region, the population of which was largely Amhara people.

The Amhara National Democratic Movement (ANDM), later renamed the Amhara Democratic Party (ADP) and the Ethiopian People's Revolutionary Democratic Front (EPRDF), had been accused of "disciplining the Amhara people instead of representing them." Even so, Amahara nationalism was a marginal force during the first 20 years of the EPRDF-led order.

Gedu Andargachew, the Amhara regional president, resigned from his position in March 2019, giving no reasons. During his farewell speech, he warned that there was an increased risk of 'narrow nationalism.'

Ambachew Mekonnen replaced Andargachew as regional president and he appointed Asaminew Tsige as Head of the Regional Security Forces . Tsige had previously been a political prisoner and was a retired general.

At the graduation ceremony of security forces members in June, Asaminew made a speech many saw as incendiary that was full of 'Amhara nationalist invective.'

The Attempt to Take Control

Explosions were both seen and heard coming from the Regional Police Commission headquarters in the early evening of June 22. Located at the headquarters were the offices of the regional legislature as well as the seat of the regional administration.

Soon afterward, gunfire was reported in Addis Ababa by witnesses, including the Embassy of the United States. According to the office of the Prime Minister, a 'hit squad' under the control of Asaminew Tsige had burst their way into a meeting of the regional cabinet and proceeded to open fire.

The meeting was regarding attempts by Asaminew to recruit ethnic militias openly.

Prime Minister Abiy Ahmed announced just after midnight on June 23 that Chief of Staff of the Ethiopian National Defense Force, General Se'are Mekonnen, had been attacked by people who were among his close entourage.

It was announced the next morning that Se'are and Magor General Gizae Aberra, his aide, had been killed. Further proclamations informed the public that Amhara Region President Ambachew Mekonnen had also been killed, and his adviser Ezez Wassie was also dead. Megbaru Kebede, the

Amhara Region Attorney general, had been injured and succumbed to his wounds on June 24.

For 36 hours, Asaminew evaded authorities until he was located and shot dead on June 24 near Bahir Dar by police. A number of people who were believed to have co-conspired with Asaminew were detained by police.

There were conflicting reports initially about the assassin. First announcements suggested he'd been arrested, but on June 24, police claimed he had committed suicide, so he wouldn't be arrested.

The Aftermath

After the attempted coup, there was a nationwide shut down of all internet access, which lasted for two days. No explanation was given officially. A call for unity by Prime Minister Abiy against the 'forces of evil' who had carried out the attempted coup and assassination was made. A national day of mourning was declared, and flags were flown at half-mast. The attempted coup was condemned by a large number of world leaders.

Terrorist Attacks in Brief

June 2

Azaz, Syria: A car bomb attack near a mosque and a market killed 22 people.

Kassel, Germany: The CDU politician Walter Lübcke was shot dead in front of his residence in Wolfhagen, Kassel. A suspect from the far-right milieu was arrested. Lübcke was famous for his pro-migrant views. Authorities suspect the incident to be a right-wing attack.

June 3

Tripoli, Lebanon: A security patrol was attacked by a militant with a bomb and firearms, resulting in the deaths of two soldiers and two policemen.

June 3-10

Khartoum, Sudan: Khartoum Massacre - protesters were ambushed by paramilitary forces and security forces over a period of days. One side claimed 118 were killed, and authorities put the figure at 62. It's impossible to be certain what the correct number was, as many bodies were dumped into the Nile River. Hundreds were injured, and many women were raped during the massacre.

June 10

Mopti Region, Mali: The village Sobane-Kou was attacked by approximately 50 men who were heavily armed. The first number of deaths given was 95, but the government revised it to a total of 35.

June 10-17

Ituri Province, the Democratic Republic of the Congo: In multiple attacks and massacres, an astonishing 240 or more people were killed during clashes between Hema and Lendu tribes. The Lendu were the main attackers and the Hema were the targets. In one mass grave in Tche, 160 bodies were found.

June 12

Abha, Saudi Arabia: A Houthi-fired rocket landed in the arrivals hall of the Abha International Airport, injuring over two dozen civilians.

Anantnag, India: Two militants attacked paramilitary soldiers while they patrolled the streets. Six were killed plus one of the attackers.

June 16

Konduga, Nigeria: Three Boko Haram suicide bombers targeted a group of people watching football in the Mandareri-Sambisa ward. Thirty were killed in addition to the bombers.

June 17

Dallas, US: A gunman attacked the Earle Cabell Federal Building and Courthouse in Dallas, Texas, United States. No law enforcement officers or civilians were injured in the shooting, though one person sustained a superficial injury when she was taking cover; the only casualty was the shooter who was shot dead by the security forces. The gunman appears to have self-radicalized online, posting memes from an incel, extremist far-right memes including ideas about the Confederate States and Nazism, combining eco-friendly and libertarian ideas with far-right authoritarianism.

June 21

Baghdad, Iraq: A suicide bomber detonated his explosives in a crowd who were worshipping at a Shia mosque, with ten killed plus the bomber.

June 22

Bahir Dar, Addis Ababa, Ethiopia: Dozens of people were killed during a failed coup d'état by Amhara militias against the regional government. In Bahir Dar, the Amhara Region President Ambachew Mekonnen, his adviser Ezez Wassie and Amharra Region Attorney General Megbaru Kebede were killed in the state offices during a meeting. In Addis Ababa Chief of Staff of the Ethiopian National Defense Force General Se'are Mekonnen and a retired general who had been visiting him were killed by a bodyguard. The militias were part of the Amhara Region's Peace and Security Bureau led by Brigadier General Asaminew Tsige, who was shot dead by security forces two days later.

June 28

Indanan, Phillippines: A military camp was attacked by two suicide bombers, leaving six people killed, including 3 soldiers. The attack was claimed by the Islamic State group.

June 30

Maruf District, Afghanistan: Humvee vehicles packed with explosives was driven by four Taliban insurgents into a government compound. The death toll was 53 and included 45 police officers.

Chapter 7:
JULY

The Torrid Tale of Jeffrey Epstein

Jeffrey Epstein, a financier, was arrested on July 6 on federal charges of sex trafficking of minors in New York and Florida. It wasn't the first time he'd faced similar charges. In turn, his arrest caused widespread condemnation and opened up the possibility of many more influential and famous people indicated in the case. Even his death in a prison cell has left many questions unanswered, and more investigations are needed to determine what exactly had happened and how he died alone in his cell.

Epstein's Background

On January 20, 1953, Epstein was born in Brooklyn to a middle-class Jewish family. In September 1974, he began working as a teacher in physics and mathematics in Manhattan. In June 1976, he was fired for poor performance.

While he'd been teaching, he was introduced to Alan Greenburg, the CEO of Bear Stearns. Eventually, Epstein was offered a job with the company due to his drive to be financially successful and his intelligence.

Epstein started as a junior assistant to a floor trader with Bear Stearns, but he quickly moved upwards to become an options trader. Within four years, Epstein became a limited partner with the company. But, in 1981, he was asked to leave, allegedly due to a 'reg d violation.'

Intercontinental Assets Group Inc. was founded by Epstein when he left Bear Stearns. He later met Steven Hoffenberg, and in 1987, the two attempted to undertake a corporate raid and take over Pan Am, but they failed.

Epstein started working as a consultant for Tower Financial Corporation the same year. He was paid a staggering $25,000 per month USD for his consulting work. The company imploded in 1993, and Hoffenberg stated in court documents that Epstein had been closely involved with their Ponzi scheme. However, Epstein had resigned in 1989 before the collapse and was never charged.

From there, he continued to work in the financial sector and traveled to numerous countries including the Middle East. In May 2007, facing charges of sex with minors, Epstein tried to negotiate a plea deal. In August 2007, the US Attorney in Miami entered into the plea agreement discussions.

During the discussions, Epstein allegedly provided certain unspecified information in exchange for a lighter sentence. The information pertained to the criminal case against the managers of the Bear Stearns hedge fund.

It was reported that Epstein had invested in the startup 'Report Homeland Security' in 2015, which was connected to the defense industry of Israel.

Hidden Video Cameras

Epstein installed numerous hidden cameras in all of his properties, so that he could record any sexual activity between prominent people who stayed at his properties with underage girls. The purpose was to use the information as blackmail, if needed.

The private island owned by Epstein in the Virgin Islands was wired completely for video recording. He began recording everyone who came to the island as a form of insurance. During a police raid in 2006 on his home in Palm Beach, two cameras were discovered.

According to Maria Farmer, who had been to Epstein's New York mansion, she'd been shown a media room where people were monitoring what was happening throughout the home by the video footage from the hidden cameras. To get into the media room, you had to access a hidden door. She said that the main focus of the cameras was on bedrooms and toilets, obviously to try and catch footage of people in their most intimate moments.

It was alleged that Epstein had 'lent' young girls to powerful individuals, so that he could gain the information to later use against them.

First Criminal Cases

A report was made to police in Palm Beach in March 2005 by a mother who claimed her stepdaughter who was only 14, had been taken to Epstein's mansion by another girl who was older. She claimed the stepdaughter was paid $300 to strip in front of Epstein and massage him.

From there, police conducted an undercover investigation of Epstein, which lasted for 13 months. The FBI became involved in the investigation; and between them and the police, they discovered Epstein had paid a number of girls to perform sexual acts with him. The youngest girl was 14, and most were under 16.

The FBI had reports on 34 confirmed minors whose allegations of sexual abuse by Epstein could be corroborated. Later around 80 victims were identified. There were further allegations that for Epstein's birthday, triplets who were only 12 years old were brought in from France then returned the next day. During the time they were with Epstein, they were sexually abused by him.

Allegedly, young girls were brought in from all over the world, including Europe, Brazil, other South American countries, and the former Soviet countries. Jean Luc Brunel's MC2 modeling agency was also allegedly supplying young girls to Epstein.

A probable cause affidavit was filed in May 2006 by the Palm Beach police that there should be four counts of unlawful sex with minors and one count of sexual abuse against Epstein.

A grand jury decision meant that Epstein would only be charged with one count of felony solicitation of prostitution, to which he pled not guilty in August 2006.

'Operation Leap Year' was instigated by the FBI in July 2006 to probe Epstein, which resulted in an indictment 53 pages long in June 2007. However, it wasn't presented to a grand jury and a plea deal was negotiated. Epstein was to receive immunity from all federal charges along with other co-conspirators. He agreed to plead guilty to two felony charges of prostitution and pay restitution to 36 victims that had been identified by the FBI. He'd also be required to register as a sex offender.

Epstein later pled guilty to a state charge of procurement of a girl under the age of 18 in June 2008. He received a prison sentence of 18 months, but he was sent to a private wing of the Palm Beach County Stockade instead of the state prison. After a few months, he was given permission to leave during the day and return to the Stockade. He ended up serving 13 months of his sentence.

A number of civil cases were filed against Epstein:

Jane Does v. Epstein - 2008

An anonymous woman filed a civil lawsuit to the value of $50 million against Epstein on February 6, 2008. She claimed that as a 16-year-old, she was recruited to provide Epstein with a massage. Once at his mansion, she said he had sexual intercourse with her and gave her $200.

Another suit similar to this one was filed by a different woman in March 2008. Both lawsuits were later dismissed, along with several others.

Victim's Rights - Jane Does v. United States - 2014

A federal civil suit was filed on December 30, 2014, in Florida by two women for violations of the Crime Victims' Rights Act for Epstein's lenient and limited state plea in 2008. As the case progressed, two more women were added.

Virginia Roberts Giuffre v. Epstein - 2015

Giuffre alleged in a sworn affidavit in January 2015 that when she was 17 years old, she'd been held by Epstein as a sex slave. She also claimed she'd been trafficked to several others, including Alan Dershowitz and Prince Andrew. She said she'd been sexually and physically abused. She'd been a sex slave from 1999 to 2002, during which time she'd helped recruit other underage girls.

Jane Doe v. Epstein and Trump - 2016

In April 2016, a federal lawsuit against Donald Trump and Epstein was filed by a woman in California who claimed she'd been sexually assaulted by them at parties at Epstein's mansion when she was only 13 years old. The suit was dismissed in May 2016.

Sarah Ransome v. Epstein and Maxwell - 2017

Ransome filed a suit in 2017 against Epstein and Maxwell. She maintained she'd been hired by Maxwell to provide massages to Epstein, who later threatened her if she didn't comply with his sexual demands. In 2018 the suit was settled.

Bradley Edwards Defamation v. Epstein - 2018

Attorney Edwards filed a state civil lawsuit against Epstein in 2018. It was settled in December 2018.

Maria Farmer v. Epstein and Maxwell - 2019

Farmer filed a sworn affidavit on April 16, 2019, in federal court in New York. She alleged that along with her sister Anne, who had been 15, they'd been sexually assaulted by both Maxwell and Epstein in 1996.

Jennifer Araoz v. Epstein - 2019

While awaiting trial, a petition was served to Epstein about a state civil lawsuit that was pending. Araoz claimed she was raped by Epstein when she was 15 years old.

Human Trafficking Charges

Epstein was arrested on July 6, 2019 on sex trafficking charges at Teterboro Airport, New Jersey. At the same time, FBI agents stormed his townhouse in Manhattan and conducted a search. They found evidence of sex trafficking and hundreds of photographs of females either nude or only partially dressed. Some of the females were confirmed as underage at the time the photographs were taken.

Numerous CDs were found in a locked safe with labels depicting what was contained on them, including nude 'girl pics.' Cash to the value of $70,000, a fraudulent Austrian passport that had expired in 1987, and 48 diamonds were also found in the safe.

The Austrian passport bore Epstein's photograph but another name, and it had multiple entry and exit stamps showing the passport had been used in Spain, France, Saudi Arabia, and the United Kingdom before it expired.

Epstein was formally charged on July 8 with sex trafficking and conspiracy to traffic minors for sex. The indictment stated that dozens of underage girls had been taken to his mansions for sex.

Despite the efforts of Epstein's lawyers to obtain bail, it was denied on July 18, as the judge deemed Epstein a danger and a serious flight risk.

Days later, on July 23, guards found Epstein lying on the cell floor at 1:30am in a semiconscious state. He had marks around his neck, and it was unclear whether he'd attempted suicide or been assaulted. His cellmate, former police officer Nicholas Tartaglione who was facing four counts of murder, denied knowing anything about what had happened to Epstein. Epstein also recalled having no knowledge of what had occurred.

Investigation in France

It was announced by the prosecutor's office in Paris, France, on August 23, 2019, that an investigation was being conducted into Epstein. The investigation was looking into possible crimes he may have committed in France and against citizens of France in other countries.

Epstein's Controversial Death

Following the first discovery of Epstein in his cell with injuries to his neck, Epstein was placed on a suicide watch. Although Epstein thought he might have been attacked by his cellmate, the staff at the prison suspected he'd tried to commit suicide.

On July 29, he was removed from suicide watch and transferred to a special housing unit. He was said to be in 'good spirits' at the time. He was given a cellmate, and the prison said they'd check in his cell every half hour.

The cellmate was moved out on August 9, and no other inmate was moved into Epstein's cell. That evening, despite the normal procedures, the guards failed to check Epstein every half hour. Apparently, the guards on duty had fallen asleep and didn't check Epstein's cell for around three hours. To cover themselves, they falsified the records. Strangely, the cameras located in front of Epstein's cell also failed to operate that night.

At 6:30 A.M. on August 10, guards found Epstein deceased in his cell. Prison staff immediately tried lifesaving measures, and emergency responders were called. He was transferred to hospital but declared dead. The prison called it a suicide.

Investigation Into His Death and Autopsy Results

The autopsy on Epstein took place on August 11. The initial report stated he'd suffered multiple fractures of the bones in his neck, including the hyoid bone, which can occur from hanging but is more common in strangulation deaths.

The New York City medical examiner, Barbara Sampson, ruled on August 16 that Epstein had died due to suicide by hanging. Epstein's lawyers weren't convinced and began conducting their own investigation. They claimed the evidence was more consistent with murder rather than suicide.

Dr. Michael Baden, a renowned forensic pathologist, was hired by the estate of Epstein to observe his autopsy. He determined in October that the injuries Epstein had were extremely unusual in hangings and much more common in homicidal strangulation. He, therefore, concluded it was more likely a homicide than suicide.

An investigation into Epstein's death was ordered by Attorney General Barr to be conducted by the Department of Justice Inspector General. The FBI was also conducting an investigation. Barr later said there were "serious irregularities" in how the prison handled Epstein and promised that there'd be some accountability.

The cameras in front of Epstein's cell that had allegedly malfunctioned were sent to an FBI crime lab to be examined.

Guards Charged

New York federal prosecutors charged prison guards Tova Noel and Michael Thomas on November 19 with creating false records, and with conspiracy. The prosecutors had obtained video footage that showed Epstein hadn't been checked in his cell for eight hours prior to being discovered dead.

Tacoma Firebombing

The Immigration and Customs Enforcement detention center in Tacoma, Washington, was firebombed on July 13. The perpetrator was shot and killed by police while trying to ignite a gas tank.

Detention Center Attacked

At 4:00 A.M. on July 13, the Northwest Detention Center for undocumented immigrants was under attack by a man throwing firebombs. When police arrived, they found the suspect carrying flares and wearing a satchel. He was also armed with a rifle and was using it to try and ignite a large propane tank. He repeatedly threw firebombs at the buildings and vehicles.

Unable to stop the suspect, and with the massive risk of the propane tank exploding, if he wasn't stopped, police opened fire and shot and killed him.

Suspect - Willem van Spronsen

The suspect was Willem van Spronsen, a carpenter of Vashon, Washington. In June 2018, he was arrested at the same location while demonstrating and had engaged in a physical altercation with a police officer. He was known to be an anarchist and he'd claimed he was associated with antifascists.

Van Spronsen's daughter had described him as an Anarchism supporter, and that she'd disagreed with his principles of using weapons and force. He'd been using the pseudonym Emma Durutti in social media, which was a combination of historic anarchists Emma Goldman and Buenaventura Durruti. Van Spronsen was involved in the Occupy Wall Street protests and was a member of the Puget Sound John Brown Gun Club. He'd previously been involved with the help group Alcoholics Anonymous.

The Manifesto

A manifesto written by van Spronsen expressed what he saw as political justification for his actions in firebombing the facility. He stated in the manifesto that "it's time to take action against the forces of evil" because of the "highly profitable detention/concentration camps and a battle over the semantics."

Northern British Columbia Murder Spree

From July 14 to July 19, two young men went on a killing spree on the Alaska Highway and Stewart-Cassiar Highway in British Columbia. During the six days, three people had been killed, and a massive manhunt was undertaken to try and find the men responsible.

Details of the Murders

Lucas Fowler of New South Wales, Australia, and his girlfriend Chynna Deese of North Carolina, America, had been on a three-week holiday around Canada when their van broke down on the Alaska Highway on July 14.

A mechanic, Curtis Broughton, and his wife Sandra had stopped to check on the young couple around 3:20 P.M. and were told that they had it under control. They'd said they were having a picnic while they waited for the van to 'unflood' and could start it again. Broughton maintained they were both happy and so they left.

On July 15, at 7:00 A.M., the bodies of the young couple were discovered by a highway worker, Trevor Pierre. They were found in a ditch near the van, their bodies a distance of five feet apart from each other, and both displayed gunshot injuries. The bodies were lying in a north direction with their heads facing towards the west. The back doors of the van were open and the windows had been smashed.

The next discovery occurred on July 19. A pickup truck that had been burnt out was found on Highway 73, South of the Stikine River Bridge. About 1.2 miles away to the South of the vehicle was the body of Leonard Dyck from Vancouver.

The two men believed to have used the pickup truck before it was burned were Kam McLeod and Bryer Schmegelsky, and initially, they were considered missing persons. A link was considered between the murder victims and the missing persons by July 22.

Suspects' Car Located

Another burning vehicle was found on July 23 near Fox Lake Cree Nation, north of Gillam in Manitoba. It was believed that the vehicle had been used by McLeod and Schmegelsky, and after the discovery, the Royal Canadian Mounted Police (RCMP) sought to have second-degree murder charges laid against the two young men.

Following public reporting of the case, a resident in Cold Lake, Alberta, told authorities that he'd assisted two young males after their vehicle got stuck on July 21. The same day, video cameras at a store in Saskatchewan captured McLeod and Schmegelsky, and the footage was given to police.

The two men had been seen twice on July 22 in Gillam, Manitoba. Later that day, they were stopped by Tataskweyak Cree Nation band constables in Split Lake and tested for alcohol use before being released. Two days later, the Emergency Response Team, air services, crisis negotiation team and canine units were sent to the area surrounding Gillam.

The search for the suspects was hindered by the environment, with swampy areas, dense forests, and wild animals all making it difficult. The search continued for almost a week with no success. A tip came in on July 28 that the two men matching the suspect's descriptions had been seen at the York Landing community landfill located southwest of Gillam.

Searches continued, and tips were coming in reporting sightings of McLeod and Schmegelsky. On August 2, a report was made to the RCMP by a local tour guide that a blue sleeping bag had been found near where the Nelson River enters Hudson Bay.

The following day a damaged boat was found on the northern shore of the river. Nearby were items that could be linked to McLeod and Schmegelsky.

Bodies Discovered

The bodies of McLeod and Schmegelsky were discovered on August 7 in northern Manitoba. They were lying in dense bush near the Nelson River, not too far from where the damaged boat was found. The autopsy report later confirmed that they'd both died due to self-inflicted gunshot wounds.

Law Enforcement Response

The RCMP commissioner formally requested the assistance of the Canadian Armed Forces on July 26, which was approved by Defense Minister Harjit Sajjan and Minister for Public Safety Ralph Goodale. By the next day, aircraft were deployed which had the ability to use high-thermal detection gear.

An Indigenous-led neighborhood watch group arrived on July 27 in Gillam after their presence was requested by the Assembly of the Manitoba Chiefs. During the manhunt, they provided volunteer services and support to the town's residents.

Arson Attack of Kyoto Animation

On the morning of July 18, the Kyoto Animation Studio in Kyoto, Japan, was attacked by an arsonist. Thirty-six people lost their lives, and a further 33 suffered injuries in the assault. It was one of the most deadly mass killings in the history of Japan since the end of World War II.

Background of the Studio

Kyoto Animation is an anime studio, with studios in a variety of locations. Studio 1 was in Fushimi, while Studios 2 and 5 were in Uji, along with the merchandise development division. Some of the most well-known titles produced by Kyoto Animation were Clannad, The Melancholy of Haruhi Suzumiya and K-On!.

Death threats had been sent to Kyoto Animation weeks before the attack, and the company president later stated it was unclear whether they were related to the subsequent arson attack due to the anonymous nature of the former threats. Police and the company's lawyers had been made aware of the threats when received.

Fiery Explosion

At approximately 10:30 A.M. on the morning of July 18, the suspect entered Studio 1 and used 40 liters of gasoline to set the building on fire. He'd carried the gasoline into the building using a platform trolley. When the gasoline mixed with the air, a massive explosion was caused.

Witnesses claimed the suspect was shouting "die" as the fire was lit. Some of the people in the building were doused with the gasoline by the suspect; and as they ignited, they fled the building, running onto the street.

The staff was trapped by the fire at the building entrance. On the third floor, 19 bodies were discovered near the stairs that lead to the roof. It seemed they'd tried to escape but were overcome by the smoke and flames.

The suspect ran from the building but collapsed on the street, suffering burn injuries himself, and he was quickly apprehended by the police. Nearby were several knives, but none had been used in the attack.

By 3:19 P.M. the fire was out, and all staff that had been in the building had been accounted for, whether they were dead or alive. The building had been completely destroyed. The lack of fire sprinklers and fire hydrants in the building certainly didn't help the situation, but legally they weren't required due to the classification as a small office.

Most of the computers and other materials were destroyed in the fire, but it was later reported that they'd been able to recover some digitized drawings from a server that hadn't been damaged.

Mass Casualties and Deaths

At the time of the arson, there were 74 people inside Studio 1. Of the 36 killed, 3 had died in hospital later due to the severity of their injuries. The nature and severity of the burns made the identification of some victims very difficult, also DNA testing had to be used.

On July 22, the autopsy results were announced, stating that most of the victims had died from burn injuries rather than smoke inhalation. This was because the fire had spread so rapidly.

At least 20 victims were women, due to a high number of female animators at Kyoto Animation.

The Kyoto Animation company president requested that the media not release the victim's names out of respect for the families. Police announced on July 25 that all of the victims had been identified and they'd begun returning them to their families. While authorities and Kyoto Animation were trying to decide how and when to identify the victims to the media, some of the relatives had already released the information concerning their deceased loved ones. When police finally released the full list of deceased victims, it was against the wishes of at least 20 of the families. But, the police stated that due to the seriousness of the event and the high attention it received, it was in the public's best interest to release the names. They were:

- Naomi Ishida, 49
- Yasuhiro Takemoto, 47
- Futoshi Nishiya, 37
- Yoshiji Kigami, 61
- Nami Iwasaki, 31
- Megumu Ono, 21
- Norie Oto, 26
- Yumi Kaneo, 22
- Sumire Kusano, 32
- Seiya Kawaguchi, 27
- Aya Sato, 43
- Sana Suzuki, 30
- Kota Sato, 28
- Hiroyuki Takahashi, 48

- Tomoka Tokimori, 22
- Miho Takechi, 25
- Takahisa Fujita, 27
- Tatsunari Maruko, 31
- Kana Matsuura, 24
- Atsushi Miyaji, 32
- Shiho Morisaki, 27
- Yuko Myoken, 29
- Sayaka Watanabe, 27
- Chitose Murayama, 49
- Kojiro Matsumoto, 25
- Yuki Omura, 23
- Junichi Uda, 34
- Yuka Kasama, 22
- Ami Kuriki, 30
- Sachie Tsuda, 41
- Keisuke Yokota, 34
- Mikiko Watanabe, 35
- Shoko Terawaki, 44
- Atsushi Ishida, 31

One victim, whose name wasn't released, died in hospital on October 4 from septic shock as a result of the burn injuries during the arson attack. This death brought the total of lost lives to 36.

Suspect Injured in the Attack

The suspect was identified as Shinji Aoba, 41, and he'd been seen by witnesses near Studio 1 days before he embarked on the arson attack. When he was apprehended near the Keihan Railway Rokujizō Station, around 330 ft. from the studio, he was suffering from severe burns. The injuries largely affected his face, chest, and legs.

While Aoba was being transported to the hospital for treatment, he admitted he was the one responsible for the fire. He accused Studio 1 of plagiarizing the novels he'd written. Kyoto Animation later revealed they'd received a draft novel from Aoba, but it hadn't passed the first stage assessment. It was confirmed that there were no similarities between the draft novel and any of their published content.

Aoba's injuries were deemed no longer life-threatening on September 5; however, he was still hooked up to a ventilator in intensive care. By September 18, he'd apparently recovered his speech. Rehabilitation started on October 8, and he was by then able to conduct short conversations and sit upright in a wheelchair.

Aoba had largely recovered from his injuries by November. He expressed remorseful feelings towards the victims and again claimed responsibility for the attack. He was also very grateful to the staff at the hospital, which he said had treated him better than anyone else had done during his entire life.

It was later reported that Aoba had suffered from mental illness, and he'd a criminal history. He was arrested and convicted in 2012 of robbing a store at knifepoint and received a jail sentence of 3.5 years. Because of his mental illness, the maximum penalty he could receive for the arson and murders could be reduced from death to life imprisonment.

Response and Impact on Production

Donations were received by Kyoto Animation for the families of the victims. The donation amount rose to US$23.1 million from businesses and fans. The company worked the best way to divide the money between the surviving victims and the families of the deceased.

The government announced on October 27 that from February 2020, anyone who wanted to purchase gasoline would have to show identification.

Due to the tragedy, the *Free!* movie publicity event planned was canceled. Other productions were delayed, including an episode of *Fire Force'* an anime about firefighters and people who died from spontaneous combustion. When it was released, it was modified to cause less distress.

Hideaki Hatta, the president of Kyoto Animation, stated that he was considering demolishing what was left of Studio 1 and instead devising a green public park with a monument in memoriam to those who died.

Kidnapping and Murder of Alexandra Măceșanu

When 15-year-old Alexandra Măceșanu was kidnapped on July 24 in Caracal, Olt County, Romania, the delay by the police to search for the young girl had devastating consequences and led to many officials being dismissed among widespread protests and public outrage at the handling of the case.

The Abduction

Măceșanu was hitchhiking from Dobrosloveni to Caracal on July 24 when she was abducted. The driver of the car, Gheorghe Dincă, was a 65-year-old mechanic, and he took the girl back to his house. Once there, he proceeded to beat and rape her and held her captive. Remarkably, she found a telephone in her captivity room and called emergency services three times.

The first phone call was made at 11:05am on July 25. Măceșanu told the operator who she was and explained she'd been kidnapped and was being held in a house in Caracal. When asked if she'd been raped, she said yes. The operator told her she'd need to tell them exactly where she was so they could locate her.

A minute later, Măceșanu made her second emergency call, explaining that she'd been abducted, blindfolded and locked in a room in a house. She thought she was in Bold, Caracal because she recalled going past a dam. She told the operator that the kidnapper's car was grey but couldn't recall the license plate. A business card she found in the house had the name Lucian Gabrial Popescu on it, but she wasn't sure if that was the actual kidnapper's name or not.

At 11:07 A.M., the police took over the phone call, and she told them what the address was on the business card. Police told Măceşanu that the address she'd given belonged to an apartment building, but she said she was captive in a house. Măceşanu called again at 11:12 A.M., asking if police were on their way and that she was frightened the kidnapper was going to return to the house.

Despite Măceşanu begging for help and telling the police and the operators that she was frightened, she was spoken to in what was described from recordings as a condescending tone.

Location Identified

The location of the house was finally identified by police around 2:00 A.M. on July 26. Sadly, the decision was made by police and prosecutors Popescu Cristian Ovidiu, Zăvoianu Cătălin Alexandru and Vasilescu Liviu, to wait for another four hours before a search warrant could be used to enter the house. There was no need under the law to wait for a warrant, and they'd the legal right to enter.

An Arrest and Confession

When Dincă was arrested, he promptly confessed to kidnapping and murdering Măceşanu and another young girl, Luiza Melencu, 18, who had been missing since April.

In a barrel at the property, multiple teeth were found. Although it was initially reported that DNA belonging to Măceşanu was found in the fragments, it was later regarded as inconclusive. Of the teeth, some showed dental work that Măceşanu hadn't had done, indicating that they might belong to someone else.

The techniques used by the forensic specialists to examine the teeth as a whole destroyed them, so it was impossible to analyze each tooth individually.

Was He Covering for Someone Else?

The families of the two murdered girls believed that they'd been killed by someone else and that Dincă was covering up for a human trafficking network. These networks were prolific in Romania, and the families also contended that the raid on the house was delayed on purpose by prosecutors to help cover up a network.

It was discovered that Prosecutor Liviu had surveillance camera footage of Dincă's car obtained before the kidnapping of Măceşanu that linked Dincă to the disappearance of Melencu. Despite having the footage, the prosecutor neither searched his property or his car, nor did he bring him in for questioning. The footage wasn't shown to other prosecutors until July 27, at which point he only revealed a still picture of the vehicle that did not indicate the license plate.

Following the raid on Dincă's home, prosecutor Ovidiu claimed that Măceşanu had been strangled to death at 2:00 A.M the morning of July 27. However, it would have been impossible for him to make those statements first of all because her body hadn't been found, and Dincă didn't make his confession until days later.

After both girls disappeared, the families received phone calls from males saying the girls would be okay. One phone call told Măceşanu's mother that she'd gotten married and had gone abroad to work. At least one of the calls was believed to be from Dincă. The family of Melencu received similar phone calls. The voices on the calls varied, suggesting there were accomplices.

Dincă had claimed to have incinerated Măceşanu's body in the barrel, but many questioned the validity of his claim. Some wondered why he'd use a method of disposal that would take at least 8 hours to burn the body when he could have disposed of it quicker and easier. Also, if he'd known she'd used his phone, he would've gotten rid of the evidence in a hurry.

Neighbors gave conflicting statements over whether or not they'd noticed any smoke or bad smells associated with the burning of a human body.

Criticism of the Case

The Directorate for Investigating Organized Crime and Terrorism was heavily criticized for investigating both cases as murders and not kidnappings and for refusing multiple requests by the lawyers acting for the families. This included conducting experiments to determine whether or not the bodies could have been incinerated as claimed. Also, suspected accomplices and witnesses weren't properly questioned.

Alexandru Cumpănașu, Măceșanu's uncle who was a businessman and had been a former talk show host, announced a week after she'd been kidnapped that he'd obtained information about where she was being held. He said he'd sent the information to several officials, asking for immediate action. One of those officials, president Klaus Iohannis, replied to the request by simply saying, "I will analyze."

Outrage spread throughout Romania when news about the circumstances of the murder of Măceșanu. A protest attended by over 2,500 people took place in Bucharest on July 27.

As a result of the case and following public outcry, the Interior Minister Nicolae Moga dismissed the National Police Chief Ioan Buda, Olt County Police Chief Cristian Voiculescu, and Olt County Prefect Petre Neacsu. A week later, the Interior Minister also resigned.

The Minister of Education Ecaterina Andronescu made a statement that "Young girls should know better than to get in cars with strangers," which resulted in the Minister being dismissed by the Prime Minister.

It was discovered that Lucian Gabrial Popescu, the man whose business card Măceșanu had found in the house, hadn't been involved in the kidnapping and murder. He'd met Dincă on one occasion but didn't actually know him.

The Nganzai Funeral Attack

As a group of mourners walked from a funeral in the Nganzai District of Borno State, Nigeria, on July 27, Boko Haram terrorists opened fire on them. The death toll was 65, and another 10 were injured.

Mourners Attacked

Multiple Boko Haram extremists approached the funeral procession in vans and on three motorbikes at around 10:30 A.M. on July 27. The mourners, all males, were returning from the funeral in Goni Abachari to their village of Badu Kuluwu when they were attacked.

Many of the mourners attempted to chase after the terrorists, but they were fired upon and were unsuccessful. In the initial attack, 23 of the 65 victims were killed, with a further 42 dying in the gunfire as they tried to pursue the terrorists.

Presidential Response

Muhammad Buhari, the Nigerian President, directed the Army and Air Force to search for the terrorists following the attack. In a statement made by Muhammad Bulama, the Nganzai local government chairman, the attack was in retaliation for the killing of 11 Boko Haram extremists by a civilian self-defense group a week earlier.

A History of Conflict

There have been repeated attacks by Boko Haram fighters in the Nganzai district. They killed 8 people and stole cattle in two villages in September 2018 after the residents of the villages tried to prevent them from taking their livestock.

An attack occurred on a camp for displaced persons outside of Maiduguri, which left two people dead. They'd burned a military base and stolen food supplies.

The jihadist conflict had been ongoing for a decade and had spilled into Cameroon, Niger, and Chad, with an estimated 27,000 lives being lost and over 2 million having to flee from the violence.

Multiple Shot at Gilroy Garlic Festival

The Gilroy Garlic Festival was taking place on July 28 in Gilroy, California, when a gunman entered the festival and began shooting. The attack resulted in the deaths of three innocent people and a further 17 were wounded. Because the gunman committed suicide, his motive is unclear.

Background of the Festival

Every year the Gilroy Garlic Festival runs for three days. It's a huge food festival, which draws crowds of up to 100,000 people from all over the United States. The family event takes place at Christmas Hill Park, Southeast of San Jose and the Silicon Valley area, in Gilroy.

Around 60,000 people populate Gilroy, and the main item produced there is garlic; hence, the name of the festival. The festival is used as a major fundraiser for nonprofit groups such as schools and clubs.

A Lone Gunman

It was the 41st annual festival this year, and on the last day, Sunday, July 28, a gunman entered the festival just before closing at 6:00pm. He'd cut through a wire fence on the boundary of the festival, so he could avoid security screening at the gate.

Armed with a WASR-10 semi-automatic rifle, the gunman fired 39 rounds into the crowd. He was carrying a 75-round drum magazine and five 40-round magazines, and the gun had been purchased a few weeks beforehand. Although that type of weapon is banned in California, he purchased it legally in Nevada.

According to witnesses, the gunman fired randomly into the crowd, not targeting anyone specifically. Someone was overheard asking him why he was doing it, and his response was that he was really angry.

Police responded within a minute as they were on the scene already, and found the gunman was wearing a bulletproof vest. They fired on him anyway, with several of the 18 rounds striking the gunman. Initially, it was reported that the gunman had been killed by one or more of the officer's gunshots, but the coroner later said he'd died after shooting himself in the head after he'd been shot by officers.

Three Killed in Shooting

The gunman shot and killed three people that day, two of whom were children. The youngest victim was Stephen Romero, who was just 6 years of age. Keyla Salazar, 13, and Trevor Deon Irby, 25, were the other two victims killed.

Nineteen patients were treated at the two hospitals in Santa Clara County. The age range of victims was from 12 to 69, and 11 had received gunshot wounds and another 8 had other types of injuries, most likely from fleeing the shooter.

Shooter Identified

Authorities identified the gunman as Santino William Legan, 19. He'd lived in Gilroy for much of his life, but months before the shooting had been living in Walker Lake, Nevada.

Four days before the shooting occurred, an Instagram account had been opened by a person of the same age and name. It said Legan was of Iranian and Italian descent. Two posts were made on the day of the shooting, one of which complained that "hordes of mestizos and Silicon Valley white twats" were congesting the countryside. The post urged people to read 'Might is Right,' a 19th-century book that is a proto-fascist manifesto. The book promotes anti-Semitism and racial violence and is commonly referred to by neo-Nazi's and white supremacists.

When police searched the car belonging to Legan, they found a shotgun inside. His father's house was searched and Legan's apartment in Walker Lake. At the apartment, officers located empty ammunition boxes for rifles and shotguns, empty boxes that had contained a rifle and shotgun, a bulletproof vest, pamphlets on guns, and a gas mask.

Unknown Motive

No motive for the attack has been uncovered by the authorities. Evidence had been found that Legan had explored some violent ideologies and had made a list of potential targets. As well as the festival, this list included courthouses, religious organizations, political institutions of both the Democratic and Republican parties, and federal buildings. Because of the list of potential targets, a domestic terrorism investigation was opened.

President Donald Trump thanked law enforcement and offered condolences on July 29. Kamala Harris, the junior U.S. senator and Democratic presidential candidate in California, also expressed gratitude towards the first responders who attended the scene.

Congressman Dan Lipinski was at the festival with his wife when the shooting occurred. He released a short statement calling for legislative action against gun violence and thanking the first responders.

During his speech in St. Peter's Square on August 4, Pope Francis condemned attacks on defenseless people and said he was close to the victims spiritually.

Markham Home Massacre

Menhaz Zaman, 23, killed his parents, his grandmother, and his sister shortly after midnight on July 28, while they were asleep in their home in

Markham, Ontario. Zaman was later arrested and charged with their murders.

Family Massacred

After a call was made to the police about people possibly being injured in the home, so they arrived on the scene and found Menhaz Zaman at the door. He'd waited until his family members were asleep, and then systematically slit the throats of all victims in their beds.

At the time, he was communicating with friends online, saying, "First mom then granny then sister and lastly dad." He further declared, "I was shaking the entire day." The conversation ended when Zaman wrote, "the police are here, goodbye."

The family members killed were:

- Moniruz Zaman, 59
- Momotaz Begum, 50
- Firoza Begum, 70
- Malesa Zaman, 21

Zaman the Perpetrator

Zaman, of Bengali descent, had claimed to be an atheist and had previously made comments against Muslims and Islam that were described as hostile. He'd left an explanation for his actions online, that said he'd begun feeling depressed and had converted to atheism following his courses failure in the second semester at university.

He dropped out of York University, where he'd been studying Mechanical Engineering after only studying for one year but kept it a secret from his family. He continued to pretend to attend University 4 days a week, and nobody knew anything different. He'd instead go to the local mall or sometimes to the community gym.

The online gamer he communicated with the night of the murders was someone he had 'met' through 'Perfect World Void,' an online adventure fantasy game.

Zaman has been charged with 4 counts of first-degree murder.

Statement from Perfect World Void

An administrator from the game released a statement saying nobody had any clue about his plans to kill his family. He'd been known as the 'troll' for a long time but hadn't shown any intention that he would commit a homicide.

The statement further said that "We thank the anonymous player who had the cleverness to trace his address and the braveness to immediately report it to the local cops. Thanks to this act, it is highly possible that some lives have been saved."

Terrorist Attacks in Brief

July 1

Kabul, Afghanistan: A defense ministry building was attacked with a car bombing and gunfire. Forty people were killed, and a further 100 were injured, which included 35 children. Responsibility was claimed by the Taliban.

July 5

Reyhanli, Turkey: A car bomb was detonated, which killed 3.

July 12

Kismayo, Somalia: Four armed men attacked the Asasey Hotel after a suicide car bomb had been detonated. The four men were killed along with 26 people. Multiple foreigners were murdered.

July 19

Kabul, Afghanistan: A bomb attack occurred at Kabul University, killing 8 and injuring 33.

July 24

Mogadishu, Somalia: The Mayor of Mogadishu was killed along with 6 others by a female suicide bomber who was also blind.

Kabul, Afghanistan: Three bombs were detonated, which murdered 15 civilians.

July 27

Nganzai, Nigeria: 65 people were killed in an attack by Boko Haram fighters at a funeral in the local government area of Nganzai, Borno State, Nigeria. Another ten people were injured, eight of them seriously.

July 28

Gilroy, US: A lone gunman opened fire against the assistants of the Gilroy Garlic Festival in Gilroy, California. Investigators have not determined the motives of the gunman, Santino William Legan, age 19, but the FBI has opened a domestic terrorism investigation into the incident.

July 31

Farah, Afghanistan: When a bomb on the roadside killed 35 and injured 27, the majority of the victims were women and children.

Chapter 8:
AUGUST

El Paso Walmart Mass Shooting

On August 3, a man walked into a Walmart store in El Paso, Texas, and began shooting randomly at the people inside the store. By the time he'd finished, 22 people were dead and another 24 injured.

Random Gunfire

The armed man entered the Walmart Supercenter near Cielo Vista Mall, eastern El Paso, at 10:40am on August 3. He was carrying what is believed to have been a semi-automatic civilian version of the AK-47. He had begun firing in the parking lot before he entered the store, crowded with shoppers. The store manager issued a 'Code Brown' signal, which informs employees that there is an active shooter.

The staff began helping customers hide or flee the gunman. Many ran to the next-door mall and hid in other stores, while some hid in shipping containers behind the building or under furniture such as tables.

Six minutes after the first emergency call was made, first responders, including paramedics, police, including off duty officers, and Texas Rangers arrived at the store. FBI agents also responded immediately to the scene. The suspect had fled; but when he reached the intersection of Viscount and Sunmount, he identified himself to Texas Rangers as the shooter and was arrested.

The Victims

Described as the deadliest attack on Latinos in recent history, 22 people were killed, and 24 suffered injuries. The deceased victims comprised of 13 Americans, 8 Mexicans and 1 man from Germany. The youngest victim was 15, and the oldest was 90.

Multiple victims were taken to the Del Sol Medical Center and the University Medical Center of El Paso. Two young children were injured, and they were transported to a children's hospital once their conditions were stable. The names of the victims were:

- Jordan Anchondo, 25
- Arturo Benavides, 67
- Andre Anchondo, 23
- Angelina Silva Englisbee, 86
- Javier Rodriguez, 15
- Leo Campos, 41
- Maribel Hernandez Loya, 56
- David Johnson, 63
- Sara Esther Regaldo Moriel, 66
- Adolfo Cerros Hernández, 68
- Jorge Calvillo García, 61
- Elsa Libera Marquez, 57
- Gloria Irma Márquez, 61
- María Eugenia Legarreta Rothe, 58
- Ivan Manzano, 41
- Maria Flores, 77
- Raul Flores, 77
- Alexander Gerhard Hoffman, 66
- Luis Alfonzo Juarez, 90
- Margie Reckard, 63
- Teresa Sanchez, 82
- Juan Velazquez, 77

Charges Laid Against the Suspect

The suspect was identified as Patrick Wood Crusius, 21, a white male who had previously been living in his family's home in Allen, Texas, around 650 miles away from El Paso.

Crusius had purchased the weapon legally but gave investigators no information about it. He stated in his first interrogation that he'd targeted Mexicans in the shooting.

On September 12, he was indicted on charges of capital murder. When he was arraigned on October 10, he pled not guilty.

The district attorney, Jaime Esparza, stated he would seek the death penalty in the case. The western district of Texas US attorney, John F. Bash, said he was considering bringing firearms and federal hat crime charges against Crusius, and that he was treating the shooting as domestic terrorism.

A former neighbor of Crusius described him as a loner who rarely interacted with anyone. A former classmate said that the other kids wouldn't work with Crusius because he had a short temper. The other kids bullied Crusius because of the way he spoke, and because it looked like he was dressed in second-hand clothing.

Cruisus had a profile on LinkedIn, which has now been removed. He referred to himself as being aimless but was mildly interested in software. He'd worked in a local supermarket as a bagger, and stated he wasn't motivated to do anything more than "what's necessary to get by."

Manifesto by Crusius

Shortly before Crusius went on the shooting spree, a manifesto called "The Inconvenient Truth" had been posted online, and police are fairly confident that it had been posted by Crusius. In another document in the same post, Crusius's name was mentioned.

Moderators of the site removed the original post quickly, but users had continued to share copies of the manifesto. The author of the document claimed to have been inspired by the Mosque shootings in Christchurch, New Zealand, earlier in the year. It further expressed support for that killer.

The manifesto also mentioned cultural and ethnic replacement, a Hispanic invasion, and environmental degradation. It promoted the 'Great Replacement,' a white nationalist and far-right conspiracy theory. The manifesto author claimed the shooting should be an incentive for Hispanics to leave the US.

Aftermath and Memorial

In the immediate aftermath, the hospitals treating the injured were rapidly running out of blood products, so the Police Department sent out a tweet to caution how blood was needed urgently and how to donate. One of the donation centers said the line of donors was stretched out the door, as people rushed to help.

Funeral services were offered for free by several funeral homes in El Paso and Mexico. A vigil was organized in Ciudad Juárez by the Rotary International chapter, during which people gathered with lit candles and cellphone lights at a park and shone them towards El Paso as a symbol of solidarity.

Walmart announced on September 3 that they'd stop selling ammunition for some assault weapons and handguns in all of its stores across America. They also pledged US$400,000 towards helping the victims.

Antonio Basco announced that anyone was welcome to attend his wife's funeral, and as a result, hundreds of people from different parts of America attended. Flowers were sent by people all around the world.

Two Hours of Terror in California

For two hours, residents in Garden Grove and Santa Ana, Orange Grove, California, were subjected to robberies and stabbings on August 7. As a result, four people were murdered and two suffered injuries. The rampage finally ended with the suspect's arrest.

The Killing Spree

The first attack occurred when the suspect robbed an apartment. When the residents discovered they'd been robbed, they notified police at just after 4:00 P.M. Around the same time as the police were called, the suspect was busy trying to rob a bakery located in Garden Grove.

A phone call was made to police at 5:04 P.M., informing them that two men had been killed at an apartment complex in Garden Grove. The suspect had stabbed the men, who happened to be the initial robbery victims who had called police earlier. One of the men died at the apartment, and the other was pronounced deceased at the hospital.

From there, the suspect tried to rob a Chevron gas station ,an insurance agency and a check-cashing business. He stabbed a woman at the insurance agency several times. He also attacked a victim at the gas station whose nose was almost amputated. In the parking lot of a Santa Ana Subway shop, the suspect stabbed another person to death.

Suspect Apprehended

The suspect was Zachary Castañeda, 33, who was living at the apartment complex in Garden Grove, where he killed the two men. Police arrested him as he left a shop in Santa Ana. As he departed the shop, he grabbed a handgun off a guard. However, when police approached him, he dropped the gun and a knife. Castañeda was on bail at the time of the killing spree and had been charged with carrying a concealed knife and drug charges. At first, it was announced that all of the victims were Hispanic, but later it was corrected all but two were Hispanic: the remaining two were white.

Police stated that Castañeda was known as a gang member and had been convicted of criminal charges 14 times.

'Not Guilty' Plea

Castañeda was charged with murder, attempted murder, assault with a deadly weapon to cause great bodily injury, robbery, burglary, and aggravated mayhem on August 9. He pled not guilty to all charges. In total, there were 11 felony counts.

Police stated he'd been uncooperative with them and he'd refused to go to court to be formally charged. In turn, he was arraigned from inside his cell.

Because he's been charged with multiple murders, he's eligible for the death penalty if found guilty.

Cairo Bombing Kills Twenty

Three cars were struck by another car set up as a bomb in Cairo on August 4. The explosive collision occurred outside the National Cancer Institute Egypt right in the center of Cairo. Twenty people were confirmed dead and 47 suffered injuries.

Hospital Targeted

At around midnight, the car bomb was traveling on a road that runs alongside the Nile River. It deliberately drove down the wrong side of the road until it collided with two other vehicles outside the hospital.

A woman who was at the hospital with her sick child was in the bathroom when the explosion occurred. She'd planned on sleeping outside for the night with her child, so they could queue early in the morning for treatment. On hearing the explosion, they ran to the main entrance but were unable to leave as it was on fire so they left through a side door.

The witness said there was panic inside the hospital, and she saw a lot of blood and body parts. She revealed it was hard to get out of the hospital due to people cramming the stairs.

Group Responsible for the Attack

The government believed the Hasm group was responsible for the bombing. The violent Hasm is an offshoot of the Islamist Muslim Brotherhood. Officials claimed a member of Hasm had been arrested in relation to the attack.

According to the ministry of health, 42 ambulances were sent to the scene, where many of the injured had suffered lacerations and burns. Around 45 victims were sent to other hospitals due to the sheer number of people needing treatment.

The ministry said they'd recorded 19 deceased victims and a "bag of body parts," and police searched the nearby Nile River in case victims had fallen after the explosion.

The front of the hospital was damaged, with broken tiles and glass covering the pavement outside. A piece of twisted metal that may have been a car bumper was hanging from the building.

President Abdel Fatah al-Sisi made a statement in which he offered condolences to the victims of the bombing. He condemned the attack, saying, "The Egyptian state is determined to confront acts of terrorism and uproot them, with all its institutions."

Hasm has denied responsibility.

Previous Attacks

In 2015 Cairo was the scene of a number of violent explosions. One car bomb had destroyed a portion of the Italian consulate that adjoined Tahrir Square. A security building had been targeted by a bomb in Shubra al-Khaima.

Four explosions rocked downtown Cairo in one night in 2014, leaving 6 people dead and 80 injured. These bombs deliberately targeted police.

Security and police institutions have been a common target by Islamist militants since the former president Mohamed Morsi was overthrown in 2013. In one attack, top prosecutor Hisham Barakat was assassinated when a car bomb hit his motorcade. This was one of the most famous, high profile assassinations in Egypt's history.

Operation to Rid Egypt of Terrorists

Sisi launched an operation in February 2018 to rid Egypt of all terrorist elements. The operation focused on the northern Sinai Peninsula, Nile Delta, and the western desert. The operation was initiated after 305 people were killed in explosions and attacks by gunmen.

Nine Shot and Killed in Dayton

As a group of people was outside the Ned Peppers Bar in Dayton, Ohio on August 4, a man approached and opened fire. Within a matter of seconds, he'd killed nine people and injured another 17. A further 10 people were injured by other means. Police officers responded within seconds and shot the perpetrator dead.

Firing Into the Crowd

The suspect had been seen going into a bar two hours before the shooting attack with a friend and a sibling in Dayton. He left the other two at around 12:13 A.M. and was captured, leaving the bar on surveillance camera.

Less than an hour later, at 1:05 A.M., a man carrying a semi-automatic firearm approached the crowd outside the entrance to Ned Peppers Bar and began shooting. The weapon contained part of a semi-automatic AM-15 in a pistol configuration and had a shortened barrel. It had a 100-round drum magazine attached.

With 20 seconds after the first shot was fired, police officers were already on the scene. The engaged the suspect and responded by shooting him. According to his autopsy report, he was struck by 30 rounds. He died at the scene.

Sixteen of the victims were sent to Miami Valley Hospital. Of those victims, one was critical and five others were admitted. Nine victims were sent to the Kettering Health Network: three were serious and three labeled in fair condition. By 10:00 A.M., of the 27 who had been hospitalized, 15 had been released.

Among those killed was the gunman's sister. It was unclear if the sibling had been intentionally shot and killed or if it was an accident. Whatever the reason, his sister was among the first of the victims killed.

The victims were:

- Megan Betts, 22
- Lois L. Oglesby, 27
- Logan Turner, 30
- Derrick R. Fudge, 57
- Nicholas P. Cumer, 25
- Beatrice N. Warren-Curtis, 36
- Thomas J. McNichols, 25
- Saeed Saleh, 38
- Monica E. Brickhouse, 39

Collateral Damage

When the autopsies were done, it was discovered that two of the victims had also been shot by the police. One woman who had been shot by the suspect had also been hit by two bullets from a police weapon. If she hadn't already received a fatal wound from the suspect, at least one of the injuries from the police weapon would have been fatal.

A second person sustained a superficial gunshot wound from a police weapon as well as multiple injuries from the suspect. The coroner ruled that both deaths were the result of the suspect's gunfire because the fatal injuries were already present before they were hit by police gunfire.

The Gunman with a Disturbing Past

The suspect, Connor Stephen Betts, 24, was from Bellbrook, Ohio, and apart from a few minor traffic infringements, he had no major criminal past. On further investigation, it was discovered he was a leftist by his own admission, and he'd made references about Satan online.

In a tweet response to the El Paso mass shooting that had happened recently, Betts had referred to the shooter as a 'terrorist' and a 'white supremacist.' He'd also liked posts about gun control.

Betts had been suspended back in high school after allegedly making lists of the students he wanted to rape and murder. The list was discovered in 2012, and police had investigated it. Betts had been bullied at school and had planned to enter the school and open fire.

In the year leading up to the shooting at Dayton, Betts had been singing in a 'pornogrind' band with the unfortunate name of 'Menstrual Munchies,' a band that played the male-dominated and misogynistic music scene. The music focused on violence, gore and necrophilia, and often had themes of sexual violence.

According to a girlfriend of Betts from high school days, he'd complained to her about experiencing psychosis and auditory and visual hallucinations. He'd told her he was scared he was developing schizophrenia.

Further Investigation

When Betts' home was searched on August 4 by the FBI and police, they found material that indicated his avid interest in mass shootings and violence. There was also evidence that he'd wanted to commit a mass shooting.

No clear motivation had been uncovered, and with Betts dead, the secret my remain with him.

When Betts carried out the attack, he was armed with hearing protection, a mask, and body armor. The weapon had been purchased online from a place in Texas, who sent it to a firearms dealer in Ohio. It had been modified to work as a rifle.

A friend of Betts was arrested on August 9 by federal agents. He was charged with 'making false statements in applying for a federal permit to purchase a weapon, and possession of a firearm by someone who illegally uses or is addicted to a controlled substance.'

The friend confessed that he had helped Betts buy the drum magazine, the upper receiver for the weapon, and the body armor. He'd also stored the items and the weapon at his home so Betts' parents wouldn't discover it. However, he wasn't suspected of knowing what Betts was planning to do that night.

Morogoro Tanker Looting and Explosion

On August 10, a fuel tanker had crashed in Morogoro, Tanzania, and what happened next, was a crime that resulted in nearly 100 deaths, as people tried to steal fuel from the crashed tanker.

Massive Lethal Explosion

After the tanker crashed and overturned while trying to avoid hitting a motorcyclist, a crowd of around 150 gathered at the scene and began to steal the fuel from the tanker, filling up yellow jerrycans. The tanker had caught fire, but the looters continued to try and steal the fuel. Suddenly, at 8:30 A.M., the tanker exploded.

Because it was such a busy road where the accident had happened, many innocent people were killed by the explosion and flames as well as those who were stealing. It was a scene of chaos as people desperately tried to rescue those who had been caught in the fire.

At least 89 people were killed in the explosion and subsequent massive fire, and a further 55 at least were injured. Many of the victims were local motorcycle taxi drivers, along with the looters. The majority of those injured suffered burns.

Official Response

The rescue was completed by 3:00 P.M. All the bodies were removed and taken to a local hospital, so the identification process could take place.

Condolences were expressed by Tanzania President John Magufuli, but he also expressed dismay at the actions of the crowd.

Foiled Plot to Kill a Prime Minister

The Samoan police announced on August 13 that they'd managed to foil a plot to kill the Prime Minister of Samoa, Tuilaepa Sailele Malielegaoi. But it wasn't the first time a plot had been planned to kill the Prime Minister; it was actually the third.

First Attempts at Assassination

Malielagoi was first appointed the Prime Minister of Samoa in 1988, was reelected in 2001, and is still in the role as of January 2020.

The first attempt to kill Malielagoi was on July 16, 1999. Eletise Leafa Vitale, 34, mistakenly killed the Minister of Public Work Luagalau Levaula Kamu instead of murdering the Prime Minister. He was charged with capital murder and conspiracy to assassinate the Prime Minister. Initially, he received a death sentence, but it was later designated to life in prison with no possibility of parole.

Police received threats in December 2010 that there was a plan to kill the Prime Minister. The police took the threats seriously since an attempt had already been made previously, but nothing came of it.

The Plot to Kill the Prime Minister

From April 2019 to the beginning of August, a plot had been formulated by at least 4 individuals to kill the Prime Minister. Police quickly apprehended 3 of the suspects, Malele Atofu, Taualai Leiloa and Lema'I Faioso Sione. They were charged with conspiracy to commit murder. The fourth suspect, Talalelei Pauga, lives in Australia and Samoa police are trying to have him extradited back to Samoa to face charges.

There were allegedly exchanges of money among the 3 men police had arrested and Pauga.

Paulo, Leiloa, and Sione appeared in court on September 9. Sione and Paulo entered pleas of not guilty, and Leiloa pled guilty. Leiloa was to be sentenced on September 30. If they're found guilty, they could spend the rest of their lives in prison.

Suspects on Trial

It was announced by the prosecution that the man convicted of the first attempt and the death of the Minister of Public Work, Eletise Leafa Vitaloe, would testify as a witness against Paulo and Sione.

Paulo and Sione appeared in court on Septemeber 21 for their bail hearings, but it was delayed until October 16, so that new legal matters relating to the case could be heard.

When they attended court on October 16, the bail hearings were delayed again because the Attorney General believed there was still a threat to the Prime Minister's life. Therefore, he requested that the bail hearings be held behind closed doors and also to prevent the media from publishing the outcome.

The closed court bail hearings were approved on October 30 by the Supreme Court of Samoa.

Taualai Leiloa Changes His Plea

The sentencing hearing for Leiloa was delayed from September 30 until October 14. At that hearing, the prosecution requested that Leiloa by represented by a lawyer due to the serious nature of his charges. Leiloa stated he couldn't afford to pay a lawyer so the sentencing hearing was postponed until November 1, to give time to find legal counsel.

At the hearing on November 1, Leiloa informed the judge that he wished to change his plea to not guilty on the advice of his new lawyer.

Killer Chased and Pinned by a Chair in Sydney

On August 13, a man attacked two people in Sydney, Australia, stabbing one to death. Although police didn't think it was terrorism, they were not ruling it out. What made this case major news, was how a bystander bravely stopped the attacker's rampage.

The Knife Attacks

In an apartment in Clarence Street, Sydney, a woman was stabbed to death. Her attacker then fled the building and out onto the street. A woman who was outside the Hotel CBD on the corner of York and King Streets was also attacked.

Video taken by a news cameraman who was present showed the perpetrator jumping on top of a car and yelling 'Allahu akbar." He then leaped off the car and was confronted by a man with a chair. He evaded him and continued to run down York Street. He chased pedestrians down the street and shouted for someone to "shoot me in the fucking head."

Bystanders Chase and Capture Suspect

A bystander who happened to be a lawyer used a chair like a circus lion tamer to try and deter the attacker away from the people in the street. This prevented the man from stabbing anyone else, and nobody was injured by trying to fight with him. Instead, he was pushed away by the chair.

Then, a number of people, including some firefighters, started chasing the attacker. Joining the group was brothers Luke and Paul O'Shaughnessy and their friend Lee Cuthbert. The group chased down the man and pinned him to the ground using a milk crate and chairs, and they kept him there until the police arrived and arrested him.

The Victims

The woman who was killed in the apartment was a 24-year-old sex worker. She had been stabbed multiple times in a frenzied attack and died at the scene.

The other victim stabbed outside the hotel was 41, and her condition was stable on arrival at the hospital.

Mert Ney - the Suspect

The knife-wielding attacker was identified as Mert Ney, 20, from west of Sydney in Marayong. It's believed he'd intended on stabbing multiple people. Police discovered Ney had been researching information on mass killings that had occurred recently, including information about the mosque shootings in Christchurch, on a USB drive he was carrying with him.

Ney was known to police and suffered from mental illness. Some reports suggested he'd escaped from a mental health facility days before he attacked, and that he had diazepam drugs on him when arrested.

On August 16, Ney was charged with one count of murder, one count of attempted murder, intentionally choking with recklessness, common assault, and wounding with the intent of causing grievous bodily harm.

Further charges were laid pertaining to Ney possessing child abuse material and having cannabis in his possession. The child abuse material was found on a USB drive in his possession.

Coatzacoalcos Nightclub Fire

A fire was started at a nightclub in Coatzacoalcos, Veracruz, Mexico, and the night of August 27. As a result of the fire, 31 people were killed. Those responsible for lighting the fire are believed to be members of the Jalisco New Generation Cartel, and they'd blocked the exits of the nightclub so people couldn't' t escape.

Setting it All on Fire

The owner of the White Horse nightclub had allegedly refused to pay the extortion demands of the Jalisco drug cartel, resulting in the attack. At first, gunmen burst their way into the bar. The owner of the bar was kidnapped, as the suspects locked all the doors and emergency exits. They poured gasoline all over the building and set it on fire.

Twenty-four of the 31 people killed had died in the fire, and the other victims died later in the hospital. The victims were 16 men and 10 women, and most of them were Mexican nationals. Two were Filipino sailors that happened to be on shore leave that night.

The Response

Andrés Manuel López Obrador, the Mexican president, had had difficulty creating an effective security strategy against criminal organizations such as the drug cartels. He stated, "This is the most inhuman thing possible. It is regrettable that organized crime acts in this manner. It is more regrettable that there may be collusion with authorities."

The resemblance of the attack to another fire at a casino 8 years ago, which was undertaken by the Los Zetas drug cartel, was pointed out by many people.

Mexico has experienced a huge record of violence in 2019, with at least 14,603 murders from the start of the year until June.

Cracking Down

Mexico has had two main challenges to deal with in the past few years: the first was trying to create an effective and large security force to crack down on organized crime gangs. The other challenge was a capable judicial system of holding the guilty accountable for their crimes. President Obrador has said that the state police force is 61% smaller than needed.

The state was supposed to get 7,200 national guard members, but many of the members were sent out on an immigration enforcement mission. This is because of the US-Mexico deal to lower the number of migrants going to the U.S. border.Other areas of Mexico have also suffered an increase in violence. For example, especially after the discovery of 19 mutilated bodies in Uruapan, believed to be carried out by drug cartels. A Catholic priest was stabbed to death in Matamoros, and 4 journalists had been killed in the past month across the country.

Veracruz governor Garcia commented, "The indications of the deplorable crime in the Coatzacoalcos bar suggest that one of the material authors is Ricardo 'N' a.k.a. 'la loca' who was detained by Veracruz security forces in July of this year and was released in less than 48 hours by the state attorney general."

State Attorney General Jorge Winckler Ortíz immediately replied, "A tragedy should not be used to distort facts and confuse public opinion." He then stated that Ricardo N. had been detained twice by the federal government and had been released both times. It became quite clear that there was an issue between state and federal authorities with both accusing the other.

The hunt for the attackers is ongoing.

Midland-Odessa Spree Shooting

On August 31, a spree shooting took place in the cities of Midland and Odessa in West Texas. Multiple victims were shot as a gunman drove by in a vehicle. This would be the third mass killing in the America in the month of August. Eight people were killed, including the perpetrator.

Drive-By Shooting Spree

At 3:17 P.M., a Texas state trooper tried to pull over a Honda for failing to signal a left turn. The man driving the Honda refused to stop and instead shot the trooper. He then proceeded into Odessa and shot another victim traveling the Interstate.

Once he arrived in Odessa, he left the Honda and hijacked a US Postal Service Dodge Caravan. He killed the driver and carried on shooting people as he drove until police were able to corner him. He was subsequently shot and killed by police in a movie theater parking lot.

Initially, there was some confusion over how many people were involved in the shooting. Multiple calls were made to emergency services and the number of victims at different locations made it seem as though there was more than one killer.

The age range of the 7 people killed was from 15 - 57 years. A further 17 wounded people were treated in hospital: with the total number of injured victims 25. Three officers were injured, including the Texas state trooper, an Odessa police officer and a Midland police officer. Of those injured, the youngest was just 17 months old.

The victims were:

- Mary Granados, 29
- Leilah Hernandez, 15
- Edwin Peregrino, 25
- Joe Griffith, 40

- Rodolfo Julio Arco, 57
- Kameron Karltess Brown, 30
- Raul Garcia, 35

Perpetrator Identified

The shooter was identified the day after the killing as Seth Aaron Ator, 36, from Lorena, Texas. At first, the authorities didn't want to release his name to the public because they didn't want him to have any notoriety.

In 2001 Ator was arrested after attempting to break into a woman's bedroom after he had threatened he would kill her brother. In 2002 he pled guilty to the charges.

Ator had been living in a metal shack that was without any plumbing or electricity and had no furniture or even a floor. Apart from a little dog, he lived by himself. A neighbor later said she'd seen him carrying a big rifle and yelling at her. He apparently would often get on the roof of his shack and shoot animals, which she'd reported to the police, but nothing was ever done about it.

Another neighbor said her family was frightened of Ator, mainly because he'd shoot rabbits at night and on one occasion, he'd banged on their door in the early hours of the morning.

Ator had attempted to purchase a gun in January 2014 but had failed the criminal background check. Because a local court had previously deemed him mentally unfit, he was flagged in the system as not being eligible to own a weapon. After the shooting, it was discovered he'd purchased the gun privately, therefore, dodging the background check.

Investigation into the Killings

FBI agent Christopher Combs stated at a press conference on September 2 that Ator had turned up to work in an enraged state. Just hours before the shooting began, he'd been fired from his job at Journey Oilfield Services.

Ator had telephoned a national tip line 15 minutes before he crossed paths with troopers and had made statements about what he considered atrocities he'd endured. At no time during the call did he make any threats. The FBI tried to identify who had made the call but ran out of time in the 15 minutes before the shooting started.

Aftermath

In the political realm, the Republicans offered their prayers and thoughts for the victims and called for cultural changes as well as pointing out issues with mental illness. The Democrats mainly urged for more gun restriction laws.

Matt Schaefer, Texas State Representative, and a Republican rejected the idea of tighter gun restrictions. He claimed he violated people's "God-given gun rights." The comments made by Schaefer drew the attention of the nation.

Democrats held five press conferences on September 4 in Dallas, Houston, Austin, San Antonio, and El Paso. A letter was delivered to Governor Abbott asking for an emergency special session regarding the protection of Texans from firearm violence. In response, Abbott's spokesman said, "Governor Abbott made clear in Odessa that all strategies are on the table that will lead to laws that make Texans safer. But that doesn't include a helter-skelter approach that hastily calls for perfunctory votes that divide legislators along party lines. Instead, the Governor seeks consensus rather than division, The Democrats who are part of today's partisan pitch can be part of the bi-partisan legislative process announced yesterday that is geared toward achieving real solutions, or they can be part of politics as usual that will accomplish nothing. Legislating on tough issues is hard and takes time. If Democrats really want to change the law, they need to stop talking to cameras and start talking to colleagues in the Capitol to reach consensus."

Texas Senator Ted Cruz made a statement to a local news station: Much of my discussions with law enforcer [sic] today was what were the warning signs that we had that this individual had a serious mental illness that posed a danger to himself or to others. What could we have done better to stop this deranged criminal from getting a gun in the first place? And that's going to be an ongoing discussion."

Stabbing Spree in Lyon

Nine people were stabbed on August 31 outside a subway station in Lyon, France. The attacker was an asylum seeker from Afghanistan and claimed he could hear voices that he said were insulting to God. He was heard by witnesses shouting religious words while he attacked. Thankfully, he was stopped by a bus driver from attacking more people.

Under Attack

On August 31, a man carrying a barbecue fork and a knife began attacking people at a metro station in Villeurbanne, Lyon. One young man, 19, was stabbed to death in the attack and a further 8 were injured. Three of the stabbing victims suffered critical injuries but survived. Twenty people who witnessed the attack were also treated for symptoms of shock.

The attacker was stopped by the bus driver and a couple of others, including Transit workers, which prevented him from entering the metro station and attacking more people. They held him in custody until the police arrived.

Suspect's Confused Statement

During questioning by police, the suspect said that he was a Muslim. He also made a statement that he'd heard voices giving him the order to kill, and insulting God. He claimed he had memories of the start of the attack but not the whole attack. He thought he knew the first victim from a dispute they had a few years prior.

He claimed he'd acted out of revenge due to the dispute. But, the police and the prosecutor said his responses were confused and incoherent. He was assessed by a psychiatrist who diagnosed him as being in a psychotic state and had paranoid delusions.

The suspect is from Afghanistan and has 2 known identities and 3 dates of birth. He holds a residence permit, which allows him to stay in France until January 31, 2020.

The Mayor's Response

Gérard Collomb, the Mayor of Lyon, rushed to the scene of the crime and asked people to refrain from speculating about the nature of the stabbing attack. He said that people who were waiting for their buses in a high traffic area were the suspect's targets.

Earlier in the year, a parcel bomb was detonated in May in the center of Lyon, resulting in 14 people being injured. Other than that attack, Lyon hasn't experienced jihadist terrorist attacks like other parts of the country.

Terrorist Attacks in Brief

August 3

El Paso, Texas, US: A mass shooting took place at a Walmart store in El Paso, Texas, United States, on the morning of August 3, 2019. Twenty-two people were killed, and 24 others were injured. A single gunman is suspected of committing the shooting. He was apprehended by police shortly afterward and arrested. The FBI is investigating the shooting as an act of domestic terrorism and a possible hate crime; no charges have been filed. The attacker released a manifesto before the attack, expressing support for and inspiration by the Christchurch mosque shootings, along with worry about the Hispanic invasion, automation, large corporations, and environmental degradation. He quoted that "Hispanics will take control of the local and state government of my beloved Texas, changing policy to better suit their needs."

August 4

Cairo, Egypt: An explosion following a crash caused by a car that drove into three other cars outside a hospital in central Cairo has left 20 people dead and 47 injured. Initially, it appeared to be an accident, but the next day the Interior Minister declared that there were explosives inside the car which were to be used in a terrorist operation. The attacker was killed in the explosion. The explosives-filled car was being driven to another part of the capital to carry out an attack when it crashed into other cars. The minister accused the Hasm Movement, but the group denied the allegations.

August 7

Kabul, Afghanistan: A Taliban suicide bombing outside a police station killed 15 and injured over 140.

Migdal Oz, West Bank: Dvir Sorek was an 18-year-old Yeshiva student who traveled to Jerusalem to buy books, but on his way back, he was stabbed to death by a Palestinian terrorist. The attack happened near a bus stop and two suspects were later arrested.

August 10

Bærum, Norway: A gunman opened fire on the Al-Noor Islamic Centre, just outside the Norwegian capital Oslo, wounding a man. Only three people were inside the building at the time of the attack. A woman was later found dead at the house of the attacker. The attack is being investigated as a terrorist attack.

August 17

Kabul, Afghanistan: A suicide bombing occurred inside a wedding hall, leaving 92 people dead and 142 injured. Responsibility was claimed by the Islamic State.

August 19

Newtownbutler, UK: A bomb exploded near the town of Newtownbutler, Northern Ireland, as police and the bomb squad was searching for a device that was reported in the area over the weekend. No one was injured in the attack which has been blamed on the New IRA.

August 23

Dolev, West Bank: A roadside bomb exploded when Rabbi Eitan Shnerb, Rina Shnerb, and her brother Dvir were hiking. Rina was killed, while her brother and father were injured. Three PFLP members were arrested.

Chapter 9:
SEPTEMBER

Another Attack on Children in China

Once again, school children in China were attacked, leaving eight dead and another two injured in Chaoyangpo village of Enshi City in Hubei province.

School Children Targeted

As the elementary school children were on their way to the first day of the new school semester, on September 3, a man approached them and attacked them. Authorities have never released the manner in which the children were attacked, including what weapon was used.

Suspect - No Clear Motive

The man responsible for the horrific attack on such innocent children has only been identified by his surname, Yu, and is 40 years old. Throughout the investigation, he hasn't provided a motive for the attack, and police are yet to uncover what it could have been.

What's known about Yu is that he'd previously been in Hubei prison for attempted murder and had been released the previous June after finishing his sentence.

Students Unsafe

There have been many serious attacks on school children in China, and they are often targeted by those who have mental health issues or those who have some kind of a grudge.

In April, 23 children were deliberately poisoned after their teacher had placed sodium nitrate in their food while at kindergarten. No motivation has been established.

In October 2018, 14 children were attacked by a man with a knife at a kindergarten in Chongqing.

Two children were stabbed to death in June 2018 outside an elementary school in Shanghai. The man had attacked the children outside the school.

In April 2018, nine students were stabbed to death at a middle school in northwestern China by a former student who had allegedly been bullied when he was at school. During the rampage, the 28-year-old assailant left another 10 people injured.

Because there are very tight restrictions on owning a gun, the most commonly weapons used in China are knives and homemade bombs.

Murder of Kathleen Jo Henry

When Kathleen Jo Henry was sexually assaulted and murdered on September 4, authorities and the public were surprised with a chance find of an SD card containing video recordings and photographs revealed who the killer was.

Who Was Kathleen Henry?

Henry was an Alaska native woman who was born in 1988 in Bethel, Alaska. She'd been incarcerated previously at the Highland Mountain Correctional Center in Anchorage, during which time she obtained her education diploma in 2012.

She'd struggled with drug addiction and had encounters with law enforcement for a number of years for mainly misdemeanor offenses. Previously married, she was single at the time of her murder.

Henry's remains were discovered along Seward Highway on October 2.

Suspect Identified by Photographs and Video

On September 30, an SD card was found on the ground near a store that contained horrifying video recording and photographs of Henry's murder. The evidence on the card showed Henry had been beaten before being strangled to death inside a hotel room. The label on the card said, "Homicide at midtown Marriott." There were a total of 12 video recordings and 39 images on the card, and the recordings had spanned 2 days, from September 4-6.

During one of the videos, a man can be seen shouting at Henry to die before laughing. It also showed she was stomped on the neck and choked.

Detectives recognized the suspect as Brian Steven Smith, a South African immigrant, from a previous investigation. He was an employee at the hotel and had rented a room at a discounted price from September 2-4.

Smith was arrested and charged with the sexual assault and murder of Henry.

Smith Charged with a Second Murder

During the investigation into Henry's murder, Smith was also linked with the killing of a second woman. He'd confessed on October 17 to killing Veronica Abouchuk, whose body was found on October 2, just South of the city in a remote area. She'd last been seen in July 2018 by her family.

Abouchuk was allegedly homeless, and she had been killed by a gunshot to the head. Smith provided police with directions to where her body had been disposed of, which matched where her skull had been found in April 2019.

Smith was arraigned on October 9 and charged with first-degree murder in Henry's death, shortly after he was indicted for first-degree murder in the killing of Abouchuk.

Deadly Riots in Johannesburg

Johannesburg, South Africa, was the scene of violent riots between September 1-5. Accordingly, 7 people were killed. The xenophobic riots targeted foreign nationals. In other African nations, riots occurred in retaliation against South African brands.

On September 8, the riots began again. The rioters looted shops and called for foreigners to leave.

Riots Break Out

Riots broke out on September 1 in Jeppestown and Johannesburg. Stores that were owned by foreign nationals were targeted and looted. The riot had begun after a taxi driver was killed after he tried to stop drug dealers.

Police had reportedly arrested 189 people for looting by September 2, and by September 5, 423 had been arrested. By then, around 10 people had died during the riot, including 2 who were foreign nations. The riot and looting then spread to Alexandra.

Approximately 50 stores and businesses that were largely owned by Africans were either destroyed or suffered damage. In the Jozi Mall, the mosque was attacked, and copies of the Quran were defiled. Every store inside the mall was attacked by looters.

Residents in Katlehong put barriers on the roads before they looted the Sontonga Mall. During the widespread looting, 2 were shot and killed, one by a store owner who was Somalian, and the other shooting occurred in Crosby.

More people were shot and killed during the rioting and the looting. Some businesses were set on fire by the looters in Alexandra, and burned corpses were found.

On September 5, 74 people were arrested in Katlehong, which brought the total of arrests up to 497. Police stated 11 people had been killed during the riots.

When the rioting resumed on September 8, Mangosuthu Buthelezi, Zulu leader, called for calm and a stop to the violence from a speech. Another person was shot and killed and more were injured. By the time all the riots had ended, more than 680 people had been arrested and at least 12 were dead.

Truck Drivers on Strike

While the riots were occurring, there was also a truck driver strike across the nation. The strike was a protest against companies hiring non-South African drivers. At the same time, Human Rights Watch made a statement that more than 200 people, predominantly foreign drivers, had been killed since March 2018 in South Africa.

How Nations Responded

A scheduled international soccer match against South Africa in Zambia was canceled by the Football Association of Zambia in response to the riots and the increased security risks.

Many South African companies halted their trading after the riots due to retaliatory attacks.

President Muhammadu Buhari of Nigeria conveyed his concerns through the South African High Commissioner to President Ramaphosa of South Africa. The African Economic Forum was set for Cape Town, but the Nigerian government decided not to participate and the embassy in South Africa was closed due to concerns about safety.

The All Progressives Congress, the ruling party of Nigeria, advocated for South African businesses to be naturalized in response to the attacks on Nigerian nationals.

Sanmatenga Attacks

On September 8, a vehicle carrying people and goods from a market drove struck an improvised explosive device in Sanmatenga Province, Burkina Faso. As a result of the explosion, 15 people on board the vehicle were killed. Around the same time, a van convoy was attacked by gunmen and left 14 dead.

Militant Attacks

Following the Libyan Civil War in 2011, there has been a steady increase in militant attacks in the region. Conflict in Azawad in nearby Mali threatened to cause a split in the country.

In 2014 there was an uprising in Burkina Faso, which led to President Blaise Compaoré's demise. Because Burkina Faso is a member of the Trans-Saharan Counterterrorism Partnership committed to peacekeeping troops in Sudan and Mali, it had become a target for the extremists in the area.

Burkina Faso had largely been free of violence until 2015, but the country was infiltrated by jihadist groups that were linked to the Islamic State and Al-Qaeda. Raids and cross-border attacks have occurred since, thus causing unrest in the countries nearby.

There have been some major attacks in the capital in the last few years. Thirty people were killed in massacres on a hotel and restaurant in 2016. In 2017, 19 were killed in similar attacks. Both had been carried out by Al-Qaeda in the Islamic Maghreb. Several armed militants attacked a number of locations on March 2, 2018, in the capital of Burkina Faso, Ouagadougou. In these attacks, 16 were killed and a further 85 suffered injuries.

Tensions between religious groups and ethnicities began in 2019 because of Islamist insurgency. The Northern areas of Burkina Faso on the border of Mali were affected more than other areas. Suicide bombings and landmines on the side of the roads were used in guerilla warfare.

Approximately 600 people have been killed to date by the insurgents using these tactics.

Sanmatenga Explosion and Gunfire

A vehicle returning from a market carrying goods and people drove over an improvised explosive device in the Barsalogho Department, Sanmatenga Province on September 8. The explosion killed 15 of the passengers in the vehicle and injured 6. To the East, a convoy of vans was transporting provisions to those who had been displaced by all the fighting, when it was attacked by gunmen. Fourteen people died in the attack.

Nobody claimed responsibility for the attacks, and the perpetrators are still unknown.

The Immediate Aftermath

Reinforcements were sent to the area immediately following the attacks. According to a military official, every effort was to be made "to ensure that humanitarian convoys in areas affected by terrorist attacks are under security escort."

Murder of Derk Wiersum

Derk Wiersum, a Dutch lawyer, was gunned down outside his home in Amsterdam on September 18. He was the lawyer of a state witness in the case against the Mocro Maffia at the time. Lawyers around the world were shocked by the killing, calling it an "attack on the rule of law."

Background of Wiersum

Wiersum began working as the lawyer for Nabil Bakkali in 2017 in the case against the Mocro Mafia, which was led by Ridouan Taghi. The case involved 16 suspects on trial for multiple murders and multiple attempted murders between the years 2015 and 2017. The leader, Ridouan Taghi, and Said Razzouki, his henchman, both were charged with giving the orders for the murders and for 'leading a criminal organization.'

On January 14, 2017, Nabil Bakkali was arrested for illegal possession of weapons. He was later arrested on September 5, when investigators believed he participated in the killing of Hakim Changachi on January 12, 2017. It's suspected he was further involved with some of the other killings.

Because Changachi had been a close friend of Bakkali, and that he wasn't the intended target to be murderees, Bakkali told Changachi's family that he'd been involved due to guit. Taghi heard about the confession, so Bakkail was put on a death list. Because Bakkali felt he wasn't safe anymore, he became a state witness. In exchange for his testimony, the deal was that his sentence would be halved.

After it had been announced that Bakkali was now a state witness, his brother Reduan Bakkali was killed on March 29.

Shot at Home

Wiersum was outside his home in Imstenrade, Buitenveldert, at around 7:40 am on September 18. A man dressed in a black hoodie Shot Wiersum then fled in a white Opel Combo. At the time of the shooting, Wiersum had been with his wife, but she wasn't injured in any way. Wiersum died at the scene.

Finding the Suspect

The first suspect arrested was believed to have been the getaway driver, and police apprehended him on October 1. It was later announced that his name was Giërmo B , and he was the co-perpetrator.

On November 20, Anouar Taghi, 26, was arrested while driving on a highway. Because he was the cousin of Ridouan Taghi, he was suspected as the one who organized the murder of Wiersum. A member of the Utrecht 'Audi-bende', Anouar Taghi, was sentenced in 2016 for a previous crime to 4 years in prison.

During the investigation, it was discovered that a number of stolen vehicles had most likely been used in the case. Two days before Wiersum was killed, a grey Volkswagen Transporter, which is normally used to transport people with disabilities, was driving around Wiersum's neighborhood for around 2 hours. It had been stolen on September 5.

Police believe the stolen vehicles had been used to surveil Wiersum in the days leading up to the murder.

Ridouan Taghi was arrested on December 16 by the Dubai Police Force in Dubai. They deported him back to the Netherlands 2 days later. Although he's still detained in custody, there's no evidence to confirm he was the one who ordered the murder of Wiersum.

Aftermath of the Lawyer's Murder

The prosecutor stated they'd continue to use state witnesses to ensure they can complete criminal cases, but he'd like there to be more options when using suspects who then become informants.

After the murder, extra security has been provided for up to 30 people who were involved in the case, including prosecutors and judges. The significance of the person's involvement in the case determines how high the level of protection is provided. Security cameras and increased police presence have also occurred.

The lawyer who has replaced Wiersum as Nabil Bakkali's lawyer has remained anonymous for safety reasons. In December, he withdrew from the case because he wasn't satisfied with the given safety measures. As of January 3, 2020, two new lawyers have been hired to represent Bakkali. Both have kept their names anonymous for their own protection. The lawyer representing Ridouan Taghi, Inez Weski, has objected to the anonymity.

Responses and Reactions

A statement by Prime Minister Mark Rutte reiterated, "Organised crime is not making it easy for us. This is a complicated fight, but one that we can win."

The Minister of Justice and Security Ferdinand Grapperhau called the murder an attack on the rule of law.

Femke Halsema, Mayor of Amsterdam, said: "A horrible murder that affects the essence of the rule of law. This is a horrible murder of a father, a lawyer, an Amsterdammer. This leads to anxiety and unrest among lawyers."

Hwaseong Serial Murders

After many years and a high number of murders, police in South Korea finally arrested the man they believed responsible on September 18. In total, the killer confessed to murdering his sister- in-law and 15 other women. The first murder occurred in 1986, and the last known murder was in 1994.

Multiple Rapes and Murders

The Hwaseong serial murders are infamous in South Korea's modern-day history and often have been compared to the crimes of the Zodiac Killer in the US. The murders and rapes were the inspiration for *Memories of Murder*, a 2003 movie.

There were 10 known rapes and murders linked between September 15, 1986, and April 3, 1991. Each victim was found gagged, bound and raped, and most of the time their own clothing had been used to strangle them to death. During the investigation, more than 21,000 men were questioned.

A bus driver who had witnessed a man board his bus just after the murder on September 7, 1988, was able to help police created a sketch of the suspect. Of the survivors who had lived through attacks by the suspect, many provided descriptions of the way the man looked and acted that matched the description given by the bus driver.

On July 27, 1989, Yoon Sang-Yeo, 22, was arrested and charged with murdering Park Sang-hee. When he was questioned, he admitted he was responsible for the young girl's death, and forensic testing of the pubic hair found at the scene was very similar to his. Police thought it had been a copycat murder, and at trial Yoon was given a sentence of life imprisonment.

Yoon appealed the sentence, claiming he had been coerced by police into giving the false confession. He stated he'd been tortured during the interrogation. But, his appeal was denied, and he spent 19.5 years in prison before being released in 2009 on parole.

When the movie Memories of Murder was released in 2003, it created new interest in the case because the movie had been inspired in part by the serial killings. Then, in 2004 a female student was killed, and the similarities sparked more interest.

There had been a 15-year statute of limitations on first-degree murder and the case was due to expire in April 2006, thus it was the subject of news headlines once again in an effort to solve it before it was too late. It was later increased to 25 years a year later and lifted altogether in 2015.

On September 26, 1989, Lee Choon-Jae broke into a home in Gwangju, Suwon, Gyeonggi Province. He had worn gloves and was armed with weapons, but was discovered by the landlord before he could complete the robbery. He was arrested and convicted, thus receiving a sentence of 18 months in prison.

Lee filed an appeal, claiming he'd only entered the house because he was running from a man who had beaten him. A second trial was held, and his sentence was suspended. He was given two years of probation, which ended in April 1990.

In December 1993, Lee's wife left him, and he invited his sister-in-law, who was 18 at the time, over to the house on January 13, 1994. He drugged her, raped her and murdered her. When her family realized she was missing, he helped his father-in-law search for her before they reported she might have been kidnapped. On January 18, Lee was arrested. He'd been questioned repeatedly, and at one point, he had asked how long the sentence was for rape and murder.

In court, Lee denied he was responsible for the girl's death, and he stated police had coerced his confession. The judge overturned his confession, but he was still convicted. Initially, he was sentenced to death but in 1995, it was reduced to life imprisonment with the possibility of parole after serving 20 years.

Identification and Confession

In 2019, police ran Lee's DNA against samples found in the underwear of one of the serial killer's victims and it was a match. It was announced on September 18, 2019, that Lee was a suspect in the serial killings. Further DNA testing linked Lee to four more of the murders.

Lee denied he was the serial killer at first, but police stated he'd finally confessed on October 2. Lee claimed to have killed 15people in total including the 10 serial murder cases that were known. The other five cases hadn't been linked to the others due to the location and circumstances of the crimes. The details of those 5 murders haven't been released as they are still being investigated.

As well as the murders, Lee confessed to committing more than 30 rapes and attempted rapes.

Police announced on November 15 that they had concluded Lee was the serial killer responsible for the 10 murders.

Wrongful Conviction

As soon as news broke that Lee had confessed to the 10 serial murders, Yoon Sang-Yeo, who had previously been convicted of one of the murders, filed for a retrial of his case on November 13.

Known Victims

Lee Wan-im, 71
Killed: September 15, 1986
Location: Taean-eup, Annyeong-ri
Evidence: Strangled by hand

- Murdered while returning to her home after visiting her daughter

Park Hyun-sook, 25
Killed: October 20, 1986
Location: Taean-eup, Jinan-ri
Evidence: Strangled by hand

- Murdered after getting off a bus

Kwon Jung-bon, 25
Killed: December 12, 1986
Location: Taean-eup, Annyeong-ri
Evidence: Strangled and gagged with her stockings

- Murdered in front of her home

Lee Kye-sook, 23
Killed: December 14, 1986
Location: Jeongnam-myeon, Gwanhang-ri
Evidence: Hands were tied; she was strangled and violated by an umbrella with a girdle left on her face

- Murdered after getting off a bus

Hong Jin-young, 19

Killed: January 10, 1987

Location: Taean-eup, Hwanggye-ri

Evidence: Hands were tied: she was also gagged with her own socks and then strangled

- Murdered after getting off a bus

Park Eun-joo, 29

Killed: May 2, 1987

Location: Taean-eup, Jinan-ri

Evidence: Strangled

- Murdered on her way to give her husband an umbrella

Ahn Gi-soon, 54

Killed: September 7, 1987

Location: Paltan-myeon, Gajae-ri

Evidence: Hands tied, gagged with her socks and handkerchief, and strangled

- Murdered after getting off a bus

Park Sang-hee, 14

Killed: September 16, 1988

Location: Taean-eup, Jinan-ri

Evidence: No evidence - wrong perpetrator initially convicted

- Murdered while sleeping in her bed

Kim Mi-jung, 14

Killed: November 15, 1990

Location: Taean-eup, Byeongjeom-dong

Evidence: Hands and feet tied, strangled, gagged with her bra, violated with a ballpoint pen, fork, spoon, and razor blade

- Murdered on her way home

Kwon Soon-sang, 69

Killed: April 3, 1991

Location: Dongtan-myeon, Bansong-ri

Evidence: Strangled and two footprint marks left behind

- Murdered after getting off a bus

Gracious David - West - Serial Killer

David-West is suspected of being a serial killer in Nigeria and is believed to have killed 15 women at least between July and September 2019: most of the murders likely happened in Port Harcourt. He was arrested on September 19 and later confessed.

Early Life of David-West

According to David-West, his childhood was hard and difficult. He said his mother had been poisoned, and that he couldn't live up to his father's expectations as the only son. David-West had attended the Lord's Chosen Church in Obigbo and had confessed to killing women to the pastor there. Instead of turning him in to authorities, the pastor invited him to attend a crusade prayer service, so he could be healed.

It was reported that David-West belonged to a fraternity group, the Deebham, who was well known for engaging in Voodoo and violent acts.

David-West was arrested during a routine stop by police as they searched the Ogoni stretch of East/West Road. He had been traveling on a commercial bus that was going from Port Harcourt to Uyo.

Nine Murders

During his confession, David-West insisted that he'd acted alone in committing the murders, despite being a member of the criminal group. Nine of the victims had been found across the city, and almost all had a white cloth wrapped around their waists and their necks. Authorities suggested they were ritual murders.

Killer's Confession

David-West told investigators that the urge to kill was irresistible, and he'd apparently search the streets every night looking for a victim. He'd find a woman and take her to a local hotel. Once there, they'd have something to eat before engaging in sex. During the night, he'd wake the woman up and use a knife to threaten her. He used cloth cut from pillowcases and tied them up, before turning up the radio or television to drown out any noise. Then he would strangle the victims manually.

He told the investigators that he'd begun killing in Lagos and had robbed the first victim of money from her bank account. Then he traveled to Port Harcourt, then Owerri, before going back to Port Harcourt.

David -West admitted, "After I kill a girl, I collect her phone, and sell the phone at Waterlines and MTN office. I met the last girl at a club in Port Harcourt."

He claimed he'd often find his victims in drinking spots and clubs. He stated, "I take a girl into the hotel, we eat, make love and sleep. Later, I wake up in the middle of the night and put a kitchen knife on her neck, ordering her not to shout. I threaten her that if she shouts that I will kill her. I promise her that if she cooperates that I will not kill her, so, the girl, out of fear, will not shout. After the girl relaxes, then, I will tear the bed's pillowcase and tie her hands and legs, so that she will not struggle. Thereafter, I strangle her."

His victims would usually beg for their lives by offering him money or would give him the details from their bank accounts. Once he had their pin numbers for their ATM cards, he'd go and take the money out and use it to get other women.

"I don't know what is making me to kill people. Immediately the urge comes, I kill, and after killing, I regret and feel sober. But later, I will still go and kill again," he recalled.

Police announced that they had arrested 3 other people suspected of being connected to David-West and the murders.

David-West Goes on Trial

Arraignment was set for October 22, but his lawyer was absent on that day. The next day, David-West pled guilty to nine murder charges. For a charge of attempted murder, he pled not guilty. He was summoned to appear in court in November.

Changes His Plea

When David-West appeared in court in November, he changed his plea to the murder charges to not guilty, despite previously confessing to carrying out the killings.

Man Opens Fire in Bar in South Carolina

In the early hours of Saturday morning, September 21, a shooting occurred at a sports bar near Lancaster, South Carolina. Ten patrons had been shot with two suffering fatal injuries.

Patrons Under Attack

At around 2:45am, patrons were still inside the Old Skool Sports Bar & Grill in Lancaster when a man began shooting. The gunfire killed two people and injured another 8. One person was injured when fleeing from the shooter.

Four of the victims were transported by air to medical centers. There were many witnesses to the shooting, but nobody was really certain as to why it occurred, and with the gunman on the run, he wasn't around to question.

An Earlier Dispute

Later that Saturday afternoon, the sheriff's office spokesman Doughlas Barfield Jr. stated that there had been a local conflict leading up to the shooting. He said, "We don't think this was a situation where a random person armed himself and went into a randomly selected location and shot a bunch of unknown people."

The Sheriff wouldn't discuss what the dispute entailed but did announce that one of the victims who had been killed was involved in it. He also stated the conflict had been ongoing for a couple of months prior.

Police knew who the suspect was and said that he wasn't allowed to own or possess a gun due to previous offenses. The two men killed were:

- Henry Lee Colvin, 29
- Aaron Harris, 28

The bar was crowded at the time and tended to draw big crowds especially on the weekends. It had been operating for at least two decades and had a history of some trouble. Police stated they'd been called to the bar due to some issues previously.

Searching for the Killer

The suspect police were hunting was Breante Deon Stevens, 31. He was a convicted felon and the public was told he was most likely armed. His previous convictions had been for robbery and drug charges, and he'd served some time in jail for them.

Suspect Apprehended

On September 29, Stevens was located and arrested in Fort Lauderdale, Florida. On October 10, he waived extradition and was returned to Lancaster County to be questioned.

Stevens was charged with 2 counts of murder and 8 counts of assault and battery of a high and aggravated nature. He was also charged with weapons violations. In court on October 11, Stevens claimed he was shot at first. He said, "If that shot that he fired would have killed me, I would have been on t-shirts."

According to arrest warrants, Stevens had gotten onto a stage at the bar before he started shooting into the crowd. It also said he'd been involved in an argument with victim Colvin at the bar. Police had obtained video surveillance footage, witness statements, and physical evidence that proved the sequence of events.

Stevens has pled not guilty to the charges; but if he's convicted of the murders, he could face the death penalty.

Police have also arrested a second person, Antonio Emmanuel Champion, 30, in connection with the shooting and he has been charged with murder. No further information about Champion is available at this time.

Terrorist Attacks in Brief

September 2

Kulp, Turkey: A vehicle transporting workers was struck by a roadside bomb, causing the deaths of 7 and injuring 10 in total.

September 8

Sanmatenga Province, Burkina Faso: Two attacks were launched in Burkina Faso. In the first attack, one vehicle transporting people and goods rode over an improvised explosive device in the Barsalogho Department, leaving at least 15 passengers dead. In the second attack, 14 people were killed after a convoy of mostly three-wheeled vehicles taking food to people displaced by fighting was attacked.

September 15

Al-Rai, Syria: A car bomb was detonated by a hospital that killed 12 and injured another 13.

September 17

Charikar, Afghanistan: A suicide bomb explosion by the Taliban near the President's election rally resulted in the deaths of 26, and another 42 were injured. The bomber was riding a motorcycle packed with explosives.

Kabul, Afghanistan: A Taliban suicide bombing killed 22 people and wounded 38 near the U.S. embassy.

September 19

Qalati Ghilji, Afghanistan: A suicide truck bombing killed 39 and injured more than 140 others outside a hospital.

September 20

Karbala, Iraq: The Islamic State bombed a minibus, killing 12 and wounding 5.

Chapter 10:
OCTOBER

Stabbing Attack at Kuopio School in Finland

On October 1, a student entered a vocational school in Kuoppio, Finland, and attacked adults and students with a saber.

The Attack

According to witnesses, the attacker entered Savo College carrying a large bag and entered the classroom. He immediately stabbed a female student in the stomach and the neck, and continued to attack other people at the school. He was armed with a gun and a saber, and the majority of people he attacked were women.

The 9 injured people ranged in age between 15 and 50, and the female student he first struck was killed in the attack. Police later believed that the woman killed was the actual target, but they don't know why.

Police were notified at 12:29pm that the attack was taking place.

Before police arrived, the attacker managed to start a small fire, but it was quickly doused after the authorities controlled the scene. The suspect was confronted by police and was shot in the leg to prevent him from escaping. Two shots were fired by police in what was later deemed a legitimate shooting.

The whole attack had lasted for around 8 minutes.

Suspect identified and Arrested

The suspect, identified as Joel Marin, 25, was a student at the school. Despite carrying an air pistol, it was not used during the attack, only the saber. Marin had apparently been the subject of bullying throughout his school life, since primary school. When police searched his apartment, they located multiple Molotov cocktails, but it was unclear what he'd planned to do with them.

Due to his injuries, he was transported to Kuopio University Hospital. A police officer was wounded as well, but it's uncertain what treatment he may have required or the nature of the injury.

At the end of October, the National Bureau of Investigation stated Marin had been moved from the public hospital to a prison infirmary at Hämeenlinna for ongoing treatment.

Marin has been remanded into pretrial custody as police continue to put a case together to charge him with murder and several counts of attempted murder.

Students Fought Back

Savo college has around 600 students enrolled and 40 staff, with many students in their late teen years and some older mature students as well. On the day of the attack, it's uncertain how many students were actually on the scene.

When Marin began attacking a teacher in the classroom, students picked up chairs and threw them at him to help them escape. The media were told by a woman at the school that she'd rendered help to a female teacher who had a deep laceration to her hand after being attacked.

Aftermath

As a sign of respect, the Finnish Parliament held a minute of silence the day following the attack. Prime Minister Antti Rinne spoke of the violence being completely unacceptable and shopping. The Prime Minister visited the scene of the attack on October 4. Flags on government buildings and institutions were flown at half-mast in honor of the victims.

Stabbing at Police Headquarters in Paris

An IT specialist at the Paris police headquarters attacked his colleagues on October 3, resulting in the deaths of three police officers and one member of support staff; and injuries to two others. The attacker was shot and killed by police.

Attacked By a Colleague

The day after police had gone on strike in France because of increasing violence against officers, an employee went on a stabbing spree in the police headquarters in Paris. Six of his work colleagues were stabbed: with three police officers died and a member of the support staff also perished.

Police responded immediately, chasing the attacker into the courtyard where he was subsequently shot to death.

The Suspect and the Investigation

Mickaël Harpon, 45, who had been deaf since he was a child, was identified as the suspect, and he had been working at the police headquarters in the intelligence unite for 16 years. Harpon held a military secrecy security clearance, which enabled him to access information that was restricted such as terrorism watch lists.

The weapon used by Harpon was a knife made of ceramic, which made it undetectable by the metal scanners at the headquarters.

At first, the suggestion was that the motive had to do with a dispute in the workplace. Then counter-terrorism was considered, and an investigation looked into whether Harpon had become a radicalized Islamist or had been involved with other terrorist groups.

It was discovered that Harpon had converted to Islam about a decade before the attack. Twice daily, he attended mosque rituals, and in 2015, fellow colleagues had reported Harpon for showing support for the Charlie Hebdo attack. Nothing had been done about the reports, however.

The investigation determined Harpon had extremist and radical religious views and no longer wore Western clothing. He also wouldn't talk to any women, unless they were family members. Police had found ties between Haropn and Salafist men.

On a USB flash drive discovered in his office was propaganda material from the Levant and the Islamic State of Iraq. There were videos of beheadings and he'd also compiled details about police officers who had been working with Harpon.

On October 14, police arrested a further 5 people who had links to Harpon. One of the men was listed as a potential security threat.

Political Reaction

The headquarters were visited by President Emmanuel Macron, Prime Minister Édouard Philippe, Interior Minister Christophe Castaner, and Mayor of Paris, Anne Hidalgo after the attack.

Castaner had been called to resign, but he refused to do so, by several prominent politicians. He stated at a press meeting that Harpon had never displayed any suspicious behavior. A day later, once it was made public that Harpon's colleagues had made a complaint about him and it wasn't investigated, Castaner admitted there had been system malfunctions that may have prevented the attack.

Murder of Devan Bracci-Selvey

In a truly shocking crime, young Devan Bracci-Selvey, 14, was stabbed to death on October 7 outside of Sir Winston Churchill Secondary School by 4 students. Tragically, he died in front of his mother.

Child Killed in Front of Mother

At approximately 1:30 P.M., Bracci-Selvey's mother had gone to the school to collect her son after he called her and said other students were bothering him. When she arrived, she noticed a group of students teasing Bracci-Selvey, and she saw them spray something on him, which was thought to be mace.

As Bracci-Selvey fled the group down the sidewalk, his mother followed him in her car. She noted a 16-year-old female student taunting him and demanding him to hit her. He refused, saying he wasn't raised to hit girls. He tried to run over to his mother's car, but the group of students swarmed around him. In turn, he was stabbed and killed.

A number of students had witnessed the incident, and some had recorded it on their phones.

Devan Bracci-Selvey

Described as quiet and shy, Bracci-Selvey had experienced extensive bullying. Despite efforts to get help for the problem, it continued. He'd dreamed of being a mechanic and was excited when he discovered he was going to be an uncle again for the second time. He was a protector and would stick up for friends without hesitation if they were being bullies.

When concerns were raised with the school about the level of bullying he was experiencing, school officials dismissed the concerns, saying there wasn't enough evidence for them to take any action. Bracci-Selvey had started to skip some of his classes, and ended up going to school part-time due to the harassment he was experiencing.

Teens Arrested

The Hamilton Police Service identified some of the suspects: 2 brothers were the first to be arrested. The boys, aged 14 and 18, were charged with first-degree murder. A third teen was arrested but released unconditionally following the interview and confirmation that he wasn't involved.

Police announced on October 8 that they'd apprehended 2 more suspects, a 16-year-old female and a 16-year-old boy. They were released on October 9, after they had been interrogated at some length. Police later stated they'd believed there was an element of planning and premeditation due to evidence uncovered.

School Response

Following the murder, a crisis response intervention team, police liaison officers, social workers, wellness counselors and staff support were sent to the school. Public anger and frustration increased at the perceived inaction of the school to deal with the issue before it progressed.

Director of Education Manny Figueiredo revealed an investigation would be done once the police investigation was finished. When asked about the bullying of Bracci-Selvey, and what had been done in response to his complaints, Figueiredo stated he wasn't aware of what had occurred before the violence. He revealed, "The schools don't live in isolation of the community... they need to take a leadership role [when it comes to bullying] because we have these students for five hours a day. We have to continue to engage our kids...if a kid turns to us, how are we responding so they see that it's safe to respond?"

Far-Right Shooting at Synagogue in Halle, Germany

On October 9, a shooting occurred in the Halle synagogue in Halle, Saxony-Anhalt, Germany which carried on into Landsberg nearby. It was the Jewish holiday of Yom Kipper. When the gunman was unable to gain entry to the synagogue, he attacked people outside. The crime was deemed an anti-Semitic and far-right attack.

Unable to Gain Entry

At around 12:00 P.M. on October 9, a gunman attempted to enter the synagogue in the Paulusviertel neighborhood of Halle. He was livestreaming at the attack at the same time.

After shooting at the lock on the door multiple times and using an explosive, he still couldn't open the door. The security system at the synagogue had recently been upgraded, which included security cameras. This enabled the people inside to see that an armed man was trying to invade.

The gunman then tried to gain entry to the yard of the synagogue, letting off homemade explosives and firing shots. An emergency call was made to the authorities at 12:03 P.M.; and within a minute, police had been notified. Federal police and rapid responders arrived in Halle at 2:40 P.M.

One of the victims killed was a woman who happened to walk by the gunman. She'd told him off for making a lot of noise; in return, she was shot multiple times near the entrance to the cemetery beside the synagogue. A man driving past stopped to check on the victim and was soon in the shooter's sights. He managed to escape, purely because the weapon failed to fire.

The gunman left the scene, drove to a kebab shop nearby, and used a shotgun to shoot through the front window. The bullets wounded a 20-year-old customer inside the shop. When the gunman entered, he shot the person again and killed the victim.

From there, the gunman went on a run, driving a rented Volkswagen vehicle. Police chased him for 50 miles, from Halle to Wiedersdorf near Landsberg. During the chase, the gunman shot at a couple and wounded them.

Eventually, the gunman was apprehended and placed under arrest in Zeitz.

Investigating the Attack

Within the first few hours after the attack, the assumption was made that there were multiple gunmen. That afternoon, Holger Stahlknecht, State Minister of the Interior, announced that there was just one gunman and confirmed how he'd been arrested. However, it was being investigated whether he'd been part of networks or a social environment.

Because the attack was a potential violation of the internal security of Germany, the Federal Prosecutor took control of the investigation. It was announced that the suspect was a German national with no previous criminal history. There were indicators of him having a right-wing extremist background.

The suspect had been living with his mother in Benndorf, close to Eisleben. Then on October 10, police undertook a search of the home. It was discovered that the gunman had used Twitch, a streaming service, to broadcast the attacks; however, because the stream wasn't listed in the site recommendations, and hadn't been made public, the only way for people to see the footage as if they were sent a direct link by someone they know.

The gunman confessed to the shooting on October 11. He further said the motive was anti-Semitic and right-wing extremist.

Gunman Stephan Balliet

Balliet, 27, had learned to use weapons while he completed his six-month military service with a Panzergrenadier battalion when he was 18. His military file showed no evidence of any right-wing beliefs.

At one point, he'd studied chemistry and molecular and structural product design at a university, but didn't complete his studies.

Balliet used Meguca, an imageboard in a chan forum, to make comments and announce plans. The posts could be completely anonymous, so anything could be said regardless of whether it was ultra-radical, inciteful, or otherwise vile.

211

Court Appearance

Balliet was sent to the federal court in Karlsruhe. He asked his court-appointed lawyer if he was Jewish and when he replied he wasn't, Balliet said he wouldn't reject him now anyway.

His lawyer told Balliet that because he'd recorded the attack, he'd provided the evidence needed for him to be convicted. Balliet told his lawyer he followed major massacres, such as the Christchurch mosque shootings and Anders Breivik's attack in Norway.

The case is still ongoing.

Truck Full of Dead Migrants Discovered in the UK

Ambulance services were called to the location of a truck at Waterglade Industrial Park in Grays, Essex, on the afternoon of October 23. Inside the truck were the bodies of 39 people, all deceased. The trailer had come from Zeebrugge, Belgium, and the truck cab had come from Northern Ireland. What ensued was a massive effort in identifying the bodies and investigating how they'd ended up in Essex.

The Dreadful Discovery

It's unknown who made the call to the ambulance service that day, but once the discovery had been made, police were notified. The avenue was closed off by police and remained almost completely closed until October 25, so that the bodies could be removed.

Police quickly realized that the people inside the truck trailer were migrants, most likely from Vietnam.

It was discovered that the truck was one of three, traveling in a convoy. Relatives of some victims had told police that 100 migrants were traveling in the trucks but only two of the trucks had arrived in the UK.

Some of the migrants had paid up to £11,000 for the trip. A young woman who had been in the truck had sent a text to her family to confirm how she was dying and unable to breathe.

The chairman of Zeebrugge port had said it was very unlikely that the migrants had entered the truck trailer there. It would've meant breaking the seal on the trailer, loading a large number of people into the trailer, and then resealing it again. To do so without being noticed would've been more or less impossible.

Arrest of Mo Robinson

Early in the investigation, police were able to identify the driver of the truck as Maurice 'Mo' Robinson, 25, from Ireland. Following his arrest, he was charged with 39 counts of manslaughter and conspiracy to traffic people.

Identifying the Dead

Identifying the victims was a long and difficult process as most of the bodies had no identification when they were found dead. People smugglers normally take away anything identifiable and are given new documents once they arrive at their destination.

At first, police thought the victims were from China, but they later discovered they were from Vietnam after the text messages from the young female victim were received by the family in Vietnam. A hotline was set up in Vietnam for families who may be missing relatives.

Eventually, after a grueling process, the victims were all identified, thanks in part to DNA testing.

The victims were:

- Nguyen Dinh Lurong, 20, male, from Ha Tinh
- Pham Thi Tra My, 26, female, from Ha Tinh
- Nguyen Huy Phong, 35, male, from Ha Tinh

- Tran Manh Hung, 37, male, from Ha Tinh
- Vo Nhan Du, 19, male, from Ha Tinh
- Tran Khanh Tho, 18, male, from Ha Tinh
- Nguyen Van Nhan, 33, male, from Ha Tinh
- Vo Van Linh, 25, male, from Ha Tinh
- Nguyen Huy Hung, 15, male, from Ha Tinh
- Bui Phan Thang, 37, male, from Ha Tinh
- Bui Thi Nhung, 19, female, from Nghe An
- Tran Thi Tho, 21, female, from Nghe An
- Vo Ngoc Nam, 28, male, from Nghe An
- Le Van Ha, 30, male, from Nghe An
- Nguyen Dinh Tu, 26, male, from Nghe An
- Tran Thi Ngoc, 19, female, from Nghe An
- Nguyen Van Hung, 33, male, from Nghe An
- Cao Tien Dung, 37, male, from Nghe An
- Hoang Van Tiep, 18, male, from Nghe An
- Cao Huy Thanh, 33, male, from Nghe An
- Nguyen Minh Quang, 20, male, from Nghe An
- Tran Thi Mai Nhung, 18, female, from Nghe An
- Le Trong Thanh, 44, male, from Dien Chau
- Pham Thi Ngoc Oanh, 28, female, from Nghe An
- Nguyen Tho Tuan, 25, male, from Nghe An
- Hoang Van Hoi, 24, male, from Nghe An
- Dang Huu Tuyen, 22, male, from Nghe An
- Nguyen Van Hiep, 24, male, from Nghe An
- Nguyen Trong Thai, 26, male, from Nghe An
- Nguyen Thi Van, 35, female, from Nghe An
- Tran Hai Loc, 35, male, from Nghe An
- Duong Minh Tuan, 27, male, from Quang Binh
- Nguyen Ngoc Ha, 32, male, from Quang Binh
- Nguyen Tien Dung, 33, male, from Quang Binh

- Nguyen Ba Vu Hung, 34, male, from Thua Tien Hue
- Phan Thi Thanh, 41, female, from Hai Phong
- Dinh Dinh Thai Quyen, 18, male, from Hai Phong
- Tran Ngoc Hieu, 17, male, from Hai Duong
- Dinh Dinh Binh, 15, male, from Hai Phong

Widespread Investigation

Police arrested a woman and a man from Warrington on suspicion of manslaughter and conspiracy to traffic people on October 25. They arrested another man at Stansted Airport in relation to the same crimes. All three were released on bail on October 27.

Mo Robinson was charged on October 26, after a period of extensive questioning. In addition to the manslaughter and trafficking charges, he was also charged with money laundering and conspiracy to assist unlawful immigration. On October 28, he appeared in court, and the Crown Prosecution Service alleged that Robinson was involved with a 'global ring' of human traffickers.

Irish law enforcement announced on October 26 that they'd detained a man at Dublin Port. The Essex Police had been interested in the man in relation to the investigation. He was later charged with offenses unrelated to the people smuggling. According to a Belgian prosecutor, he was the man who had been captured on CCTV multiple times at Zeebrugge, dropping off the trailer.

Two brothers from Armagh, Northern Ireland, were detained on October 29 by Essex Police. One of the brothers owned the company that had been operating the truck cab. The brothers were being questioned on suspicion of manslaughter and human trafficking.

After a European Arrest Warrant was issued in the UK, a man who had previously been questioned was arrested again on November 1. He was charged with 41 offenses, which included 39 counts of manslaughter, and extradition proceedings launched.

Eight suspects who were believed to be involved at the Vietnamese end were arrested by Vietnamese police on November 4.

On November 25, Robinson pled guilty to conspiring to assist illegal immigration over the period between May 1, 2018, and October 24, 2019. He wasn't required to plead to the manslaughter charges in this hearing.

The investigation into the ring of traffickers stretches across Europe and is still ongoing. It has been a widespread effort to track the truck's and trailer's travels before the bodies of the victims were discovered.

Child Charged with Five Murders

When a 9-year-old boy was charged with 5 counts of murder in Illinois on October 23, opinions were divided on whether this was an appropriate action to take against someone so young. It brought up questions regarding the ability of a child to know that what he or she doing could lead to deaths. But, how normal is it for a child to wait until people are incapacitated and then calculatingly do something that would take the lives of so many?

A Deadly Fire is Lit

On April 6, Kyle Alwood waited until his family was asleep then set fire to their mobile home. Only one other family member managed to escape, Katie Alwood, Kyle's mother. She stood outside the mobile home, listening to the screams of her fiancé, children, and her grandmother, as they perished in the home.

Autopsies later showed that all the victims had died due to smoke inhalation.

The Victims

The victims included three toddlers, making the situation even more tragic. Ariel Wall, 1, and Daemeon Wall, 2, were Kyle's half-siblings. Rose Alwood, 2, was his cousin.

Jason Wall, 34, was Kyle's stepfather, and Kathryn Murray, 69, was his great grandmother.

During an interview with media, Katie Alwood said, "I don't know what's worse. Hearing him scream or when it stopped," referring to her fiancé Jason Wall.

Little Boy Lost

Since the tragedy, Kyle's mother has claimed the boy was diagnosed with some form of schizophrenia, bipolar disorder and ADHD. She revealed that Kyle was a 'loving' child and that he deserved a second chance. His aunt Samantha, however, whose daughter Rose was killed in the fire, thinks he deserves severe punishment.

She insisted, "I think he should go somewhere until he's the legal age to go to juvie. Then I think he should go to juvie. And then from juvie to prison. Because at the end of the day, whether he meant to or not, he knew what fire did."

His mother says she has forgiven Kyle for what he had done and loved him regardless of his actions. He's currently living with his grandparents because he cannot be detained due to his age.

Legalities of Charging a Child with Murder

Prosecutors believe Kyle set the fire deliberately and defended their decision to charge such a young child with murder. If he's convicted, he'll most likely only face a period of probation and be ordered to undertake treatment or counseling.

During a court hearing recently, it was reported that Kyle seemed confused. He understood what was going on but had trouble understanding some of the terms and language used. His lawyer had to explain to him what the words meant throughout the hearing.

As he was taken from the courtroom by his grandparents, Kyle cried.

Next, he'll undergo an expert evaluation to determine if he's fit to stand trial. Kyle's lawyer, Peter Dulksi, has said that because of his age and what he's seen during his interactions with Kyle, he thinks it's unlikely Kyle will be fit to stand trial.

His next court appearance is scheduled for February 2020.

Russian Soldier Shoots Ten Colleagues

A soldier in Gorny, Zabaykalsky Krai, Russia, went on a shooting spree at a military base on October 25. The attack left eight soldiers dead and two others with injuries.

How the Attack Took Place

At around 6:20 P.M., the Russian soldier who had just received an assault rifle shot and killed Captain Yevseyev. A few soldiers were able to hide behind an armored truck nearby, but the majority of the soldiers were unarmed and unable to flee.

The soldiers were forced to lie down on the ground, as the gunman shot each one in the head. Six more soldiers were killed, and three initially survived their injuries. One of the wounded soldiers died not long after arriving in hospital. The other surviving victims suffered multiple gunshot injuries to the head, stomach and arm.

There had been 30 rounds in the magazine, and 26 of them were fired in the attack. The noise of the gunshots could be heard in a radius of a few miles surrounding the base.

Afterward, the suspect ran into a neighborhood nearby, resulting in school children being sent home and stores closing.

Within two minutes of the start of the onslaught, the Russian SWAT team, the Spetsnaz, arrived. The suspect surrendered immediately as soon as he saw the Spetsnaz. He announced that he "didn't regret anything."

Those Killed and Injured

Killed

- Vladimir Yevseyev, 1989 - Captain.
- Daniil Pyankov, 1990 - Senior lieutenant
- Roman Kovalyov Роман , 1998 - Sergeant
- Yegor Bogomolov, 1999 - Private
- A.V. Nikishin 1998 - Private
- Alexey Andreyev , 2000 - Yefreytor. He was badly injured and later died in the hospital.
- Andrey Dmitriyevich Pokotilo, 1999 - Private
- A.S. Kuropov, 1998 - Private

Injured

- V.R Shpak - Private
- A.A. Grafov - Private

Investigation and Suspect

The suspect was Pvt. Ramil Salengalovich Shamsutdinov from Vagay Village, Tyumen Oblast. His father was a retired military commander. Shamsutdinov, 20, had initiated the attack during the changing of the guard. After first killing his captain, the other victims were shot in the head and then 'finished off' by 'control shots.'

He was arrested by the Chita military court; and if he's found guilty, he could receive a sentence of life imprisonment.

Mental Health Motive

It has been suggested that the shooting attack was due to Shamsutdinov suffering a nervous breakdown. It was added that the breakdown was due to personal issues and not a result of his military service.

Shamsutdinov had been at the remote Siberian base for only four months before he attacked his colleagues.

Contents of Serial Killer Ivan Milat's Final Letter

Many celebrated the death of one of Australia's worst serial killers in history, Ivan Milat. Known as the 'Backpack Killer,' the story of Milat and his crimes has been told repeatedly because of the horrific nature of his crimes. When he was struck down with cancer, some saw it as karma for his terrible actions, Milat would have the last word, in the form of a letter to his brother, and that last word was 'innocent.'

The Backpacker Killer

Between 1989 and 1993, Milat committed a number of murders in New South Wales, Australia. Seven bodies were found partially buried in the Belanglo State Forest, just over 9 miles from the town of Berrima.

The victims ranged in age from 19 to 22 years, and five were tourists from overseas. Three were from Germany, and two were from the UK.

Milat was captured and convicted of the murders and was sentenced to life in prison on each count of murder without any possibility of parole. One of his victims had managed to escape, so Milat was also convicted of attempted murder, robbery and false imprisonment, receiving another six years in prison for each count.

Milat throughout had claimed he was innocent, but the amount of evidence against him was staggering. Some have theorized he didn't act alone, but this has failed to be proven to date.

Known victims were:

- Deborah Everist, 19
- James Gibson, 19
- Simone Schmidl, 21
- Anja Habschied, 20
- Gabor Neugebauer, 21
- Joanne Walters, 22
- Caroline Clarke, 21

Terminal Illness and Death

Milat was diagnosed with terminal esophageal cancer in May 2019 after he was transferred to the Prince of Wales Hospital in Randwick for investigation. He received treatment and was moved to Long Bay Correctional Center for the continuation of his sentence.

After losing 20 kg in weight in a matter of weeks, Milat was transferred to a secure unit at the Prince of Wales Hospital on August 9. Despite also having a high fever, his condition was not reported to be life-threatening at that time. He was given treatment then sent back to Long Bay.

Milat died at 4:07 A.M. On October 27 in the infirmary of Long Bay Correctional Center. He was aged 74 years at the time of his death.

Milat's Final Letter

Many saw Milat's last letter as a final insult. The letter was written to Bill Milat, his brother, who, like most of the family, had always believed Milat was innocent. While Bill read some of the letter to the media, it was noted Milat had wanted his funeral to be funded by the taxpayer.

The letter also requested that Bill receive all of his belongings after Milat's death.

The Letter in Full

"Hello and may all be well with both of you and your family.

Things are fairly crook with me but while in mind and senses I would like you to know that years ago you were nominated as my next of kin contact person by CS NSW, that's Corrective Services New South Wales.

Due to my health issues, I wish to leave you all I have.

All funds, moneys held in my prison account and to possessions of all other items of property, legal and trial and appeal reviews documents held on my behalf by Corrective Services NSW. Above all I request be given to William [Address] I thank you for this.

I realise and am aware that this letter my wishes may not be legal will and testament CS NSW Government Services and probate procedures may come into play I believe.

But hope this letter may clearly show my intentions and wishes that you Bill receive my funds and legal documents.

Keep this letter to show it to your solicitor that you may sole beneficiary.

Please don't pay for my funeral services or contribute in any way.

CS NSW to fund it all.

A pauper's burial or whatever is suitable. I have assured the commissioner of CS of NSW of my wishes.

I am innocent of the crimes convicted of.

24/10/2019

Ivan Milat

Innocent"

Orlinda Mass Shooting

On October 31, in Orinda, California, a mass shooting took place at a house party that resulted in 5 people killed and another 4 injured.

Airbnb House Party

The house where the incident occurred was an Airbnb residential house that had been rented by a woman. The owner of the property had been told that the house was needed for a family reunion and that only 12 people would present. The excuse for gathering there instead of at their own house was that some of the family members had asthma and at that time, the Kincade Fire was burning North of Orinda.

Because it was only for one night and Halloween, the renter was told by the property owner that they weren't allowed to have any parties at the house.

Multiple Gunshots Fired

There were at least 100 people at the house during the party. Numerous calls had been placed to the police by neighbors of the property complaining about the noise. Police officers were sent to the house around 9:00 P.M. When reports came in of gunshots being heard at the house at 10:45 P.M., police rushed to the scene.

When police arrived, many party attenders were fleeing from the property. One of those attending the party said that there had been no argument, no physical fight or warning before the shots were fired.

As a result of the shooting, 4 men were killed: all in their 20s and a 19-year-old female died the next day from the injuries she sustained. Many others were injured; again, some from gunshots; while others were injured in the rush to escape.

The Investigation

The investigation led police to consider the possibility of links between 2 of the victims, and the Page Street Mob gang. There could also be a link with a quadruple homicide that occurred in 2015.

Five suspects were eventually arrested, and 4 were charged with murder and conspiracy to commit murder. The fifth suspect was charged as being an accessory to the crime. However, the country district attorney declined to pursue the charges without further investigation and the suspects were released on November 18.

Two further suspects were arrested on November 21 on charges relating to weapons and child endangerment. They'd seized a firearm that could be linked to the shooting and several more.

The Response

A large memorial was created outside the rental home that contained notes to those who had died, photos of the victims, and flowers.

As a result of the incident, CEO of Airbnb, Brian Chesky, announced that there would be a company policy change as of November 2 that would mean a site-wide ban on party houses. They'd also implement a screening and flagging system for potentially high-risk reservations. A dedicated rapid response team would also be developed to take action immediately against those who violate the policies.

A special hearing was held by council members to discuss if there needed to be new regulations regarding rentals and parties. A short-term ordinance was passed banning short-term rentals. If someone was planning to rent a house or a room for less than 30 days, he or she now had to register with the council.

Some of those who lived in Orinda felt that the response to the shooting was focused on Airbnb policy more than showing empathy for the victims.

Terrorist Attacks in Brief

October 3

Paris, France: A radicalized Islamist stabbed four people to death and injured two others at the central police headquarters in Paris. He was an administrative worker and had been recently converting to Salafist Islam. The perpetrator was shot instantly dead by other officers.

October 4

Arbinda Department, Burkina Faso: A shooting attack at a gold mine killed 20 people. The number of injured is unknown.

October 7

Jalalabad, Afghanistan: A suicide bomb attack on a minibus carrying new recruits for security forces resulted in the deaths of 14, and a further 37 were injured.

October 9

Halle and Landsberg, Germany: Two people were killed when a man wearing military-style clothing attempted to enter a synagogue by force and attacked a kebab shop in Halle, Saxony-Anhalt, Germany. The attacker fled the scene in a car and wounded a man and a woman while stealing a Taxicab from a garage in the Landsberg region. A few hours later, he had an accident near Zeitz and was arrested. The attacker had a far-right terror motive and streamed the attack on Twitch for 35 minutes, where he explained his motives for the attack and expressed racist comments on Jews and non-white people.

October 10

Banten Province, Indonesia: Wiranto, a 72-year-old Indonesian politician, is stabbed two times in his stomach by an Islamic State member. He survived the attack and is in a stable condition. Three other people, including a police officer, were stabbed and wounded. The two attackers, a man and a woman, were arrested.

October 11

Oudalan Province, Burkina Faso: The Grand Mosque in Salmossi was attacked by gunmen who opened fire, killing 16 people.

October 18

Nangarhar Province, Afghanistan: Two bombings at a mosque during Friday prayer resulted in the deaths of 73 people, and an additional 36 were wounded.

October 28

Pobe-Mengao Department, Burkina Faso: After people in the village refused to purchase ammunition for Islamists, they shot and killed 16 of them.

October 29

Kulgam District, India: Kashmiri separatists are believed to be behind an attack on Bengali Muslin laborers in their home, resulting in 7 deaths.

Chapter 11:
NOVEMBER

LeBarón Family Massacre

In a horrific attack on November 4, south of the Mexico-United States border, three carloads of family members from the La Mora community were attacked by gunmen. The cars were ignited and many of the victims were burned alive. Nine people, including children, were killed. In sum, the common belief is that a drug cartel was responsible.

A Religious Community

The victims of the attack had all come from rancho La Mora, Sonora. The population is around 150 people, the ranch the size of about 1,000 acres. The victims' religious affiliation was different from the Church of the Firstborn which has its headquarters at Colonia Le Baron, Chihuahua, but the groups do intermarry with each other.

The groups contain independent fundamentalist Mormons as well as the Church of the Firstborn members, and some follow the Latter-day Saints. The victims were descended from settlers who founded Rancho Oaxaca, formerly Colonia Oaxaca in the late 19th century.

It has been reported that the La Mora community had some type of understanding with the Los Salazar, del Cartel de Sinaloa, a dominant outlaw band. The overlord is El Chapo, who is incarcerated in the U.S.

The Sinaloa told residents not to buy fuel across the Chihuahua state lines, and new enforcers unfamiliar with the agreement often pointed guns at the La Mora residents using the road.

Two Attacks on Three Vehicles

As three SUVs carrying LeBaron family members were traveling along the main road en route to attend a wedding in Le Baron, gunmen opened fire on the vehicles. The LeBaron's, American Mexicans, were traveling about 70 miles when they were ambushed in Bavispe.

The first car had left around 10:00 A.M. that morning, and onboard were Rhonita Miller and her children. The next two vehicles left closer to 11:00 A.M. Dawna Ray Langford drove one of the vehicles with nine children onboard, and the other was driven by Christina Marie Langford Johnson and her baby daughter.

When Johnson's car was stopped, she jumped out and was waving her hands to signify, she wasn't a threat. Her body was found 15 yards from the car, shot to death. Her baby was left in the car and was not injured.

Another car was located 11 miles away from the other vehicles. It had been burned out, and inside were the bodies of Miller and her children. It's believed she had broken down with a flat tire before being attacked.

Two surviving children, aged 13 and 9, managed to escape to get help. It took the 13-year-old boy more than 6 hours to walk to the family compound. He'd hidden the other surviving children in bushes before he left the scene, and when he didn't come back before nightfall, the 9-year-old girl started to seek help and also walked for 6 hours.

From 6:00 P.M., the search began to find the survivors, with the hidden children found at 8:30 P.M. The 9-year-old who had gone for help was located at 9:45pm. She had gone down the wrong road but was found through her footprints.

Victims and Survivors

Nine members of the group were killed, 6 of who were children. All of the victims held dual US and Mexico citizenship. Five children were injured in the attack, and 3 remarkably escaped any injury. All of the injuries were from gunshots.

- Titus Miller, 8-month-old twin
- Tiana Miller, 8-month-old twin
- Rogan Langford, 2
- Krystal Miller, 10
- Trevor Langford, 11
- Howard Miller, 12
- Christina Marie Langford Johnson, 29
- Rhonita Miller, 30
- Dawna Langford, 43

The Mexican Army later escorted family members to the massacre scene. The funerals began on November 7, and all were buried in La Mora and Colonia LeBaron.

Investigation into Criminal Cartel

Authorities announced that they believed the attack was as a result of the family being mistaken for a convoy of cartel vehicles. There had been a shootout earlier in the day between two rival cartels. However, others felt that activism by some extended family members who condemned criminal groups might have made them a target.

The first suspect was arrested on November 5, but authorities announced that the person hadn't been involved in the massacre the following day. Some claimed that the new Los Jaguares cartels, who were an offshoot of Sinaloa, may have been responsible.

Marcelo Ebrard, Mexican Foreign Affairs Secretary, invited the FBI to help with the investigation as the victims were joint citizens.

The Mexican police later obtained video footage of around a dozen men dressed in black with rifles going towards the vehicles. The footage lasted less than a minute and was likely taken by a phone belonging to a suspect.

On December 1, it was announced that several suspects had been arrested.

Response

One of the community members stated he believed the attack was targeted, and that there couldn't have been a case of mistaken identity because one of the children who survived said that one of the women had tried to identify herself before she was shot.

The Church of Jesus Christ of Latter-day Saints expressed love, sympathies, and prayers to the victims and their families and noted that they understood the victims weren't members of the church.

President Donald Trump offered military support to Mexico to help defeat the drug cartels, but the offer was declined. President Andrés Manuel López Obrador cited he'd discuss security cooperation with Trump, however.

Another School Shooting in California

Saugus High School, located in Santa Clarita, California, was the scene of a school shooting on November 14. Two students were killed and 3 were injured before the shooter committed suicide.

Student Shoots at Fellow Students

On the day of the shooting, classes hadn't begun, and the students were largely on the quad or in the outside courtyard. One of their fellow students retrieved a handgun from his bag and began shooting at the students.

The shooter fired one round, and then the pistol seemed to jam. He fixed it before shooting another 4 students. The last round in the pistol was used to shoot himself in the head.

During the shooting, many students ran: some left the campus altogether, and shouted at other students and teachers to run. Students were moved into classrooms by teachers to escape the danger. A student who had been shot ran and hid in the choir room, which the teacher secured by barricading the door.

The students who were barricaded inside rooms utilized skills they'd learned from drills on how to protect themselves in a shooting situation. Scissors were handed out to the students, as recommended in one of the drills.

The whole attack had lasted just 16 seconds, and it was captured on surveillance camera footage.

First on the Scene

That day, 3 off-duty police officers were first on the scene as they had just dropped people off at the school. One was a Los Angeles County Sheriff's Department detective, and the other 2 were officers from Los Angeles and Inglewood. Within about a minute, other deputies arrived on the scene.

The Casualties

The 2 fatalities were a 14-year-old boy and a 15-year-old girl. The injured victims included a boy, 14, and two girls, aged 14 and 15. Four were hospitalized at the Henry Mayo Newhall Memorial Hospital, which included the shooter. Two victims were sent to Providence Holy Cross Medical Center.

Despite all of the victims and the shooter being from the same school, they apparently had no personal connections with each other.

Shooter Had Turned 16 the Same Day

The shooter was Nathaniel Tennosuke Berhow, who was turning 16 on the day of the attack. He died from his self-inflicted injury the day after the attack.

Berhow's parents had been divorced since 2016, and he'd been living with his mother and sister. It A neighbor recalled that he seemed to have struggled after the death of his father in 2017. He was also having problems with his girlfriend.

Those who knew him at school described Berhow as quiet and seemed like a regular teen. He was involved in sports and was in a junior varsity cross country group. He'd been a Boy Scout and was a good student in an Advanced Placement class.

Investigating Berhow

Berhow was below the legal age to own a firearm, and detectives worked with the Federal Bureau of Alcohol, Tobacco, Firearms, and Explosives to determine it was a kit weapon, one that was made by purchasing parts individually.

But, when the family home was searched, several weapons were discovered, and some of them hadn't been registered. It's believed that may have been his father's, who had been a keen hunter.

Later it was announced by the sheriff that the murder weapon was a 'ghost gun,' put together using interchangeable parts that had no serial numbers. Police believe he'd done this himself, as there was no evidence to suggest he'd been helped by anyone.

There was nothing in Berhow's home to indicate what his motive may have been. Because of his knowledge of the weapon and the speed at which he executed the shooting, the sheriff believed Berhow had planned it.

Response and Aftermath

The way the school had taught the students how to react to an active shooter situation was heavily praised. Parents also stated that the alert system had kept them updated regularly about the attack.

Other schools in the district were closed until the next week, and Saugus High was closed until December.

A memorial was created outside the school, and a banner was put up that people could write messages on to those who had died in the shooting. The victims were commemorated at a football game on November 15 with a moment of silence, the release of balloons, stickers and signs, and by chanting 'Saugus Strong!'

A number of vigils were attended by hundreds.

Fresno Football Party Shooting

While a large group of people was gathered at a home on November 17 to watch football, they were attacked by two males sneaking through the backyard and opening fire on them. Four people were shot and killed, and six more were injured in the attack. It had been the third mass shooting in less than one week in California.

A Deadly Gathering

On the day of the attack, around 35 to 40 family members and friends had gathered together in the backyard of a home in Fresno, California, to watch the football game between the Chicago Bears and the Los Angeles Rams.

During the game, all the women and children present had decided to go inside and watch television. There were sixteen men that continued to watch the football game from outside.

At close to 6:00 P.M., two men snuck into the backyard through a gate that was unlocked and began firing on the group of men. They shot at the men randomly before fleeing on foot.

Those Killed and Injured

The four men killed were between the ages of 23 and 40, and three were pronounced dead at the scene. The fourth man was transported to the hospital, where he later died due to his injuries. Two of the men who were killed were acclaimed singers from Southeast Asia.

One of the injured survivors was taken to one hospital while the others were treated at the same hospital where the other man had died. The survivors ranged in age from 28 to 36 years. They were all members of the Hmong community and those killed were:

- Xy Lee, 23
- Kou Xiong, 38
- Phia Vang, 31
- Kalaxang Thao, 40

Unknown Identities, Unknown Motive

To date, the investigation by the Fresno Police Department with assistance from the US Bureau of Alcohol, Tobacco, Firearms and Explosives, has yet to uncover who was responsible for the shooting. They haven't yet determined the motive, but they believe the group was targeted specifically.

An 'Asian Gang Task Force' was mobilized to investigate the possibility that the shooting could have been related to an increase in violence being committed by Asian Gangs at the time.

The Hmong people are from Southeast Asia, typically living in Laos, Vietnam, and Southern China. Fresno has the largest Hmong population in California and is the second largest in America.

Dresden Royal Jewelry Heist

Although a crime without violence, the heist of the Dresden royal jewelry on November 25 was a remarkable piece of planning that shouldn't have been able to occur. The estimated value of the jewelry was €1 billion.

The Green Vault Museum

The royal jewelry had been stored at one of the oldest European museums, the Green Vault in Dresden, Germany. The Vault had been created in 1723. Plus, at the time of the robbery, there were around 4,000 pieces of jewelry and other treasurable items. Most were decorated with precious metals and stones, including gold, silver, pearl, and ivory, as well as gemstones.

The most impressive piece housed at the Green Vault was the Dresden Green Diamond, a beautiful 41-carat stone that fortunately was out on loan to the Metropolitan Museum of Art in New York at the time.

A Clever Plan

Near the museum is the Augustus Bridge. At around 4:00 A.M. on November 25, a small fire was started on the bridge, destroying a power box that caused an outage. The outage caused security alarms to be disabled, but CCTV cameras were still operating.

The next step was the cutting of the iron bars surrounding a window of the Jewel Room in the museum. A smallish hole was created, making police believe that the thieves must have been small in stature to accommodate. Two thieves were caught by CCTV inside the vaults. The displays, which were made out of glass, were smashed with an ax so the thieves could access the jewels.

In the heist, they tried to remove three 18th-century jewelry sets. Each set was made of 37 parts and contained diamonds, emeralds, rubies and sapphires. Because some of the parts were attached to the cabinet by being sewn into the surface, several pieces were left behind.

Once they had grabbed what they could, the thieves left the same way they came, through the small hole in the window. The placed the bars they'd cut back into a position to try and delay the discovery of the robbery.

Just before 5:00 A.M., security guards discovered the heist and notified police, who sent 16 police cars to the scene.

Precious Pieces Stolen

Of the pieces stolen, one was an epee, a small sword that was made of gold and silver. The hilt of the sword contained 9 large diamonds and 770 smaller diamonds. Another piece was a brooch type jewel that had once been worn by Queen Amalie Auguste. It was comprised of 660 precious gemstones.

The Dresden White Diamond was taken: with a value of around €10 million. A diamond epaulet and a bejeweled Polish White Eagle Order were stolen, as well as an Order of the White Eagle breast star, which contained a 20-carat diamond in the center and rubies in the shape of the Maltese Cross. A hat clasp with 15 large and 100 small diamonds was also taken, with the largest stone measuring 16-carats.

The total estimated value of the stolen jewels is more than €1 billion, which is equivalent to US$1.1 billion. This made it the largest museum heist in world history. The director of Dresden State Art Collections, Marion Ackermann, stated the value of some of the items would be near impossible to price due to their historic-cultural value.

Still Under Investigation

By the time police arrived at the museum after they were alerted by security guards, the thieves had already fled the scene. Roadblocks were set up in the surrounding area, but because the museum was close to the autobahn, the thieves had most likely escaped the area quickly.

It's believed by police that there were actually 4 thieves, despite only 2 being seen on camera. An Audi A6 was found on fire later in an underground parking lot, and police think this was the escape vehicle.

A reward of €500,000 was put up by police to try and flush out information about who the thieves were and how to find them.

There's a large concern that the thieves may dismantle the jewels or melt the precious metals down so they could be sold on the black market. They couldn't sell them as they were because they were too renowned.

To date, no suspects have been identified, and the jewels have yet to be found.

Hyderabad Gang Rape and Murder

A young female veterinary doctor was gang-raped and murdered in November which caused outrage right across India. The suspects were arrested fairly quickly, and the harshest possible sentence was rendered.

A Violent and Abhorrent Attack

On November 27, Disha (real name protected), 26, parked her scooter close to the Tondupally toll plaza. She got into a taxi at 6:15pm and went to see a dermatologist in Hyderabad.

She was noticed by 2 truck drivers and their assistants, and while she was away from her scooter, they deflated one of the tires. On her return at approximately 9:15pm, she noticed the flat tire and placed a call to her sister for help.

The men grabbed Disha and pushed her into bushes nearby, turning off her phone. She started screaming for help so to make her quiet they poured whiskey into her mouth. The men stripped off her clothes and took turns raping her. She was bleeding and became unconscious.

When she regained consciousness, they smothered her. They wrapped her up in a blanket and loaded her body into the truck. They drove to an area near the interchange on Hyderabad Outer Ring Road. Then sometime between 2:00 A.M. and 2:30 A.M. they burned her body. They'd purchased petrol and diesel for the sole purpose of burning the body.

Her body was discarded underneath Chatanpally Bridge in Shadnagar and was discovered the following day. Her body had 70% burns, and her belongings were found near the toll booth.

Four Men Arrested

Using footage from CCTV cameras along with a witness statement and Disha's phone, police were able to identify the four attackers and arrest them within 24 hours. They were sent to Cherlapally Central Jail for 14 days, and a fast track court was ordered by the Telangana Chief Minister.

Executed in Police Custody

On December 6, the four suspects were taken to the scene of the murder so the crime scene could be reconstructed, according to reports by police. They claimed that 2 of the suspects grabbed guns off the officers and attacked them. As a result, a shootout occurred, and all 4 suspects were shot and killed.

Second Body Found

Close to where the body of Disha was found, another body was located. The woman's body was half burnt, similar to what had been done to Disha. An investigation was launched on December 1. However, police are uncertain if it's another murder case or if it was a case of self-immolation. No link has been found between the 2 cases.

Local and Global Response

Numerous protests took place throughout the country due to the serious outrage the crime caused. Calls were made for stricter laws against rapists. When the suspects were in custody, people protested outside the police station calling for the men to be shot or hanged.

Following the deaths of the suspects, thousands of people celebrated. Even celebrities and politicians thanked the police for the 'encounter' - a term used for extrajudicial justice in India.

Human rights organizations, though condemned the killing of the suspects. Activists believed the case should have gone down the normal legal route, but without a trial, nobody would know if they were actually guilty or innocent.

An investigation was started by the National Human Rights Commission of India into the suspect's deaths, and news agencies have questioned if the 'encounter' was in fact, staged.

Disha's family, although happy with the killing of the suspects, were unhappy about the response by the Hyderabad police, believing that if they'd responded quicker, she might still be alive. Her father had contacted the police at 11:00 P.M. the night she was killed because she was missing. The police instead of looking for Disha spent a lot of time trying to work out the applicability of the jurisdiction of the police station. The family also claimed they asked inappropriate questions to the family members. They finally went looking at 3:00 A.M. with the family.

The following day, 3 policemen were suspended for negligence and the delay in registering her disappearance as a missing person case.

Stabbing on London Bridge

During a terror attack in Central London on November 29, five people received stab wounds by a single attacker. Two people were killed, and it was bystanders that helped to stop so many more from being attacked.

Prisoner Rehabilitation Conference

At the time of the attack, a Prisoner Rehabilitation Conference was taking place at the Fishmonger's Hall, located at the northern end of London Bridge. The conference was celebrating the fifth anniversary of a program called Learning Together, which helps offenders reintegrate back into society once they've been released from prison.

The program is run by the Cambridge Institute of Criminology, and a former prisoner who was invited to attend was Usman Khan. He'd previously undertaken the program. Khan was prohibited from entering London due to his release terms but was granted an exemption for the day so he could attend the conference.

Killer Khan Unleashes Terror

Police were called at 1:58 P.M. to attend the Fishmonger's Hall because Khan had threatened to use his fake suicide vest to blow up the hall. He'd taped two kitchen knives to his wrists, and he began to stab people inside the hall.

A number of people in the hall fought back against Khan. One of these people was a chef who was working at the hall who took a long narwhal tusk, 1.5m long, off the wall to use as a weapon. Another who tried to help was a convicted murderer who was out on day leave to attend the conference.

Khan fled the building and began to attack pedestrians out on the bridge. Several were injured by Khan until a plainclothes British Transport Police officer and members of the public were able to restrain him and take away his knives. Another bystander used a fire extinguisher to keep Khan back by spraying at him.

Armed police officers arrived at the bridge around 2:03pm, and found Khan restrained by a bystander. The police surrounded Khan: and after pulling the bystander away, they shot twice at Khan and killed him.

Innocent Victims

Jack Merritt, 25, was a graduate of law and criminology and had been working as an administration officer for the University of Cambridge when he was killed by Khan. The other fatality was Saskia Jones, 23, who was a former student at the University of Cambridge.

As part of Merritt's administration role, he was the course coordinator for the Learning Together program. Jones was volunteering at the event.

Two women received serious injuries from Khan, and the chef that grabbed the narwhal tusk suffered less serious stabbing injuries.

Usman Khan and Terrorism

Usman Khan, 28, was a British national of Pakistani descent. Part of his teenage years was spent in Pakistan, and he'd left school without obtaining any qualifications. He was known by police to have links to Islamist extremist groups, and when he was released from prison in December 2018, he had been serving a 16-year sentence for terrorism charges.

The previous terrorism charge stemmed from a plot that Khan was part of that had been inspired by Al-Qaeda. His plan was to create a terrorist camp on land in Kashmir owned by his family and to eventually attack the London Stock Exchange with a bomb.

His plan was foiled by MI5 and the police, and he was convicted. There had been 9 men involved in the plot and Khan was just 19 years old at the time. During the trial, Khan was identified as one of the 'more serious jihadis.'

Khan was allegedly a supporter of extremist group Al-Muhajiroun, and he was a friend and student of terrorism and Islamist supporter, Anjem Choudary.

The Hague Stabbing Attack

On November 29, three teenagers were attacked by a man wielding a knife on a busy shopping street in The Hague. Nobody was killed in the attack, but it left the city in fear of violence.

A Violent Spree

The streets were filled with Black Friday shoppers on the evening of November 29. The Grote Markstraat is one of the busiest streets in The Hague, especially during sales seasons.

Three teenagers were at the Hudson's Bay store when a man with a knife attacked them at 7:45 P.M. The victims included a local boy, 13, a girl from Leiderdorp, 15, and another girl from Alphen aan den Rijn, 15. None of the victims knew each other. The injuries weren't life-threatening and all were discharged from hospital quickly.

People ran in all directions in a panic to get away from the attacker.

Suspect Arrested

The attacker was apprehended in the center of The Hague soon after the attack had occurred. He was a homeless man aged 35, but his name has not been released. He was taken to the local police station for questioning.

Is There a Possible Link to the Earlier London Attack?

The stabbing attack had occurred just hours following the attack on London Bridge. This led many to consider if the attacks were linked somehow. With the London Bridge attack labeled as terrorism, it posed a great concern that this attack at The Hague may be terrorism as well.

Police said it was too early to determine if it was terrorism or not, but they weren't ruling it out until their investigation was complete. The suspect remained in custody in the interim.

Terrorist Attacks in Brief

November 1

Ménaka Region, Mali: A military post was attacked by suspected Islamic gunmen, resulting in 54 being killed. The gunmen fled the scene, and the Islamic State claimed responsibility.

November 2

Tell Abyad, Syria: A car bomb explosion in a marketplace killed 13 and wounded more than 30. The PNK was suspected.

November 6

Fada N'gourma, Burkina Faso: A Canadian based mining company was attacked by Islamic militants, using bombs and gunfire. The attack left 37 dead, possibly more, and more than 65 injured.

Yala Province, Thailand: Islamic militants opened fire on a security checkpoint, killing 15 people and wounding 5.

November 10

Tell Abyad, Syria: A car bomb explosion resulted in 8 deaths and 26 injured.

November 11

Qamishli, Syria: Car bombs were detonated near a hotel and in a commercial district, killing 6 and wounding 21. Responsibility was claimed by the Islamic State and the Levant.

November 13

Kabul, Afghanistan: A suicide car bomb exploded a Canadian private security convoy, killing 12 and injuring more than 20.

Medan, Indonesia: A suicide bomber blew himself up near the Medan Police's headquarters. Only the attacker was killed. Four police officers and two civilians became injured. The attacker had connections with Islamic State-affiliated Jamaah Ansharut Daulah (JAD).

November 16

Al-Bab, Syria: Multiple car bombs exploded near a bus terminal resulting in the deaths of 19 and more than 50 injured.

November 18

Gao Region, Mali: Terrorists ambushed a convoy of Malian soldiers, killing 43 and wounding 29. 17 of the terrorists were also killed. Responsibility was claimed by the Islamic State.

November 23

Tell Abyad, Syria: A car bomb was detonated in the main street, killing 10 and wounding 25.

November 26

Tell Halaf, Syria: After a car bomb was detonated, 17 people were killed, and 20 were injured.

November 29

London, UK: A mass stabbing at London Bridge results in two civilians killed and three others injured. The attacker, 28-year-old convicted terrorist Usman Khan who was wearing a fake explosive belt, was shot dead by police. The stabbing was confirmed as a terrorist attack. The Islamic State claimed responsibility for the attack without giving evidence.

Chapter 12:
DECEMBER

Ten People Fired Upon in New Orleans

In a mass shooting in the French Quarter, New Orleans on December 1, ten people were injured but remarkably nobody was killed. There was a lot of police presence in the area at the time due to the Bayou Classic football game. No motive has been uncovered, and the hunt is still on for the perpetrator.

Public Shooting

There was a huge turnout of tourists on Canal Street on December 1 due to the Bayou Classic football game. Because of the increased crowds, extra police were on patrol.

At around 3:25 A.M., shots were fired in the 700 block of Canal Street, and officers responded immediately. They were just a few feet away, and at first thought they were being shot at. Because of the huge amount of people trying to escape the area, police had trouble trying to figure out where the shots were coming from.

Most of the shooting incident was recorded by surveillance cameras. Of the 10 people shot, 2 were critical. The ages of the victims ranged from 16 to 36 years, and there were five females and five males.

Unknown Perpetrator

Both state and federal officials are helping the New Orleans police gather evidence to try and determine who was responsible for the shooting. A reward was announced by Crimestoppers, which was raised higher to $10,000.

A person was detained not long after the incident, but it was released. Police did, however, locate a weapon at the scene.

It's believed by investigators that the shooting was the result of a feud that had occurred outside of New Orleans. They infer that the shooting was carried out by visitors to the area who were from Louisiana.

Mayor's Response

The Mayor of New Orleans, LaToya Cantrell, responded to the incident by focusing on the crime rate that was declining in the city. She said, "The city of New Orleans will not allow incidents like this to derail the progress we have made or further disrupt our community. This tragedy will not define us, and it will not deter us from moving our city forward and keeping our people safe."

Shooting at Pearl Harbor

On December 4, a US Navy sailor opened fire on colleagues at the historic Pearl Harbor base in Hawaii. Two men were killed, and a third was treated at a hospital nearby for his injuries. Immediately after the shooting, the gunman took his own life.

A Historical Place

The Pearl Harbor Naval Shipyard is a military base on the island of Oahu, Hawaii. It was the site of an attack by the Imperial Japanese Navy 78 years prior, which killed over 2,000 Americans and destroyed a large number of US airplanes and battleships. It's also the home of the USS Arizona Memorial which is visited by almost 2 million people each year.

The base is home to both Navy and Air Force units, and there were more than 66,000 people living there as of 2015.

U.S. Sailor Turns Killer

Around 2:30 P.M. on December 4, a sailor began shooting on the base. It was 3 days before the National Pearl Harbor Remembrance Day was to take place. During the shooting, 2 civilian workers were killed, and another was injured. The gunman then turned his gun on himself and pulled the trigger, killing himself.

Witnesses stated that from the start to the finish of the shooting, it had taken just 23 seconds.

The gunman was identified as Machinist's Mate Auxiliary Fireman Gabrial Antonio Romero, 22. He'd been in the Navy for less than 2 years. After graduating from the Recruit Training Command in Illinois, and Navy Submarine School in Connecticut, he was assigned to the USS Columbia attack submarine. At the time of the shooting, the submarine was in a dry dock at the base for maintenance.

Since the shooting, numerous questions have been raised about the status of his mental health leading up to the attack. Concerns were presented that Romero had sought out counseling and that he'd been targeted by an informal hearing 'tied to non-judicial punishment proceedings' and then was given loaded weapons for guard duty.

Unknown Motive

A motive for the attack is still being investigated, with no clear evidence to suggest what drove Romero to shoot the others and then take his own life. It's believed his victims were random, and there was no personal agenda to kill anyone specific.

Officials don't concede that the attack was an act of terrorism.

Robbery, Chase and Shootout in Miramar

Following the robbery of a jewelry store in Miramar, Florida, on December 5, a chase ensued which resulted in a shootout between the robbers and police. During the gunfire exchange, the robbers were killed along with 2 innocent people.

Robbery of the Jewelry Store

At around 4:14 P.M. on December 5, two suspects entered the Regent Jeweler store at Miracle Mile, Coral Gables, Florida. The cashier at the store was held at gunpoint while the robbers stole diamonds. When confronted by the owner of the store, gunfire was exchanged, resulting in one store worker being injured. One of the bullets struck City Hall, so the building was locked down.

The store had a silent alarm; and when it went off, police responded, arriving in less than 2 minutes. On arrival, the officers were fired upon by the gunmen, and the officers returned fire.

The gunmen jumped into a U-Haul van and fled. The vehicle was dumped a mile away in a suburban neighborhood. They then carjacked a UPS delivery truck, holding the driver hostage at gunpoint as they continued their escape, heading on to Interstate 75 into Broward County.

Deadly Shootout

Multiple police cars chased the suspects until the rush hour traffic caused the UPS truck to be boxed in, forcing it to stop. Officers ducked down behind bystander's cars and began firing on the suspects.

Nineteen police officers were involved in the chase and shootout with the robbers. Thirteen of the officers were from the Miami-Dade Police Department and the others from the Miramar Police Department and the Pembroke Pines Police Department. The whole event was broadcast on television live by news' helicopters.

Victims

The shootout resulted in the deaths of four people. Both suspects were killed by the police. The UPS driver, 27, who had been hijacked, was killed;

and a 70-year-old member of the public who had been in a car was also killed.

The UPS driver was Frank Ordonez, and the elderly driver killed was Richard Cutshaw. Cutshaw's car was in front of the UPS truck.

Perpetrators

The suspects were identified as Ronnie Jerome Hill, 41, and Lamar Alexander, 41, and both were from Miami-Dade County. They were cousins, and both had criminal records. Alexander was the father of 3 children. Hill was the father of 2, one of which had special needs.

Alexander had previously been convicted of a robbery in 1996 and a burglary in 1997, which resulted in a probation sentence. In the 2000s, he was arrested 5 times but wasn't convicted. Then in 2008, he was incarcerated for an armed robbery and was released on parole in 2017.

Hill had been imprisoned twice. He'd been convicted of burglary and robbery in the 1990s, then more recently had been convicted of 5 burglaries.

The family thought Alexander had turned a new leaf, as he'd been working for a garbage collection company before the robbery in Miramar. Likewise, with Hill's family, since he'd been working as a driver for a cabinetry company.

Officers Stood Down

All of the police officers involved in the shooting were relieved of duty while the incident is investigated by the FBI. Questions have been asked whether the situation was handled appropriately by police.

It hasn't been released if the bullets that struck and killed Frank Ordonez came from police weapons or the suspects. It also isn't clear how Richard Cutshaw was shot and killed when his car was in front of the UPS truck.

Family Response

The sister of frank Ordonez voiced her anger regarding the handling of the situation by police on her Twitter account. She believed police should have tried to negotiate with the robbers instead of resorting to gunfire so quickly. She believes that her brother may still be alive if the police had handled it differently.

Gunman Opens Fire at Naval Air Station Pensacola

A mass shooting occurred at the Naval Air Station Pensacola on December 6 in Pensacola, Florida. A shooter killed 3 people and injured a further 8 before he was killed by police deputies. The suspect was a Saudi Arabian aviation student and terrorism was a potential motive.

Under Fire

The gunman opened fire in a classroom building, and the first report was made at 6:51 A.M. He'd managed to move through two floors, firing as he fled. One of the wounded victims managed to escape and alert the first response team. They were informed who the shooter was and given more details about what was happening.

At 7:45 A.M. Escambia County Sheriff's Office deputies engaged the suspect, and a shootout ensued, resulting in the death of the suspect. During the shooting, a student from Saudi Arabia had been filming the building. He'd been at a dinner party hosted by the suspect before the attack.

Those Who Were Shot

The 2 deputies who had arrived on the scene and killed the gunman were injured during the exchange of gunfire. They then received wounds to their limbs, and were treated in hospital. Two of the people killed were declared deceased at the scene and the third died at the hospital.

One of the victims was a high school track star from St. Petersburg, Florida, and the victim who perished at the hospital was a graduate of the United States Naval Academy and had come to the base 2 weeks prior to start flight training.

The Gunman is Identified

The FBI refused to release the gunman's name during a news conference the night of the attack, and they wouldn't comment on any potential motives. However, the identity of the gunman was released by officials anonymously, as Mohammed Saeed Alshamrani, who was a second lieutenant in the Royal Saudi Air Force.

Alshamrani had started aviation training at the station in August 2017, and he was meant to finish in August 2020. The program included basic aviation, initial pilot training, and English-language.

According to SITE Intelligence Group, a manifesto was released by Alshamrani before the shooting, which "attacked what it calls an American 'war of attrition' waged on Muslins around the world."

During the dinner party Alshamrani hosted right before the shooting, he'd watched mass shootings videos along with 3 other Saudi students.

The investigation includes looking for signs he may have been radicalized and whether the shooting was a terrorist act. Defense Secretary Mark Esper opened another investigation about the measures taken to vet foreign nationals into military training programs in the U.S.

New Jersey Mass Shooting

On December 10, at a kosher grocery store in Jersey City, a mass shooting occurred, leaving 5 people dead, including the 2 suspects. Just before the shooting, a police detective was killed at a cemetery nearby.

Shootings Begin

At around 12:30 P.M., Police Detective Joseph Seals walked towards 2 persons at the Bayview Cemetery to speak to them about an investigation he was undertaking. Apparently, the van the suspects were in had been related to a murder in Bayonne the weekend prior. He was going to confiscate weapons that were in the van when he was shot dead.

The suspects stole a U-Haul vehicle and fled the scene, driving to the kosher grocery store in Greenville, Jersey City, New Jersey. Inside they shot and killed 3 people, and when police arrived, gunfire was exchanged for more than an hour. Eventually, the suspects were shot and killed by police. When they searched the vehicle they'd occupied, a live pipe bomb was discovered.

The Killed and the Injured

Detective Joseph Seals had been with the Jersey City Police Department since 2006. He was married and had 5 children. Mindy Ferencz, who co-managed the store with her husband, was killed. Douglas Miguel Rodriguez was working at the store that day when he was killed. The other fatality was Moshe Deutsch, a rabbinical student.

- Police Detective Joseph Seals,39
- Mindy Ferencz, 31,
- Moshe Deutsch, 24-
- Douglas Miguel Rodriguez, 49

Suspects Identified

The identity of the suspects was made public on December 11. David Anderson, 47, and Francine Graham, 50, who was Anderson's girlfriend, were the suspects. The investigation showed that it had been a targeted attack and that Anderson was involved with the Black Hebrew Israelite Movement. Postings on his social media page were connected to anti-Jewish and anti-police writings.

The Black Hebrew Israelites believe they're the true descendants of ancient Israelites. They believe that anyone else claiming to be Jewish was impostors. A short manifesto was located in the van Anderson and Graham had been driving, but there was no specific motive or rational explanation for the attack.

Anderson and Graham were also suspected in a murder in Bayonne the weekend prior when an Uber driver was killed.

Hate Crime

Steven Fulop, the Mayor of Jersey City, sent a tweet out on Twitter that Anderson and Graham had targeted the location of the attack specifically. He referred to the shooting as a hate crime.

The Aftermath

Because of the shootout, the Sacred Heart Church, the Jersey City Medical Center, and 12 schools were put on lockdown until the situation ended. Almost 100 children were held next to the market until it was safe. Buses and the light rail services were suspended, and the turnpike was closed temporarily.

President Trump expressed his condolences to the families and the victims through Twitter. Governor of New Jersey Phil Murphy also used Twitter to express his thoughts, prayers, and condolences for all those affected. He also praised Detective Seals for his service.

Gunman Takes Aim in Hospital Waiting Room

A gunman opened fire on people while they sat in a hospital waiting room in Ostrava, Czech Republic, on December 10. Six people were killed, and three suffered injuries. As police closed in on the suspect later that day, he committed suicide.

The Last Thing Anyone Expected

At around 7:15 A.M. on the morning of December 10, the suspect walked into the waiting room of the Faculty Hospital in Ostrava. He carried a CZ 75B pistol, which was an illegal weapon. At that time, there were around 30 people in the waiting room on the third floor of the building where trauma was treated.

At first, the suspect stood quietly holding the pistol down by his leg. He pointed the pistol at his own head but didn't fire. He then aimed at the people in the room and began shooting. He aimed the weapon at the necks and heads of the victims, killing 6 adults. Of the 3 injured victims, 2 had suffered serious injuries.

After the shooting, the suspect fled the hospital, driving to his mother's home. He then confessed to her what he'd done and said he was going to commit suicide.

Police Arrive Within Three Minutes of Emergency Call

The first call to emergency services was made at 7:19 A.M., just a few minutes after the shooting had begun. Three minutes after the call was received, the police arrived at the hospital.

Of note, police officers in the Czech Republic are always armed, carrying pistols, and there's usually at least an automatic rifle in each patrol car.

By the time the police arrived, the gunman had already fled. But they knew the car he was driving and utilized a police helicopter to locate it. The suspect was tracked down three and a half hours after the shooting had taken place, in Děhylov, 5 miles from the hospital.

As police approached the house, the gunman, who was sitting in his car, shot himself in the head. Resuscitation attempts were made immediately, but half an hour later, the suspect was pronounced dead.

The Gunman

The gunman was named as Ctirad Vitusek, 42, a construction engineer. His work colleagues told police that he'd recently taken 2 weeks of sick leave as he was seriously ill. He'd been treated at the hemato-oncology department of the hospital, which addressed blood cancers. In sum, he felt that nobody could help cure him or help with his illness.

Vitusek had previously been convicted 3 times, one of which was for a violent crime, which made him unable to possess a firearm legally. Investigations are ongoing as to how he was able to obtain the firearm used in the shooting, and what his possible motive was for killing innocent patients waiting for surgery.

The Murder of Tessa Majors

Tessa Majors was murdered on December 11 by a group of teenagers, the oldest of which was just 14 years old. They'd planned to rob her but ended up stabbing her numerous times resulting in her death. The case made major headlines not just for the brutality of the murder, but because the perpetrators were so young.

Fatal Robbery

Majors, 18, was a student at Barnard College. On the afternoon of December 11, she was walking through Morningside Park, Manhattan. Just before 5:30 P.M, she was attacked by a group of people on a staircase. She was grabbed, and one of the offenders put her in a chokehold while they took what they could from her pockets.

It's believed Majors bit one of the attackers, which enraged him, leading to her being stabbed multiple times. As the attackers fled from the scene, Majors managed to stagger up the staircase. She was found by a security guard who called 911.

Majors was then transported to Mount Sinai Hospital where she was pronounced dead. The fatal wounds were sustained in her torso.

Investigation and Suspects

The first suspect arrested was Zyairr Davis, 13, who was apprehended after trespassing elsewhere, and the clothes he was wearing matched the description given by a witness. While being questioned by police, he confessed that he was involved in Majors' murder.

He told police that he'd picked up the knife that was later used to kill Majors. He'd apparently watched while the other 2 involved had grabbed Majors and how one had put her in a chokehold. Then one of them slashed her with the knife while she was screaming for help.

The trial date for Davis has been set for March 16, 2020. His lawyers had asked for him to be released into the care of his uncle and aunt due to his age, but the judge refused because of the serious nature of the charges.

Police later arrested a second suspect, but because they didn't have enough information to charge him, he was released.

The third suspect, aged 14, had fled before the police had a chance to question him about the murder. Photographs of him were released by police in an effort to locate him. He was subsequently arrested on December 26 in the Bronx.

The investigation is ongoing to find the required evidence to enable police to charge the 14-year-old suspects. DNA testing has been done, and investigators are awaiting the results.

Tessa Rane Majors

Majors was born in 2001 and was originally from Charlottesville in Virginia. She was in her freshman year at Barnard College, which is a private female-only school located in Manhattan.

She played the bass and sang in a band called Patient 0, who had released an album before her death. They'd played their first gig and had two more lined up for the winter.

Majors was interested in journalism and was involved in the creative writing club when she was in high school. In spring 2019, she'd interned at *Augusta Free Press*. Her father is an English professor.

The Aftermath

Improved security measures were put in place at Morningside Park after the murder of Majors. Guard booths weren't staffed 24 hours a day outside the park. Even the safety shuttle bus that ran in the evenings had an extended operation period.

Hanukkah Stabbing in Monsey

On the seventh night of Hanukkah, December 28, the home of a Hasidic rabbi in Monsey, New York, was invaded by a masked man carrying a large machete or knife. Several people were injured, some critically, as they fought back against the attacker. Besides the attempted murder charges, the attacker was also charged with a federal hate crime.

Background of Monsey

Monsey is a hamlet of Rockland County and has the largest number of Jewish residents per capita of any other county in the US. Large Hasidic communities are based in Monsey, and they continue to grow in population.

Attack on Rabbi's House

Rabbi Chaim Rottenberg was hosting a Hanukkah party at his home on the seventh night of Hanukkah., Nearly 100 people had come together to watch the Rabbi light the candles as part of the celebration.

At approximately 10:00pm, a man came into the house with a scarf covering his face. He was carrying either a machete or some type of large knife and immediately began attacking the people at the party. Five people were injured: one person suffered a fractured skull and was rendered unconscious.

One of the injured victims was the rabbi's son. People at the party fought back against the intruder, using furniture to fend him off accordingly. The whole attack went on for about 2 minutes, after which the intruder ran from the house. He then tried to get into the synagogue next door, the Congregation Netzach Yisroel. He was unable to enter the locked doors, and so left in a vehicle. His escape was witnessed and his license plate number was given to the police.

On the George Washington Bridge, a license plate reader picked up on the vehicle at 11:45 P.M. as he was entering New York City. The car was stopped by police in Harlem, and the attacker was arrested just after midnight. When he was apprehended, he allegedly smelled like bleach and had blood on his clothing. He was transported back to Monsey and handed over to the Ramapo police.

Suspect - Grafton E. Thomas

The intruder was African-American Grafton E. Thomas, who was living in Greenwood Lake, which is Northwest of Monsey. His father had entered as an illegal immigrant and was granted amnesty under the Immigration Reform and Control Act of 1986, so he was then able to reside in the US legally.

Since 2001, Thomas had been arrested 7 times. The charges included killing or injuring a police animal, assault, resisting arrest, possession of controlled substances, meaning a police officer, and driving under the influence. In 2013 he spent a short period in jail for the possession of a controlled substance. The charge of killing or injuring a police animal came from an incident when Thomas had punched a police horse.

In 2018 Thomas was charged for endangerment, weapon possession, and menacing a police officer.

Under Investigation

During the investigation, police uncovered journals Thoams had written about anti-Semitic thoughts and views. They also contained drawings of a swastika, the Star of David, and material about the Nazi culture and Adolf Hitler.

There seemed to be references to the Black Hebrew Israelites, and Thomas had sated that Hebrew Israelites had taken from the Ebinoid Israelites. The browser on his mobile phone had been used prior to the attack to look at an article about increased police presence in Jewish neighborhoods.

He'd also searched for certain phrases through the browser, including "Why did Hitler hate the Jews," German Jewish Temples near me," and "Zionist Temples" in the local area.

Police are also investigating Thomas as a possible suspect in a stabbing attack that happened on November 20. The victim, an Orthodox Jew, was on his way to early prayer at 5:30 A.M. when he was attacked and stabbed. He sustained critical injuries.

The lawyer representing Thomas stated that Thomas' family declined any known history of belonging to hate groups or antisemitism. But, they claimed he'd a history of mental illness requiring hospitalizations. Medical records confirmed he'd been received treatment for schizophrenia, so in that instance, the family members were correct.

Legal Proceedings

On December 29, Thomas was arraigned on five counts of attempted murder and one count of first-degree burglary, and he pleaded not guilty to all charged. The court set his bail at US$5 million.

A criminal complaint against Thomas was filed by the United States Attorney for the Southern District of New York. The complaint charged Thomas with five counts of "obstruction of free exercise of religious beliefs involving an attempt to kill and use of a dangerous weapon and resulting in bodily injury," a federal hate crime.

Political Impact

The attack by Thomas had resulted in a discussion about recent New York State bail reforms and their impact. The new reforms require the courts to release offenders on non-monetary conditions for nearly all misdemeanors, burglary and robbery in the second degree and non-violent felonies. This includes whether it was a hate crime or not. It was found that Thomas had been released previously following arrests for several minor violent crimes.

West Freeway Church of Christ Shooting

During a live-streaming of the service at the West Freeway Church of Christ on December 29, a gunman entered the church and started shooting. The whole attack was streamed live in real-time, with multiple videos and social media posts showing the crime as it happened. The most surprising facet of the whole event was that the gunman probably didn't consider that a number of people in the church were also armed with guns.

An Unexpected Shooting

When the suspect started shooting, he managed to kill members of the church. Another church member, Jack Wilson, Head of Security, fired back, and the gunman was fatally shot within 6 seconds of firing the first shot. Wilson, a firearms instructor, and previously been a reserve deputy sheriff in Hood County, Texas.

The parishioners who were killed were Richard White,67, and Anton Wallace, 64.

Around 5 people stood up, armed with guns when the shooting began. It's shocking how many people in Texas carry weapons into a church service.

The Gunman

The suspect was Keith Thomas Kinnunen, 43, who lived in River Oaks in Texas. At the time of the shooting, he was wearing a wig and a fake beard, which made the security deacons of the church suspicious.

Kinnunen had been arrested and convicted several times over the last 10 years and at one point, was homeless. He'd been ordered to stay away from an ex-wife who said he was paranoid and violent back in 2012.

He was charged in 2008 with felony aggravated assault with a deadly weapon. It was later dropped to a charge of misdemeanor deadly conduct, and in 2009, he was convicted. He was sentenced to jail for 90 days.

Kinnunen was arrested in Tuttle, Oklahoma, in 2011, for assaulting an employee of a store. He'd also set fire to a number of things around the town including tampons soaked with oil, tree branches that had been doused with gasoline and a football that had been soak in lamp oi. He was convicted of misdemeanor assault and battery and misdemeanor property damage and sentenced to another 90 days for the assault and 1 year in jail for the property charge.

Over the years, Kinnunen had been treated for a number of mental illnesses, including depression and forms of psychosis. An evaluation of his mental status in 2012 stated, Kinnunen "displayed several signs of mental illness, including 'apathy, long latency of response to questions and an impaired ability to attend, concentrate and focus.'"

Further evaluation in 2013 stated that his "expressed thoughts were noted to be marked by 'latency of response,' but 'otherwise...coherent.'" Also, that "he does not currently evidence significant cognitive impairment or mental illness."

He was arrested again in 2013 by Fort Worth police for theft. Then following his conviction in January 2014, he received a 30-day jail sentence. His next charge was in 2016, in New Jersey, for unlawful possession of a weapon. He received a sentence of time served.

Kinnunen had been to the West Freeway Church of Christ on several occasions, and it was difficult to ascertain what his motive was on the day of the shooting. However, Kinnunen's sister alleged that Sunday was the birthday of their younger brother who had killed himself in 2009.

Reaction

Because Kinnunen had been shot and killed by an armed church member who was carrying a concealed weapon, the gun rights advocates are using the incident as an example of how private citizens armed with firearms are beneficial.

Terrorist Attacks in Brief

December 1

Est Region, Burkina Faso: A shooting attack at a church killed 14 and wounded many others.

December 4

Jalalabad, Afghanistan: Gunmen ambushed a vehicle carrying a Japanese doctor, Tetsu Nakamura, the head of Peace Japan Medical Services, and five Afghans, including the driver, a colleague of the doctor and 3 bodyguards. All were killed.

December 6

Wajir County, Kenya: A bus was ambushed by gunmen near the Somalian border. Of the 11 killed, one was a doctor, and 7 were police officers. Non-Somalis were attacked specifically by the gunmen. Responsibility was claimed by Al-Shabaab.

Pensacola, US: A Saudi student opened fire at a U.S. naval base in Pensacola, Florida. The attack left at least three killed and eight injured, including two deputies. The police are investigating a 'terrorist motive' in the deadly shooting.

December 10

Jersey City, US: A man and a woman opened fire at a kosher grocery store. Three civilians were killed, and another civilian and two police officers were wounded. Before the attack, the shooters killed a police detective at a nearby cemetery. During a shootout with the police, the two attackers were killed. They acted due to anti-Semitic and anti-police motives.

December 11

Bagram Airfield, Afghanistan: Taliban militants attacked Bagram Airfield using car bombings and gunfire, leaving 2 dead and 80 wounded.

Inates, Niger: A military post was attacked by Islamic State militants with bombs, mortars, and gunfire. The attacked killed 71 soldiers, and dozens more were injured and kidnapped. After the attack, 30 soldiers were missing.

December 15

Beni, the Democratic Republic of the Congo: ADF militants stabbed and killed 22 civilians in Beni, DRC.

December 24

Arbinda, Burkina Faso: Jihadists attacked an army outpost in northern Burkina Faso, causing the deaths of 7 soldiers and 80 militants. At the same time, dozens of militants attacked civilians in the nearby town of Arbinda, killing 35, including 31 women. Islamic State claimed responsibility, but only for the killing of the soldiers.

December 28

Mogadishu, Somalia: A suicide truck bombing at a checkpoint killed at least 84 people, including at least 15 university students, several police officers, and two Turkish engineers. At least 150 other people were wounded, many critically. Al-Shabaab claimed responsibility for the attack on December 30.

Monsey, US: A man stabbed and injured 5 people in the home of a rabbi where a Hanukkah party was underway. The suspect fled the scene and was arrested in New York City after midnight. New York Governor Andrew M. Cuomo described the attack as an "act of domestic terrorism."

Conclusion

In essence, it's important to look back on the year that has passed and remember the violent crimes that have occurred for a number of reasons. Firstly, it makes you appreciate what you have and where you live compared to some of the countries that are facing wars, conflicts, and horrific bombings and massacres.

It's also critical to understand what's going on around the world. Like when studying history, looking back can enable you to discover the keys to moving forward. Perhaps you start to notice things that you didn't detect before? Maybe the clues on how to prevent some of these crimes are in the understanding of what has already taken place?

Crime is always going to be there, whether it's non-violent or violent, and there will never be a way to stop all of it. As the population around the world continues to grow, so will the incidences of crime, as we've seen over the last century.

It's a sad fact that serial killings and suicide bombings are so commonplace now that we barely notice them anymore. But they're there, and they aren't going away. It's clear by this book content that terrorism is on the rise, and everyone should be vigilant.

We're now in 2020, a year that we once thought would bring flying cars. Wouldn't it be great if instead, we found the key in preventing some of these horrific crimes from happening in the years to come?

More Books By Jack Rosewood

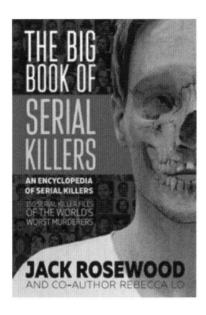

There is little more terrifying than those who hunt, stalk and snatch their prey under the cloak of darkness. These hunters search not for animals, but for the touch, taste, and empowerment of human flesh. They are cannibals, vampires and monsters, and they walk among us.

These serial killers are not mythical beasts with horns and shaggy hair. They are people living among society, going about their day to day activities until nightfall. They are the Dennis Rader's, the fathers, husbands, church going members of the community.

This A-Z encyclopedia of 150 serial killers is the ideal reference book. Included are the most famous true crime serial killers, like Jeffrey Dahmer, John Wayne Gacy, and Richard Ramirez, and not to mention the women who kill, such as Aileen Wuornos and Martha Rendell. There are also lesser known serial killers, covering many countries around the world, so the range is broad.

Each of the serial killer files includes information on when and how they killed the victims, the background of each killer, or the suspects in some cases such as the Zodiac killer, their trials and punishments. For some there are chilling quotes by the killers themselves. The Big Book of Serial Killers is an easy to follow collection of information on the world's most heinous murderers.

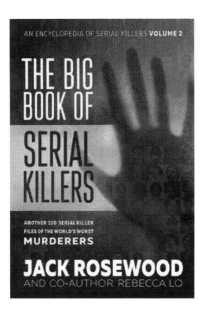

Our first volume caused such an impact that we've decided to bring you the long-awaited Volume 2 of the most comprehensive Serial Killer encyclopedia ever published!

Murderers or monsters, normal people turned bad or people born with the desire to kill; it doesn't matter where they come from, serial killers strike dread into our hearts with a single mention of their names. Hunting in broad daylight or stalking from the shadows, we are their prey and their hunt is never done until they are caught or killed.

With a worrying number of them living in our communities, working alongside us at our places of employment and sharing the same spaces where we spend time with our families, serial killers are typically just another neighbor that we barely think about. A worrying thought, to be honest.

In The Big Book of Serial Killers Volume 2 we go through the lives of 150 serial killers who allowed themselves to fall under the influence of their darkest desires and took the lives anywhere from one to one hundred victims; we speak of their motives and how their stories ended (*if* they ended...), and remind you of the fear and pain that they left behind.

But what can you expect from **The Big Book of Serial Killers Volume 2?**

You will find such things as:

- An excellent A-Z list of all of these deadly killers, allowing you to reference the encyclopedia whenever you need to find out more about any single murderer.
- All of the uncensored details of their crimes, with much effort taking into account to describe their horrific acts.
- Important information on their date and place of birth, date of arrest and number of victims, among other facts.
- A list of Trivia facts for each killer, allowing you to learn more about their personalities and any films or documentaries made about them.

So, with nothing more to add – it's only time now for you purchase this book and begin learning about 150 of the sickest, most dangerous serial killers in world history.

This is the next level in murder: are you ready to learn about the evilest men and women in history?

Manufactured by Amazon.ca
Bolton, ON

15501946R00162